# Martin Luther King Jr.

**Recent Titles in Black History Lives**

W.E.B. Du Bois: A Life in American History
*Charisse Burden-Stelly and Gerald Horne*

Thurgood Marshall: A Life in American History
*Spencer R. Crew*

Barack Obama: A Life in American History
*F. Erik Brooks and MaCherie M. Placide*

Harriet Tubman: A Life in American History
*Kerry Walters*

Zora Neale Hurston: A Life in American History
*Stephanie Li*

Rosa Parks: A Life in American History
*Darryl Mace*

Jackie Robinson: A Life in American History
*Courtney Michelle Smith*

Booker T. Washington: A Life in American History
*Mark Christian*

Jesse Owens: A Life in American History
*F. Erik Brooks and Kevin M. Jones*

# Martin Luther King Jr.

## A LIFE IN AMERICAN HISTORY

Jamie J. Wilson

**Black History Lives**

BLOOMSBURY ACADEMIC
NEW YORK • LONDON • OXFORD • NEW DELHI • SYDNEY

ABC-CLIO
Bloomsbury Publishing Inc
1385 Broadway, New York, NY 10018, USA
50 Bedford Square, London, WC1B 3DP, UK
29 Earlsfort Terrace, Dublin 2, Ireland

ABC-CLIO, the ABC-CLIO logo, BLOOMSBURY and the Diana logo are trademarks of Bloomsbury Publishing Plc

First published in the United States of America 2023

Copyright © Bloomsbury Publishing Inc, 2023

Cover image © LOC Photo/Alamy Stock Photo

All rights reserved. No part of this publication may be reproduced or transmitted in any form or by any means, electronic or mechanical, including photocopying, recording, or any information storage or retrieval system, without prior permission in writing from the publishers.

Bloomsbury Publishing Inc does not have any control over, or responsibility for, any third-party websites referred to or in this book. All internet addresses given in this book were correct at the time of going to press. The author and publisher regret any inconvenience caused if addresses have changed or sites have ceased to exist, but can accept no responsibility for any such changes.

**Library of Congress Cataloging in Publication Control Number: 2023011855**

ISBN: HB: 978-1-4408-6400-1
PB: 979-8-2163-9676-5
ePDF: 978-1-4408-6401-8
eBook: 979-8-216-17199-7

Series: Black History Lives

Typeset by Amnet ContentSource

To find out more about our authors and books visit www.bloomsbury.com and sign up for our newsletters.

# Contents

*Series Foreword  vii*

*Preface  ix*

*Acknowledgments  xi*

**CHAPTER 1**
King's Early Years and Education  *1*

**CHAPTER 2**
Becoming a Leader  *19*

**CHAPTER 3**
Challenging the Nation  *37*

**CHAPTER 4**
Embracing a Larger Movement  *55*

**CHAPTER 5**
The Nation and the World Are Listening  *73*

**CHAPTER 6**
People to People and People in Action  *89*

**CHAPTER 7**
Birmingham and Standing before God  *105*

**CHAPTER 8**
The Man of the Year and the Nobel Prize Laureate  *123*

**CHAPTER 9**
Going to Chicago  *141*

**CHAPTER 10**
Beyond Vietnam to Memphis  *159*

*Why Martin Luther King Jr. Matters  179*

*Timeline  187*

*Primary Documents  193*

*Bibliography  205*

*Index  219*

# Series Foreword

The Black History Lives biography series explores and examines the lives of the most iconic figures in African American history, with supplementary material that highlights the subject's significance in our contemporary world. Volumes in this series will offer far more than a simple retelling of a subject's life by providing readers with a greater understanding of the outside events and influences that shaped each subject's world, from familial relationships to political and cultural developments.

Each volume includes chronological chapters that detail events of the subject's life. The final chapter explores the cultural and historical significance of the individual and places their actions and beliefs within an overall historical context. Books in the series highlight important information about the individual through sidebars that connect readers to the larger context of social, political, intellectual, and pop culture in American history; a timeline listing significant events; key primary source excerpts; and a comprehensive bibliography for further research.

# Preface

I wrote this book hoping that it will introduce Martin Luther King Jr. to a new generation. It is by no means an exhaustive study, but it provides the lay reader with a meaningful discussion of one of the most important civil rights leaders of the twentieth century. L. D. Reddick, King's friend, adviser, and confidante, released the first biography of King in 1959 before he emerged as a national and international leader. Five years later, in 1964, Lerone Bennett Jr. published *What Manner of Man*, which ends with King's Nobel Peace Prize lecture. David Levering Lewis's *Martin Luther King, Jr.: A Biography* was issued in 1978, a decade after King's death. Four years later, Stephen Oates's *Let the Trumpet Sound* appeared and offered a thoughtful and well-researched look at King. In 2002, Marshall Frady published a reader-friendly biography of King titled *Martin Luther King Jr.: A Life*, which is a brief primer on the late leader. Paul Harvey's *Martin Luther King: A Religious Life* examines King's life and work "through his religious visions for a moral transformation in American society" (Harvey 2021, 3). One would think there would be many more published biographies of King, given his place in the United States and African American history. Instead, historians and writers have elaborated on certain aspects of his political life and theology and offered important insights, such as Thomas Jackson's *From Civil Rights to Human Rights: Martin Luther King, Jr., and the Struggle for Economic Justice*, Michael Honey's *Going Down Jericho Road: The Memphis Strike, Martin Luther King's Last Campaign*, and David Garrow's marvelous studies about the SCLC (Southern Christian Leadership Conference) and the FBI's surveillance of King. Branch Taylor's award-winning, multivolume collection *America in the King Years* is a must-read for anyone wanting to understand the complexities of the civil rights movement era.

This work synthesizes material from a variety of published sources and unpublished material, and I am indebted to the work of the Martin Luther King, Jr. Research and Education Institute at Stanford University and the King Center in Atlanta, Georgia. Staff at the Research and Education Institute spent decades collecting material by and about King and published seven comprehensive volumes that include his major speeches, sermons, and correspondence. Parts of this book could not have been written without their labor of love and meticulous work.

Ten chronological chapters are offered here, with twenty sidebars that place King within the larger cultural, social, and political context of the time: "The Origins of Jim Crow," "The Great Migration," "The Murder of Emmett Till, 1955" "Highlander Folk School," "*Jet* Magazine," "Rock and Roll," "*Ebony*," "Historically Black Colleges and Universities," "The Motown Sound," "Ku Klux Klan," "White Citizens' Council," "Black Rock and Roll: The Early 1960s," "Cold War and Civil Rights," "Civil Rights Music," "COINTELPRO [Counter Intelligence Program]," "The Free Speech Movement," "Long, Hot Summer Riots, 1965–1967" "Hippies," "The Black Arts Movement," and "The Shrine of the Black Madonna." Also included are primary sources by individuals who remember King's life and legacy, including former president Barack Obama. The book ends with a consideration of "Why Martin Luther King Jr. Matters" wherein I argue that he matters in our twenty-first century world because in the areas of education, poverty, war, racism, housing, police brutality, and white supremacy, his social and political agenda has largely been unfulfilled.

The historian Vincent Harding called him an "inconvenient hero," a title that is most appropriate for King. King did not always want to lead or be a symbol of the black freedom struggle. Challenging the status quo is never convenient, and when one attempt to shake the very social foundation of the nation, as he did, support comes and goes, while scorn and rebuke are just around the corner. Throughout the book, the reader will hear King's thoughts about God, humanity, racism, war, poverty, and social injustice as well as the actions he took to bring about the world he dreamed of. His work and his ministry capture the spirit of the civil rights song, "Ain't Gonna Let Nobody Turn Us Around."

# Acknowledgments

I am thankful for the opportunity to write this book and think about King's tireless work, but it almost did not happen. When I contracted to write this book, I had just finished *The Black Panther Party: A Guide to an American Subculture* and was working on an edited collection. When the collection was finished, I was burned out. By the time my writing spirit returned, the COVID-19 pandemic befell us. My university had to pivot to online learning, and my children were out of school for about a month before we realized they were not going back to in-person learning for a while. We were without guidance from our school district for at least a month, and my then third and fourth graders needed guidance, so I reached back into my elementary teacher education training and developed daily curricula for both of them in multiple subjects for most of spring 2020.

In fall 2020, my children, then fourth and fifth graders, did not return to in-person learning, so from September 2020 to April 2021, I spent my days teaching and/or supporting elementary school math, English language arts, science, and social studies. Interspersed throughout the school day, I filled several other important roles: the lunch lady (because they ate lunch at completely different times), the IT troubleshooter, the custodian, and the timekeeper. Perhaps the most important role I assumed was that of the hype man. I had to keep the family's momentum going and buoy my children's spirit during the isolation of the pandemic and increased tensions in race relations. It was exhausting.

The pandemic also affected the buying and selling of books, so we were unclear if or when this book would be published. I learned that my initial editor left the project, then the second, then the third editor. We were in a holding pattern until when, to my surprise, my fourth editor, Thomas Krause appeared. With a gentleman's grace, he brought this book to publication. Thank you, Thomas.

I also want to express my gratitude to my dear wife, Staci, who supported me through this project. On my teaching days, she packs my lunch and leaves me a note in my lunch bag. One day as the deadline approached, she left a note that read "You are 25.2 miles into the race. Put your head down and finish it." Thank you, Taya and Tamya, my daughters. They both helped clean up the piles of books and papers that occupied the dining room, "Pipa's Work Space," and told anyone who would listen that "my dad is finishing his book." They are good souls.

# 1

## King's Early Years and Education

Martin Luther King Jr. was the second of Martin Luther King Sr. and Alberta Williams King's three children and was born in his maternal grandparent's home in Atlanta, Georgia, on January 15, 1929. His maternal grandfather was Reverend Adam Daniel (A. D.) Williams. The son of slaves, Williams was a social activist and began his tenure as pastor of Ebenezer Baptist Church in 1894. During the late nineteenth and early twentieth centuries, he strategically increased Ebenezer's membership and stature in Atlanta's segregated, black section and was active in the Young Men's Christian Association (YMCA), the National Association for the Advancement of Colored People (NAACP), the Atlanta Baptist Ministers Union (ABMU), the General State Baptist Convention (GSPC), the Georgia Equal Rights League (GERL), and other civil rights organizations in the state. Jennie Celeste Williams (née Jennie Celeste Parks) was King's maternal grandmother. The daughter of William and Fannie Parks, she was a devout woman, a foundational figure at Ebenezer Baptist Church, and would become a confidante for King as he aged. A. D. Williams died on March 21, 1931. Celeste Williams died ten years later, on May 18, 1941. Her death caused such a despondency in the twelve-year-old King that he contemplated suicide.

King's father, Martin Luther King Sr., known as Daddy King, was a prominent Atlanta Baptist minister in his own right before he assumed the pastorate at Ebenezer Baptist Church in 1931 shortly after A. D. Williams's death. As the new pastor, he continued to promote Williams's notions of a black Christianity that challenged legal barriers, social injustices, and economic discrimination faced by African Americans throughout Georgia and the South under Jim Crow. King's mother was an only child and received one of the best educations an African American woman could receive in the American South during the late nineteenth and early twentieth centuries. Before her marriage to Daddy King, Alberta worked as an elementary school teacher. At Ebenezer and throughout black Baptist circles, she was a well-known and sought-out pianist, organist, and choir director. Along with his older sister Christine and his younger brother Alfred Daniel (A. D.), Martin Luther King Jr. grew up in the bosom of the Baptist church and, with his father's salary, the comfort and stability of the black middle class.

As a child of a black preacher and a former elementary school teacher, King was surrounded by books even at a young age. His formal education, however, began in the first grade at Yonge Street Elementary School, the first modern, brick school building for African American children in Atlanta. Toward the middle of the school year, his precocious intellect had so impressed his teachers that he was moved into the second grade. King attended David T. Howard Elementary School from the third grade to the sixth grade. The school was named after the former slave who, according to his obituary in the *Atlanta Daily World*, was "Atlanta's most beloved citizen and the city's pioneer businessmen" (Gibson 2017).

After elementary school, King attended Atlanta University's Laboratory High School. Atlanta University opened its doors in 1869 under the aegis of the American Missionary Association to train black teachers. In 1930, it opened its Laboratory School by merging youth-centered educational programs sponsored by Spelman College, Morehouse College, and Atlanta University. It was a "laboratory" in that it was the primary student-teaching facility for Atlanta University's student teachers. By the late 1930s, the school had garnered the attention of the black intelligentsia. In May 1939, W. E. B. Du Bois, the renowned historian, sociologist, and activist, visited the school and addressed the school's Honor Society candidates. King was in ninth grade and was not a candidate and may not have been part of the listening crowd on that late spring day to hear Du Bois, but according to Maudestine Dangerfield, an educator at the school, Du Bois's address had a profound effect on the entire school. When the Laboratory High School closed in 1942, King transferred to Booker T. Washington High School. Named after the former slave and founder of Tuskegee Institute in Alabama, Booker T. Washington High School was the first black public secondary school in Atlanta, and King graduated from there at the age of fifteen in 1944.

King's parents and community sought to protect the King children from the daily and ever-present degradations of racism, but their protection could only go so far. King had a white playmate from ages three to six, the son of a white couple who owned and operated a store across the street from the King's residence. When King entered school at age six, the boy's parents forbade their son from playing with him because he was black. It was perhaps the first time the young King became aware of racism and the limitations it placed on black and white people. One day, while shopping downtown with the young Martin, his father was told that he would have to try on a pair of shoes in the back of the store. Refusing to accept such treatment, the elder King left the store without buying shoes, declaring, "We'll either buy shoes sitting here or won't buy any shoes at all" (Frady 2002, 15). Later, despite his five years delivering papers for the *Atlanta Journal*, King was denied a manager position because he was black. As a teenager, he left his position at Railway Express, a package delivery company, after his supervisor kept using racial epithets toward him and his fellow black workers.

In May 1944, when he was a high school junior, King delivered his address "The Negro and the Constitution" in Dublin, Georgia, at the First Baptist Church. The speech calls attention to and questions the contradictions of American race relations, and in it, King highlights Marian Anderson, the famous African American contralto who had performed throughout the United States and Europe to show that "even winners of our highest honors face the class color bar." Anderson was invited to perform in Washington, DC, by Howard University, but the university's performance spaces were too small to accommodate the large audiences who wanted to see her. In 1939, Howard University officials approached the Daughters of the American Revolution, the owners of Constitutional Hall, one of the largest venues in the city, but they refused to let Anderson perform on their stage because of their strict white-artists-only policy. Rather than cancel her Washington appearance, NAACP executive secretary Walter White worked with Secretary of the Interior Harold Ickes to allow Anderson to perform at the Lincoln Memorial on April 9, 1939, before a crowd of seventy-five thousand people. Through her performance, King said, Anderson brought forth a "new baptism of liberty, equality, and fraternity" for the nation, but she still could not stay at a decent hotel throughout the nation because she was black (Carson, Luker, and Russell 1992, 110). King would experience his own contradiction with American race relations. After delivering his first public address, during which he calls for racial equality, he was forced to relinquish his seat to a white passenger and stood the 135-mile journey back to Atlanta. It was through events such as these, and another completely opposite of them, that led King to abhor racial segregation.

> **CULTURAL CONNECTION: THE ORIGINS OF JIM CROW**
>
> The term Jim Crow comes from the 1828 minstrel song and dance "Jump Jim Crow," made popular by Thomas Rice, a white comedian. As a system, it was meant to codify white supremacy and to politically, socially, and economically subordinate African Americans living in the South. In the immediate postemancipation years of the late 1860s and 1870s, Jim Crow laws were introduced and supported by newly formed governments throughout the former Confederacy. Jim Crow determined one's residence and educational opportunities, dictated one's behavior and demeanor, denied African Americans the right to serve on juries, suppressed black voting rights, curtailed black economic development, and stripped most blacks of any political rights. In Virginia, blacks and white had separate almshouses. Mississippi health officials created separate and unequal public health facilities for blacks. Tennessee legislators passed laws forcing blacks and whites to attend separate public schools. In North Carolina, cemeteries were segregated. Throughout Georgia, whites and blacks took oaths on separate Bibles.
>
> Upheld by the U.S. Supreme Court's *Plessy v. Ferguson* (1896) decision, Jim Crow directly affected the lives of generations of African Americans and shaped race relations for millions of blacks and whites in northern and southern states from the late nineteenth to the mid-twentieth centuries.

After graduating from high school, King spent the months of June, July, and August working on the Cullman Brothers tobacco farm in Simsbury, Connecticut, a town in Hartford County about eleven miles from Hartford, the state capital. Labor shortages associated with World War II led Connecticut tobacco farms to recruit seasonal labor from southern black colleges and black towns. King was an eager teenager wanting to earn money for tuition and to get away from the South. It was his first time staying away from home for an extended period and his first time experiencing racial relations so dramatically dissimilar from the segregated South. When he transferred trains in Washington, DC, he could sit anywhere he wanted throughout the train rather than in a "colored" section. He found work in the farm's kitchen and earned enough to send home twenty-five dollars per week. In Simsbury, he worshipped with white coreligionists on an equal basis and, as the head of the religious department, regularly delivered sermons to over one hundred men working on the farm. While on a visit to the nearby city of Hartford, he attended several shows and ate at local restaurants without any segregation.

King left Simsbury in mid-September 1944 and began studies at Morehouse College. Morehouse was founded as the Atlanta Baptist College in 1867, two years after the Civil War. In 1906, it was renamed Morehouse

College after Henry Lyman Morehouse, a member of the Atlanta Baptist Home Mission Society. For over 150 years, Morehouse has been devoted to providing young African American men with a broad-based liberal arts education. When Martin began his education at Morehouse, he was following his father's and grandfather's footsteps and became part of a rich intellectual and activist tradition. For Daddy King, his son's career as a minister was inevitable: at five years old the young King was baptized and joined the church by professing his belief in Jesus and accepting the fundamentalist teachings and theology of his parents and church community. The teenager had rejected the physical resurrection of Jesus, but he was still destined to be a preacher, his father thought. During his first three years at Morehouse, however, King was not sure what profession he wanted to pursue, majored in sociology, and considered becoming a doctor or a lawyer.

King was active on campus in the glee club, the student council, minister's union, debate team, and the sociology club, but there was nothing academically remarkable about him. According to George D. Kelsey, a professor and director of the Morehouse School of Religion, King's academic record at Morehouse was "short of what may be called good" (Carson et al. 1992, 155). Benjamin Mays, the president of Morehouse, considered King a good citizen at the college but not a particularly brilliant student. Overall, King performed better in his junior and senior years than in his freshman and sophomore years. He received thirteen Cs, seven Bs, and took eight classes pass/fail, all of which he passed in his first two years. As an upperclassman, King took three classes on a pass/fail basis, earned thirteen Bs, five Cs, a D, an A, and one incomplete. When he graduated with his bachelor of arts degree in sociology in 1948, he had a 2.48 grade point average, making him a slightly above-average student (Carson et al. 1992, 38–39, 157).

By his senior year of college, after soul-searching, at age eighteen, King decided to join the clergy. In June 1947, he was licensed to preach and became the associate pastor at his father's church. He delivered his first sermon as a licensed preacher in fall 1947 to a large, attentive audience. His sister remembers that "young ministers [usually] preached their trial sermons in the basement of the church, but [Martin's address] was delivered in the overflowing sanctuary because of the number of people who wanted to hear him speak" (Farris 1986, 57). King was ordained in February 1948, and his father wanted him to become the copastor at Ebenezer once he graduated from Morehouse. Instead, King entered Crozer Theological Seminary that fall.

Located in Upland, Pennsylvania, a short distance from Philadelphia, Crozer was a liberal seminary with Baptist roots and a student body of around one hundred students. Most of the students were male, the majority were from southern states, and about 25 percent were black. Its interracial student body was completely alien to King, but he took an immediate liking to the school and excelled. The social scene was completely different from Morehouse. In Atlanta, he lived at home under the watchful eyes of his parents and commuted to the Morehouse campus. At Crozer, he lived in the main dormitory, and like his time in Simsbury, Connecticut, he was on his own. This time, however, he was a college graduate and a self-assured young man. King enjoyed the camaraderie at Crozer but loved Philadelphia and nearby Camden, New Jersey, more. With their vibrant African American communities, he frequented the two cities to attend house parties and sporting events. During his first semester, he bragged to his mother about how a "fine chick" in Philadelphia had become enamored with him. More importantly, Crozer provided him the space to explore ideas beyond the religious fundamentalism of Ebenezer.

He consulted various religious perspectives in Protestantism, Buddhism, Jainism, and Islam and systemically engaged ideas that few African American or white ministers had ever heard of in the mid-twentieth century. His professors challenged King, encouraged him to read broadly, think deeply, and cultivate his personal theology. He learned about Zoroastrianism's and Greek mythology's influence on Christianity, and in an essay "Light on the Old Testament from the Ancient Near East," written for his Introduction to the Old Testament course, he questions the historical accuracy of the Pentateuch—Genesis, Exodus, Leviticus, Numbers, and Deuteronomy. Using contemporary approaches of biblical criticism, King argues that Christians can extract moral truths from the Pentateuch without scriptural literalism, or acceptance of the stories told within it as accurate, historical facts.

King departed from black Baptist, fundamentalist teachings of Jesus's inherent divinity and agreed with William Adam Brown's description of Jesus in his Christian theology course. Brown, a liberal Christian theologian and author of *How to Think of Christ*, writes that "Jesus is a true man, bone of our bone, flesh of our flesh, in all points tempered as we are" (Brown 1948, 6–7). Understanding and describing Jesus as human, Clayborne Carson, a noted King biographer, suggests that it allowed King the "possibility of progressive improvement in earthly society through individual action" (Carson et al. 1992, 257). King combined this new perspective with a nuanced understanding of the Christian prophets. In "The Significant Contributions of Jeremiah to Religious Thought," an essay for his Old Testament course, he analyzes the life and times of the prophet Jeremiah. He finds Jeremiah to be a prophetic martyr and an exemplar of spiritual fortitude whose unwavering faith in God led him to challenge religious and political orthodoxy in his own time.

In "The Place of Reason and Experience in Finding God," another essay for his Christian theology class, King juxtaposes Karl Barth's theology with that of Edgar S. Brightman. Karl Barth was a noted Swiss theologian and author of *Epistle to the Romans* who argued that God was transcendent and supreme and was impossible to know through science, philosophy, intellect, or culture. Brightman, an American Methodist theologian, Borden Parker Bowne Professor of Philosophy at Boston University, and author of *The Finding of God*, disagreed with Barth and maintained that it was possible for an individual to know God through reason and their own personal religious experiences. King supported his position by consulting the ideas of Edwin Aubrey and Rufus Jones. Aubrey was a Baptist theologian, president of Crozer Theological Seminary from 1944 to 1949, and author of *Man's Search for Himself.* He also established the department of religious thought at the University of Pennsylvania. Aubrey rejected a blind faith in science or in the Bible and argued for a middle ground for Christianity between supernaturalism and rationalism wherein science and religion reinforced each other to improve humanity. Rufus Jones, a Quaker mystic and founder of the American Friends Service Committee (AFSC), believed that religion could not exist without science because the natural sciences made religion more easily understood and that every person possessed the light of God in their souls. After careful consideration, King concludes that anyone, from the "simplehearted believer to the philosophical intellectual giant may find God through religious experience" and that reason is a "supreme road" to God (Carson et al. 1992, 234, 236).

King's time at Crozer also introduced him to the teachings of Mahatma Gandhi, the nonviolent activist who inspired the Indian people to oppose British rule and gain their independence in 1947. In 1950, King attended an event at the Fellowship House in Philadelphia, where he heard Mordecai W. Johnson speak about his recent experiences in India. Johnson graduated from Morehouse College in 1911 and Harvard University Theological School in 1922. In 1928, he earned his doctor of divinity degree from Gammon Theological Seminary. In 1926, Johnson became president of Howard University in Washington, DC, a position he would hold for thirty-four years until his retirement in 1960. Under Johnson's leadership, Howard became the capstone of black higher education. He expanded its educational opportunities by upgrading Freedmen's Hospital, a critical training center for African American physicians, and established a law school that would train attorneys who would go on to challenge Jim Crow laws throughout the South—including Supreme Court Justice Thurgood Marshall. By 1950, when King met Johnson, he had become one of the most influential African American Christian ministers in the United States and had been part of a multiracial delegation of religious leaders who spent close to two months traveling around India and speaking with its citizens. During his travels, Johnson began to better understand the power of Gandhi's message of nonviolence and his influence among everyday Indians. More importantly, Johnson connected Gandhi's message to African Americans' struggle against racism and segregation. Johnson's newfound commitment to Gandhi's pacifism inspired King, who voraciously read and shared anything he could get about Gandhi and his nonviolent philosophy.

In fact, when discussing the ways God works in the world, in an assignment for his Christian Theology Today course, King argued that God's spirit works in individuals who use it to improve society. Gandhi was among those individuals he highlighted whose life and work "reveal the working of the Spirit of God." Other spirit-filled people were David Livingstone, the nineteenth-century Scottish physician and missionary; Albert Schweitzer, the Nobel laureate; and Jesus (Carson et al. 1992, 249). Gandhi's pacifism and the growing Cold War led King to begin to consider his own stances toward nonviolence. In an essay for his Christianity and Society course, King rejects absolute pacifism and moves toward a contingent or conditional pacifism. Absolute pacifism rejects violence and war in all forms, including self-defense. Contingent or conditional pacifism opposes war and predatory violence but also accepts the idea that war can be a necessity to prevent future violence and the unnecessary, wanton taking of human life. King does not embrace war and expresses a desire to see it disappear from the earth but rejects absolute pacifism because it "results in anarchy" (435). King connected intellectually with Gandhian ideas, but he would have to leave seminary and start his public ministry before he would truly understand its practical application to social struggle.

Throughout his career at Morehouse College, King had been a slightly above-average student. Less than five years later, when he graduated from Crozer with a bachelor of divinity, he was class president and valedictorian. Despite certain aloof and snobbish tendencies in his church-based fieldwork, King was respected by his classmates, and the faculty showered him with accolades. Charles Batten, the dean at Crozer, called him "brilliant" and a "real leader" (Carson et al. 1992, 406). Morton Scott Enslin, King's New Testament professor, referred to his student as being "conscientious, industrious, and with more than usual insight" who would "probably become a big strong man among his people" (Carson et al. 1992, 354, 382). He received the Pearl Ruth Plafker Award for being the "outstanding member of the graduating class" of 1951 and the J. Lewis Crozer Fellowship, an award that included a $1,200 scholarship for graduate school (441).

After graduation, King wanted to continue his education and pursue the doctor of philosophy in systematic theology with hopes of becoming a professor of religion. He applied to and was accepted at Edinburgh

University (Edinburgh, Scotland) and Boston University. He also applied to Yale University but was denied admission due, in part, to his poor performance on the Graduate Record Examination. In fall 1951, King was twenty-two years old with two bachelor's degrees, enthusiasm, what seemed to be unlimited potential, and a green Chevrolet that his parents purchased for him as a graduation gift from Crozer. He drove over one thousand miles from Atlanta, Georgia, to Boston, Massachusetts, to begin his graduate work at Boston University's School of Theology.

In the early 1950s, city life in Boston was completely different from the town culture of Upland, Pennsylvania, and outside of the classroom, King enjoyed all that Boston had to offer. Boston was small in comparison to New York City, its closest metropolis, and it suffered from the crippling injustices of racism and discrimination for black residents but not in the same ways that southern states did. King walked the streets of Boston and its environs without being concerned about moving aside when a white person passed or lowering his gaze to be unassuming as he would have done in Atlanta, Georgia. He attended parties and other social functions with his classmates, and while he may not have been the class president, he was a popular classmate and liked by almost everyone. His apartment became the meeting place for the Dialectical Society, a group of theological students who debated and analyzed important philosophical positions as they related to modern society. In an attempt to improve his preaching ability and connect with local black Bostonians, King attended and spoke regularly at Twelfth Baptist Church in Roxbury, the city's predominantly African American neighborhood.

Boston University provided King with opportunities to deepen and clarify his theological perspective by examining some of the most important philosophers and theologians of the Western world, especially Edgar S. Brightman, who taught at the school. His doctoral program required the successful completion of forty-eight hours of graduate level coursework, four qualifying exams, and a dissertation. For two academic years, from fall 1951 to spring 1953, King took nineteen graduate courses in systematic and historical theology, philosophy of religion, the Old and New Testaments, modern philosophy, recent philosophy, the history of philosophy, the philosophy of Plato, Christian Doctrine I and II, and the philosophy of Alfred North Whitehead. Sixteen of the courses were taken at Boston University, and three were completed at Harvard University, in nearby Cambridge. Of the sixteen courses taken at Boston University, eight were taken with L. Harold DeWolf, and two were taken with Edgar S. Brightman. The two professors would have a profound impact on King's intellectual development.

Brightman was a towering philosopher. He obtained his bachelor's and master's degrees from Brown University in 1906 and 1908, respectively.

In 1910, Brightman earned his bachelor of sacred theology from Boston University and a doctorate, under the tutelage of philosopher and Methodist theologian Borden Parker Bowne in 1912. When he died in 1953, he had published fourteen books, including the often-cited *Problem of God* (1930) and *Philosophy of Religion* (1940), authored over six hundred scholarly articles, and mastered several languages. DeWolf earned his bachelor's degree in 1924 and his bachelor of sacred theology in 1926 from Nebraska Wesleyan University. In 1935, with mentoring from Brightman, he earned his doctorate from Boston University, where he would teach ethics and systematic theology until 1965 and authored several books, including *The Religious Revolt against Reason* (1949). Both men were personalist in their theological perspective. Personalism or personal idealism is a liberal religious philosophy that posits that human persons are critical to understanding and experiencing God.

Throughout his coursework, King examined and compared personalism with other theologies to explain and understand the human/God relationship and clarify why evil exists in the world despite God's omnipotence and inherent goodness. In a fall 1951 term paper, he contrasted the philosophies of William Ernest Hocking, J. M. E. McTaggart, and Brightman. Hocking was an American philosopher and author of *The Meaning of God and Human Experience* (1912). McTaggart was an English philosopher and the author of *Some Dogmas of Religion* (1906). Perhaps not surprisingly, King agreed with Brightman on all major theological arguments. He found Brightman's philosophy of religion more compelling than Hocking's, and Brightman's notions of immortality more convincing than Hocking's and McTaggart's. On the issue of religious experience, King appreciated both Hocking's and Brightman's views that religious worship is a useful vehicle "to find the ultimate powerful reality to which man must adjust himself and by which he is judged" (Carson et al. 1994, 87). On the doctrine of God, King dismisses McTaggart's thesis as atheism and Hocking's notions as "antilogical" theism. Only Brightman's ideas of modified theism that sees the finite nature of God's power and the infinite power of God's goodness were suitable for understanding the relationship between humans and God. During spring 1952, in a paper for his systematic theology course with DeWolf, King revisited Karl Barth and, armed with his new enthusiasm for personalism, dismisses Barth's notions of a transcendent, unknowable God and argues for an "immanent" God who is ever present in the universe and whose "creative genius" sustains the world and humanity (Carson et al. 1994, 104).

DeWolf and Brightman challenged King. Besides Brightman and Hocking, DeWolf encouraged him to examine the theologies of other contemporary American theologians and philosophers, such as Reinhold Niebuhr, as well as contemporary European intellectuals, including Russian philosopher Nicholas Berdyaev, the French Catholic philosopher Jacques Maritain, and the Swedish Lutheran theologian Anders Nygren whose notions of Christian love in *Agape and Eros* would be constant themes in King's ministry. King also studied the ideas and contributions of German Protestant theologian Martin Luther and of John Calvin, the French Protestant reformer. Under DeWolf's guidance, King poured over the Christian Old Testament, especially Jeremiah, Amos, Isaiah, and Psalms, to gather lessons of what it meant to be human and commune with God. In Brightman's two-semester course on German idealist philosopher George Wilhelm Friedrich Hegel, King read Hegel's most influential works.

King was an excellent student and a gregarious classmate and found time to socialize outside of the classroom. In early 1952, he and Philip Lenud, a black student at Tufts University and Morehouse alumnus, moved into a spacious apartment in the Roxbury neighborhood of Boston, which became a popular social space for black students from surrounding colleges and universities. They continued hosting meetings of the Dialectical Society. King would also frequent some of the local nightspots, such as the Totem Pole Ballroom, a popular dance hall on Commonwealth Avenue in the nearby city of Newton, Massachusetts. Perhaps the Totem Pole was where King took his dates. According to his autobiography, he "had met quite a few girls" in Boston that he was not "particularly fond of," that is, until he met Coretta Scott (Carson 1998, 34).

The third child of Bernice McMurray and Obadiah Scott, Coretta Scott was born on April 27, 1927, in Heiberger, Alabama. As a child, when she was not attending the segregated elementary schools three miles from her home, she was working as a cotton picker or at other odd jobs to contribute to the family's income. Her father owned a chicken farm and hauled lumber independently, and after the family saved enough money, he purchased a sawmill and opened a grocery store. In 1939, Coretta Scott started at Lincoln High School, a school run by the American Missionary Association, in Marion, Alabama. Its interracial faculty created a rigorous curriculum of sciences and arts, including music. Scott took advantage of the music curriculum; she enrolled in music classes and took trumpet, piano, and voice lessons with Olive J. Williams. When she was not taking lessons, she was performing in the school choir and the Mount Tabor African Methodist Episcopal Zion Church youth choir, where she was a sought-after soloist.

After graduating valedictorian of her class in 1945, Scott attended Antioch College in Yellow Springs, Ohio, where she majored in music and elementary education. The college was founded in 1850, with Horace Mann, the nineteenth-century public education advocate and reformer, as its first president and was one of the first nonsectarian institutions of higher education to offer equal educational opportunities to women and

African Americans. Scott was a budding activist at Antioch and joined the school's NAACP chapter. In 1948, she traveled to Philadelphia and attended the Progressive Party national convention to support Henry A. Wallace's bid for the presidency. She graduated from Antioch with a bachelor of arts degree in the spring of 1951. The following fall, she was a student at the New England Conservatory in Boston, Massachusetts, with the hopes of being a concert singer.

King must have grown tired of the dating scene and meeting girls his friend H. Edward Whitaker called "one-time wreckers" (Carson et al. 1994, 159). In January 1952, he asked Mary Powell, a student from Atlanta studying in Boston, if she could introduce him to any of her friends. Powell gave him Scott's telephone number, and after an enchanting telephone conversation, Scott agreed to see King. During their first date, they shared a meal at Sharaf's Cafeteria, an eatery on Massachusetts Avenue, discussed their love of music and what it was like to be a student in Boston. King was immediately smitten by Scott, and through the winter and spring of 1952, they saw each other regularly to study together, dine, or take long car rides.

For a young twentysomething of good, black Atlanta pedigree, King had learned about the importance of marriage and social standing from his parents and church community. Both Scott and King saw in each other qualities that made them compatible. Scott visited Atlanta in August 1952 to meet the Kings formally. Initially, it seems that King's parents opposed their son's relationship with Scott. She was a Methodist, not a Baptist, and did not belong to one of the many affluent black families of Atlanta. In time, however, Daddy King and Alberta's opposition gave way to love and the hope that their son would start a family. King Jr. and Scott were engaged to be married in April 1953. On June 18, 1953, at the age of twenty-four and twenty-six, respectively, standing before God and Heiberger's black community, they married in her parents' garden. King Sr. performed the ceremony. The day after their wedding, the bride and groom were back in Atlanta to be received by the Ebenezer Church family at a wedding reception.

In late June, King's parents went on vacation and put him in charge of the church during their absence, so the newlyweds spent the remainder of the summer in Atlanta. Coretta Scott King worked at a local black-owned bank as a clerk while her husband fulfilled his many pastoral duties. Ebenezer kept King busy, and he delivered eleven sermons at Ebenezer and surrounding churches before they left to attend the National Baptist Convention in Miami, Florida, in early September. The trip was not a honeymoon, but it was as close to one as the couple would get. The two spent a week in Miami, the cultural center of southern Florida, attending meetings, seeing old friends, and getting ready to go back to Boston.

## CULTURAL CONNECTION: THE GREAT MIGRATION

From the turn of the twentieth century to 1960, millions of African Americans left towns and cities in the South for destinations on the West Coast, the Midwest, and the Northeast. Known as the Great Migration, the black internal migration changed local and state demographics, politics, and regional cultures nationwide. In a fifty-year period, from 1910 to 1960, the African American population increased by about nine million. In 1910, 90 percent of African Americans lived in the South. In 1960, only 60 percent did.

Both push and pull factors set migrants moving. Push factors are problems in the migrants' home location that make remaining there challenging, while pull factors are positive developments of a place people are migrating to that encourage them to move there. There were a variety of factors that pushed and pulled black migrants from the South, but they broadly fit into two categories: economic reasons and social reasons.

Black workers were mostly agricultural workers in the South at the beginning of the twentieth century, and many were sharecroppers. In the early 1900s, a boll weevil infestation decreased cotton productions, and an economic system that kept African Americans indebted to white landowners became an even less tenable way of making a living. Having no other viable employment opportunities available to them, African Americans left the homes of their birth for better economic opportunities in the North and Midwest. World War I and World War II created employment opportunities in midwestern and northern cities, pulling African Americans there as factories turned from making peacetime consumer goods to producing goods for American soldiers and allied forces. Jim Crow laws and lynching were social reasons that pushed African Americans out of the South. Between 1882 and 1961, 3,446 African Americans were killed by violent white mobs. During the Red Summer of 1919, whites initiated race riots and targeted blacks.

The North also had social pull factors for black migrants. Since slavery it was considered "the promised land." Segregation laws in cities and towns outside the South were not as extensive and in some cases a matter of custom, not law. As the Great Migration continued, cities such as Harlem, New York; Philadelphia, Pennsylvania; Chicago, Illinois; and Los Angeles, California had within them the best of both worlds for migrants. Southern migrants brought with them their foodways, music, and traditions and re-created home in a new place.

New cities and surroundings, however, failed to live up to migrants' and their children's expectations. Over time, poor local and state leadership, a nationwide divestment from urban areas, house discrimination, deindustrialization, and poverty changed black enclaves to black ghettos. The North had not lived up to its promise.

Upon their return to Boston, Scott King and King, moved into a comfortable apartment in Boston's South End neighborhood. She completed degree requirements at the conservatory. He spent the fall preparing for his qualifying exams and taking care of their new home. Qualifying examinations are a series of written tests created by a panel of advisers to prepare the candidate for scholarly research and help the student develop a depth and breadth of knowledge within and outside of their specialty. King was required to complete exams in four fields and chose theology of the Bible, history of doctrine, systematic theology, and history of philosophy.

He wrote his first exam on theology of the Bible in early November 1953 and was asked to discuss Christian hope as well as Old and New Testament perspectives on sin and evil. In late November, before the Thanksgiving recess, he took his second exam, this time on the history of doctrine, in which he discussed the ways Christian beliefs were interpreted and taught by philosophers and theologians from the second and third centuries to the mid-twentieth century. His answers synthesized a variety of perspectives including that of Paul of Samosta, an early Christian thinker from the third century; Augustine of Hippo, from the late fourth and early fifth centuries; medieval European Scholasticism; Protestant reformist John Calvin; Quaker George Fox; Karl Barth; and Reinhold Neibuhr. King took his qualifying exam in systematic theology in mid-December, a week before Christmas. Through a series of essays, he discussed and clarified his positions on the salient points of Christian theology: the proper understanding and role of religious scriptures, how to understand and explain God, sin and the nature of humanity, the importance of redemption, and the role of the church to the individual and society. King's exams were daunting and took months of concentrated study to master material that was at times obscure, but the budding scholar received high marks on all his exams.

He began preliminary research on his dissertation in fall 1953, and since he was not tied to Boston University, and Scott King was finished classes in early 1954 when he completed his qualifying exams, he began looking for pastor positions. Dexter Avenue Baptist Church in Montgomery, Alabama, and First Baptist Church of Chattanooga, Tennessee, had expressed interest in King assuming their pastorate as early as November 1953. He gave a trial sermon at First Baptist on January 17 and another one a week later at Dexter on January 24.

On January 24, 1954, he stood at the pulpit of Dexter Avenue Baptist in Montgomery, Alabama, a college town, and delivered "The Three Dimensions of a Complete Life," a sermon he would expand upon and deliver to a variety of audiences for over a decade. Using Revelations 21:16, King applies the writer's vision of God's new city to human personality. "And the city lieth foursquare, and the length is as large as the breadth. . . . The length and the breadth and the height of it are equal" (Revelations 21:16, King

James Version). The three dimensions of a complete life, according to King, are length, breadth, and height. Length referred to one's concern for their personal well-being. Breadth is a concern for other people. The height of life is the "upward reach for God" (Carson and Holloran 2000, 122). King enjoyed meeting the Dexter's congregation, and according to Roosevelt Crockett, one of Dexter's deacons in the audience that day, members of the congregation were "still praising [King's] name" weeks after the sermon (Carson et al. 1994, 240).

While he was waiting to hear from First Baptist and Dexter, King completed his fourth qualifying exam on February 24 on the history of philosophy and prepared for speaking engagements. He received an A– on the exam, which surveyed major problems in ancient Greek philosophy and the primary contributions of major European scholars, including British intellectual John Locke, Irish philosopher George Berkeley, German transcendental idealist Immanuel Kant, Scottish Enlightenment skeptic David Hume, German idealist Johann Gottlieb Fichte, and nineteenth-century German philosopher Arthur Schopenhauer. Several days later, he traveled to Lansing, Michigan, to speak at both the Union Baptist Church, where his paternal uncle Joel Lawrence King was pastor, and at the local chapter of the NAACP. He also delivered a sermon, "Rediscovering Lost Values," at Second Baptist Church in Detroit, which was broadcast on *Hour of Faith*, a radio program at WMPC, a local AM Christian station.

The sermon uses Luke 2: 41–52 as the scriptural text. When Jesus was twelve years old, his father and mother, Joseph and Mary, took him to Jerusalem to celebrate the feast of Passover. When the feast ended and the celebrations were over, they left Jerusalem to return to Nazareth. After traveling for a day or so, they realized they had forgotten Jesus in Jerusalem and had to return to get him. They go backward to find or "rediscover" Jesus, a "mighty precious value," so they can go forward to Nazareth (Carson et al. 1994, 251). For humanity to move forward and rid itself of injustice, corruption, hatred, and selfishness, King maintained, it must go back and reclaim two important values or principles that have been lost: "moral foundations" and "spiritual control" (Carson et al. 1994, 251, 253). By moral foundations, King meant that God was just and created a universe based on ethical laws that were not relative to the changing tides of political opinions or intellectual fashions. Spiritual control means that God is actively involved in the unfolding and expansion of the universe, including human lives. To reclaim the second value, humans must recognize the importance of God in their lives. "Rediscovering Lost Values," like "The Three Dimensions of a Complete Life," would be a staple sermon for King in the years to come.

First Baptist Church did not offer King the pastorate, fearing that the young minister lacked experience, and hired Rev. H. H. Battle, who would go on to lead the church for over forty years. Dexter's members, a large portion of whom were college educated, middle-class professionals and professors at Alabama State College, in Montgomery, were captivated by the young preacher's intellect and unanimously voted to offer him the pastorate with a $4,200 annual salary. Such a salary made him the highest-paid African American minister in all of Montgomery. He accepted the call to lead the church in mid-April but would not begin his position until September 1, 1954.

In the spring of 1954, King began to research his dissertation, negotiated the terms of employment at Dexter, learned more about the congregation he was about to lead, and preached at different congregations throughout the South, Northeast, and Midwest. On April 25, he preached at Vine Memorial Baptist Church in Philadelphia, Pennsylvania, at the request of Reverend Leonard Carr, who founded the church in 1933 during the Great Depression. Three weeks later, he was the guest minister at Union Baptist Church in Cambridge, Massachusetts, where he delivered a sermon titled "What Is Man?" At the end of May, he was back at Dexter Baptist Church, where he delivered "Loving Your Enemies" and ordained church deacons.

"What Is Man?" maintains that a person is "an animal with a material body" and "spiritual being" whose purpose is to have a relationship with God (Carson et al. 2007, 175, 178). In "Loving Your Enemies," King expands upon the idea of love mentioned in Matthew 5:43–45 (KJV): "Ye have heard that it hath been said, Thou shalt love thy neighbor, and hate thine enemy. But I say unto you, Love your enemies, bless them that curse you, do good to them that hate you, and pray for them which despitefully use you, and persecute you; That ye may be the children of your Father which is in heaven: for he maketh his sun to rise on the evil and on the good, and sendeth rain on the just and on the unjust." Hate, he argues, warps one's personality, and when one succumbs to it, one unwittingly allows it to strengthen throughout the universe. King provides a practical approach to help his listeners love their enemy. The first is to critically examine oneself to determine whether one's action had turned someone into an enemy, take personal responsibility for creating an enemy, and then change the personality trait that may be effrontery. In order to love your enemies, you must begin by analyzing yourself. The second approach is to "find the element of good" in one's enemy. The third approach is to resist the temptation to get the better of one's enemy if the opportunity presents itself. In the end, King declares that love "will save our world and our civilization, love even for enemies" (Carson and Holloran 2000, 42).

On June 13, King was in Harlem, New York, preaching at Friendship Baptist Church. Almost one month later, he was back at Dexter celebrating Men's Day with his new congregation. During his various engagements, he practiced his preaching skills, made political and religious connections, inspired his audiences, and became an up-and-coming minister in his ordaining body, the National Baptist Convention.

On September 1, 1954, at age twenty-five, King assumed the pastorate at Dexter and delivered his homily "Recommendations to the Dexter Avenue Baptist Church for the Fiscal Year 1954–1955." The sermon included thirty-four recommendations, among them, increasing the church's revenue, creating new religious education opportunities for adults and children, building a religious education, ensuring that every member of the congregation was a registered voter, and overhauling the institutional checks and balances to provide him more decision-making power, including church committee appointments, above and beyond the board of directors or the church deacons. It was a bold move for a young, new minister to ask for so much from the older congregants. For some, such drastic requests may have seemed like a coup. But the church wanted bold, new leadership, and on October 31, he was officially installed as the pastor of Dexter. His father gave the sermon, and his mother directed Atlanta's Ebenezer Baptist Church choir.

At twenty-five years old, King was a recently married man with a promising future as the pastor of a politically progressive black church in segregated Alabama, but he was also a doctoral student and had to write his dissertation to complete his degree. During the summer of 1954 and the early months of his pastorate, he pieced together time to write a dissertation, "A Comparison of the Conceptions of God in the Thinking of Paul Tillich and Henry Nelson Wieman."

Paul Tillich was a German-born philosopher and theologian who immigrated to the United States in the early 1930s. From 1933 to 1965, he taught at Union Theological Seminary in New York City, Harvard University, and the University of Chicago and wrote extensively in the field of systematic theology. He authored several important theological works that would influence King's development, including *Systematic Theology* in three volumes (1951–1963) and *The Courage to Be* (1952). Henry Nelson Wieman was a Harvard-educated, American-born philosopher and theologian who wrote about the nature of God and taught at Occidental College, the University of Chicago, the University of Oregon, and the University of West Virginia, for almost fifty years. He authored *Source of Human Good* (1946), "God Is More Than We Can Think," published in *Christendom* (1936), and "Values: Primary Data for Religious Inquiry," published in the *Journal of Religion* (1936).

Both Tillich and Wieman were influenced by contemporary developments in psychology and the social sciences and presented an idea of God as an impersonal force that permeates the universe yet stands outside of humanity. Wieman understood God as the source of human good.

Tillich's God "is not the kind of being who can be spoken of in the same terms as one of his creatures" (Thiselton 1974). According to King, Tillich's and Wieman's concepts of God were not useful methods to speak about or understand God. King countered both theologians with his own idea of a personal God, who can be related to and communicated with on a daily, moment-to-moment basis, who does not stand beyond the daily interactions of human and humanity but is inextricably involved with them. By forwarding the notion of an impersonal God, King believed Tillich and Wieman rejected the "rationality, goodness and love of God in the sense of the words" (Carson et al. 1994, 25). King's dissertation readers, DeWolfe and S. Paul Schilling, approved his dissertation, and after making the necessary corrections, he received his doctorate in June 1955.

Boston University faculty passed King and conferred his degree, but King's dissertation was not without its problems. Years after his death, it was discovered that he had plagiarized major portions of his dissertation. His dissertation took large portions from books and dissertations written by many authors, including Tillich and Wieman, without properly citing his sources. In most instances, he copied materials verbatim. It is unclear whether King knew what he was doing. He had sloppily and improperly footnoted his sources in many of his course papers at Crozer without penalty and was busy being pastor at Dexter Avenue Baptist Church in Montgomery, Alabama, when he was writing his dissertation. Perhaps he did not devote the necessary time and intellectual energy to the project. No matter what the reason—hubris, ignorance, or exhaustion—King's project was not an original work of scholarship.

Although he had a keen mind and was able to understand complicated theological positions, King was not called to be a scholar. History called King to be a leader in the black civil rights movement, and his upbringing, parentage, education, and new wife had prepared him and gave him space to do that.

# 2

## Becoming a Leader

In late fall of 1955, the preacher who had thought he would be a college professor of religion was pulled in a completely different direction. King was a sought-after speaker, a young pastor, and with the birth of Yolanda Denise King on November 17, he was also a new father. He had developed into a vibrant, popular preacher among black Baptists and became increasingly concerned with the plight of all Americans who had not, up to that point, benefited from the American dream. Unbeknownst to him, he would be soon thrust into the national spotlight.

On Thursday, December 1, Rosa Parks, a local, forty-two-year-old, black Montgomery resident was returning home from her seamstress job at the local Montgomery Fair Department store. Shortly after boarding the city bus, its white driver, J. P. Blake, told Parks to relinquish her seat to a white passenger and move to the back. Parks refused and was arrested for violating local and state codes requiring segregation on all public conveyances. At police headquarters, Parks was processed and jailed. She was later released on bail to E. D. Nixon. Nixon was a fifty-six-year-old, local activist. In the 1920s, he worked as a Pullman porter and became active in the Brotherhood of Sleeping Car Porters (BSCP), a black union organized by A. Philip Randolph, who inspired Nixon to become the leader of the Montgomery BSCP branch. During the 1940s, Nixon and other black activists formed the Alabama Voters League to increase the number of black registered voters. In 1944, he was elected president of the Montgomery chapter

### Cultural Connection: The Murder of Emmett Till, 1955

Emmett Till, the only child of Mamie and Louis Till, was born in Chicago on July 25, 1941. His father was conscripted into the U.S. Army and died in Europe in 1942, leaving him to be raised by his mother and extended family. According to those who remembered him, Till was a gregarious boy with an infectious smile who attended an integrated public school with a lot of friends from different racial and ethnic groups. When he was fourteen in August 1955, he and his sixteen-year-old cousin, Wheeler Parker, boarded a train bound for Money, Mississippi, to stay with their uncle Moses Wright and visit relatives.

Shortly after their arrival, Wright, Till, Parker, and several of Till's cousins went to the Bryant Grocery and Meat Market to buy groceries and sundries. While he was alone in the store, Till and Carolyn Bryant, the white twenty-one-year-old wife of store owner Roy Bryant, had an interaction. No one knows exactly what transpired between Till and Bryant. One story is that Till asked Bryant on a date. Another is that Till whistled at her to show that he found her attractive. A third story is that Till purchased his goods quietly, and then when his transaction with Carolyn Bryant was completed, he said "Bye, baby" as he walked out the door. According to an interview Bryant gave in 2007 at the age of seventy-two, Till said nothing to her, and if he did, she did not remember. While it may be impossible to come to a conclusion as to what happened between Bryant and Till, one fact is clear: Till was slain because of it.

When Roy Bryant returned home from a Texas business trip, Carolyn Bryant told him a story about her interaction with Till. Roy Bryant and J. W. Milam, his brother-in-law, drove to Moses Wright's home early Saturday morning, August 28, 1955, and kidnapped, beat, and murdered Till by shooting him in the head. To hide what they had done, they tied a piece of heavy farm equipment around Till's neck with barbed wire and dumped his lifeless body into the Tallahatchie River. Till's body was found several days later by a fisherman. His body was transported back to Chicago for an open-casket funeral and burial. Twenty-five thousand people viewed Till's body for four days and *Jet* magazine, an African American periodical, published images of Till's body.

Roy Bryant and J. W. Milam were arrested and charged with the abduction and murder of Emmett Till. Both were found not guilty by an all-white jury. Later, Bryant and Milam admitted that they killed Till in an article written by William Bradford Huie for the January 1956 issue of *Look* magazine. Because they had been tried and found not guilty, they could not be tried again.

Hundreds of thousands of people were moved by the images they saw in *Jet* and the subsequent reporting on the case in black newspapers and other magazines. Southern lynching and white antiblack violence were exposed, and black and white activists saw in Till's murder a call to action. His death was not in vain; instead, it was a watershed moment in the civil rights movement.

of the National Association for the Advancement of Colored People (NAACP) and two years later was elected NAACP state president. Nixon had worked with Parks in the BSCP and the NAACP and was convinced that he could use her act of civil disobedience to end segregation in public transportation.

Earlier that year, on March 2, Claudette Colvin, a teenager, loudly and vociferously refused to give her seat to a white passenger and was dragged off the bus kicking and screaming. Not only was she charged with violating segregation laws but she was also charged with assault and disorderly conduct. A group of clergymen, including Martin Luther King Jr., and activists formed a committee to bring attention to Colvin's case. The committee met with city and bus officials and asked for a humane form of segregation where drivers would treat black riders and white riders with more respect and where black riders entered the bus from the rear and whites entered the bus from the front. The plan was dismissed, and the old segregation laws continued to be enforced. At her trial on May 6, Colvin was only found guilty of assault and was forced to pay a small fine. The black Montgomery community was not prepared to support Colvin in the same way they would Rosa Parks. Colvin was an unwed, pregnant teenager prone to loud public tirades who had a father with substance abuse issues and an unstable home.

Rosa Parks, however, was a married church member, had worked on various political campaigns in Alabama, had attended Highlander Folk School in 1954 and 1955, and had connections with influential, white Montgomery residents. Nixon asked Parks and her family to consider appealing her case to challenge bus segregation. Such an appeal, they knew, might involve violent reprisals from local whites. After some debate, Parks agreed, saying to Nixon, "If you think it will mean something to Montgomery and do some good, I'll be happy to go along with it" (Branch 1998, 131).

In addition to appealing Parks's case, Nixon started planning a one-day boycott of the buses and immediately called Jo Ann Robinson. Robinson moved to Montgomery in 1949, when she accepted a job as an English professor at Alabama State College. That same year, Mary Fair Burks, the chairperson of Alabama State College's English department, organized the Women's Political Council (WPC), a black women's political organization that worked with and advocated for black Montgomery. Burks encouraged Robinson to join and serve as its president in 1950. In 1953, the WPC met with city officials and the city's bus line to complain about black mistreatment on the buses, but their concerns were dismissed, and Robinson began to consider what a bus boycott would look like. So when Nixon called her about his idea of a one-day bus boycott for Monday, December 5, to coincide with Rosa Parks's trial, she agreed to help. Robinson stayed up all

> ### CULTURAL CONNECTION: HIGHLANDER FOLK SCHOOL
>
> Highlander Folk School was a nontraditional school where its interracial student body could "learn how to challenge the traditional problems of the South" including "segregation, discrimination, racism, and ignorance" (Hughes 1985). It was founded in 1932 near Monteagle, Tennessee, by Myles Horton, a Tennessee native who studied at Cumberland College, Union Theological Seminary, and the University of Chicago. In 1931, he went to Denmark to learn strategies to assist those living in Tennessee's poor Appalachian region. In the 1950s, he was the school's director of workshops. Septima Clark was an activist and educator and became the school's director of education. Her years teaching African Americans in her home state of South Carolina and throughout the South earned her title "teacher to a movement."
>
> During the 1930s, Highlander's work primarily focused on the problems of unemployment and educational programming connected to the demands of labor unions. The 1954 U.S. Supreme Court *Brown v. Board of Education* decision led Highlander to focus its work on issues surrounding desegregation. Between 1953 and 1957, it conducted workshops for white and black educators and activists to help them develop leadership skills and strategies to help implement *Brown* during white southern resistance to the decision.
>
> From 1954 to 1961, Highlander trained African American and white college students to challenge racial discrimination and improve race relations in the South. In May 1960, it convened a conference to examine "The Place of the White Southerner in the Current Struggle." Over one hundred students from twenty colleges met at Highlander in November 1960 during the sit-in movement to discuss nonviolent tactics and strategies to break down segregation laws. Some of those students would later become founders of the Student Nonviolent Coordinating Committee (SNCC).
>
> During the same period, Septima Clark and Bernice Robinson created Citizenship Schools on the Sea Islands around Charleston, South Carolina, that focused on developing local black political leaders through adult literacy programs. The program was three months long and required adult participants to attend two nights per week for two hours per session. During the three months, students learned basic literacy, how to sign their names, and how to use the mail to register to vote. Through its programming and development of local community leaders, Highlander Folk School was integral in redefining the social justice agenda in many southern communities during the 1950s and 1960s.

night making copies and distributing leaflets to Montgomery's black residents throughout the weekend. The leaflet requested "every Negro to stay off the buses on Monday in protest of the arrest and trial. Don't ride the buses to work, to town, to school, or anywhere on Monday.... If you work take a cab or walk" (Robinson 1987, 46).

To make the boycott effective, Nixon needed the support of Montgomery's black religious leaders, including newly arrived Martin Luther King

Jr., especially since Dexter Avenue Baptist Church was centrally located and easier to get to for those working downtown who wanted to attend an evening mass meeting. When Nixon called King on Friday morning, December 2, to get his support for an emerging boycott, King was cautious and told Nixon that he would have to think about it. He was understandably trepidatious. Being new to the community and a first-time father, and having never participated in a massive opposition to segregation, he was unsure how the boycott would affect his career in Montgomery. By that evening, after considering his and Dexter's position and potential influence on the emerging campaign, King committed to the boycott and agreed to have a meeting of black leaders in his church.

Led by Rev. L. Roy Bennett, the president of the Montgomery Interdenominational Ministerial Alliance, roughly fifty black leaders attended the meeting in Dexter's basement until midnight, amending the WPC's leaflet, making copies, and sorting through the various details associated with a boycott. Pastors agreed to support the boycott and announce it from their pulpits on Sunday. All agreed to attend and conduct a mass meeting on Monday, December 5, at 7:00 p.m. at Holt Street Baptist Church.

On Saturday, leaflets continued to be distributed, and African American–owned media outlets announced boycott plans. As promised, black pastors informed their congregants of the boycott and the importance of their staying off the buses on Sunday. On Monday, December 5, the bus boycott appeared to be successful. Despite lost wages and fears of white reprisals, the vast majority of black Montgomerians stayed off the buses. That morning at her trial, standing before Judge John B. Scott, Rosa Parks pleaded not guilty but was convicted and fined. The fine was a small $14, but her attorney Fred D. Gray appealed her conviction to the state court of appeals. Gray was a twenty-five-year-old attorney and minister at the Holt Street Church of Christ. He was born in Montgomery, graduated from Alabama State College, and later earned his law degree from Case Western Reserve University in Cleveland, Ohio. For Gray, Parks's case was personal, as he had endured segregation and abuse on city buses. Again, she was released after Nixon posted her bond.

Almost 90 percent of the usual black riders refused to ride the bus that day. With the buses remaining empty throughout the morning and early afternoon, it was clear that blacks were motivated to make a change in their city. King and seventeen other black leaders met at Mount Zion Baptist Church that afternoon to determine next steps and what would happen at that evening's mass meeting. It was determined that a protest committee, the Montgomery Improvement Association (MIA), be formed to direct the citywide civil disobedience, create a list of demands, and negotiate with city officials. King was elected its chairperson. Rev. L. Roy Bennett, the pastor at Mount Zion African Methodist Episcopal (AME) Zion Church was elected to serve as its vice chairman. Rev. Uriah J. Fields, pastor of the Bell Street Baptist Church, was chosen to be recording secretary. Rev. Edgar Nathaniel French, pastor of the Hilliard Chapel AME Zion Church, was elected to be corresponding secretary. Mrs. Erna Dungee, the secretary of the WPC, was selected to be financial secretary. E. D. Nixon was voted treasurer. Before it adjourned its first meeting, the MIA declared that the boycott go on "until conditions are improved" and created an agenda for the upcoming mass meeting (Carson et al. 1994, 70).

King arrived home to Coretta and Yolanda tired and in a rush to prepare his speech to be delivered at the mass meeting that was to start at 7:00 p.m. Without sitting down for supper, King entered his study to jot down a few notes and pray. By the time he arrived at Holt Street Baptist Church, it was a little past seven. The church was filled, and the audience was energetic and euphoric from their successful boycott. Hundreds of people stood outside the church for several blocks waiting to hear speeches and the fate of the boycott over loudspeakers.

As the chairman of the MIA, King presided over the meeting and offered one of his first recorded public speeches. First, the audience sang "Onward Christian Soldiers" and "Leaning on the Everlasting Arms." "Onward Christian Soldier" is a nineteenth-century English hymn adapted by many African American denominations in the late nineteenth and early twentieth centuries. Its refrain is an encouraging call for action: "Onward, Christian soldiers, marching as to war, with the cross of Jesus going on before." For those singing it that night, it was a call for spiritual and moral warfare against southern racism and discrimination. But these antiracist warriors were not going into battle alone; they were going with God as "Leaning on the Everlasting Arms" suggests. Its last verse comforts the singers: "What have I to dread, what have I to fear, leaning on the everlasting arms? I have blessed peace with my Lord so near, leaning on the everlasting arms."

Next, Rev. William Frank Alford, the pastor of Beulah Baptist Church, delivered the opening prayer followed by a scripture reading, Psalm 34, by Rev. Uriah J. Fields, the interim pastor at Bell Street Baptist Church. Like the opening hymns, Psalm 34 was chosen carefully to encourage the crowd in its fight for justice. It reminds the reader that there is hope and power by depending on God. "I sought the LORD, and he heard me, and delivered me from all my fears. They looked unto him, and were lightened: and their faces were not ashamed. This poor man cried, and the LORD heard him, and saved him out of all his trouble" (Psalm 34: 4–6, King James Version).

King followed Fields and offered a thoughtful address that described the many abuses endured by black Montgomery bus riders and justified the protest on moral and political grounds. As Christians who advocated nonviolence as Jesus did, he noted that the only weapon they had "is the weapon of protest," and as American citizens, it was their "right to protest for right" (Carson et al. 1997, 72–73). He assured the protesters that their united efforts and hardships were not in vain and would eventually topple segregation on city buses.

When the crowd finished applauding King, Rev. French took to the pulpit to introduce the crowd to Rosa Parks and Fred Daniel, a local activist at Alabama State College. Rev. Ralph Abernathy, the pastor of First Baptist Church, read the MIA's resolution that reiterated the unfair treatment meted out to black bus riders and declared that the boycott would continue until the city bus company and an MIA delegation meet to "discuss their grievances and to work out a solution for the same" (Carson et al. 1997, 78). After the resolution was passed by those present, King politely dismissed himself, transferred his presiding duties to another minister present, and left Holt to deliver an address at the Montgomery Young Men's Christian Association's (YMCA's) father-son banquet.

Over the next several days, King and MIA board members met to clarify strategies and next steps. On the morning of December 8, they met with members of the Alabama Council on Human Relations (ACHR), a nonprofit advocacy group; James H. Bagley, the manager of Montgomery city buses; Jack Crenshaw, legal representative for the Montgomery City Lines; William A. "Tacky" Gayle, Montgomery's mayor; Frank Warren Parks, commissioner of public works; and Clyde Chapman Sellers, commissioner of public safety. King and his associates made three proposals similar to the ones made months before in the Claudette Colvin case. The first proposal called for better treatment by bus drivers. The second proposal called for seating black passengers from the back to the front of the bus and seating white passengers from the front of the bus with no seats reserved for blacks or whites. The third recommendation called for the hiring of black bus drivers in African American neighborhoods. After four hours, negotiations broke down without any agreement. Disappointed with the stalemate, King called Rev. Theodore Judson Jemison in Baton Rouge, Louisiana, seeking advice on how the MIA should proceed. Jemison was the pastor at Mount Zion Baptist Church in Baton Rouge and one of the primary organizers behind African Americans' eight-day bus boycott there in 1953. He suggested that King and his associates create a private carpool to transport black residents throughout the city. The MIA also sent a letter to National City Lines in Chicago, Illinois. Montgomery City Lines was a franchise of National City Lines, and King and MIA leaders hoped that the national office could influence its subsidiary. The Chicago office refused to force the Montgomery bus line to change its segregation policies, maintaining that racial segregation in Alabama was state law.

That night at the second mass meeting over which King presided, he proposed the idea of a carpool to those present. The idea was positively received, and by the end of the meeting, over 150 people had volunteered their automobiles to be included in the pool. After ministers informed their congregations of the carpool that Sunday, even more drivers enlisted their vehicles. In the interim, King and the MIA continued to negotiate with the bus line, using a technicality in the Montgomery City Code. The code, they admitted, required the segregation of races, but it did not require a black rider to vacate their seat for a white rider. Instead, it only required a black rider to vacate their seat if one was available in the black section of the bus. Having blacks seated from the rear to the front and whites seated from the front to the rear of the bus on a first come, first served basis, they reasoned, could be accommodated under the law. Further, they noted, since Alabama state law provided individual bus companies with a certain amount of discretion as to how they should enforce segregation codes, negotiations between the MIA and the bus line should continue in good faith without legal obstacles. The bus line and city officials rejected the MIA's argument, believing instead that their intransigence would break the boycott.

At the boycott's beginning, King was mulling over an academic position. Earlier in December, Milton Cornelius Ballenger, the dean at Shurtleff College, contacted King and offered him a position on the faculty. Shurtleff, which provided a liberal arts education, was Baptist in affiliation, coeducational, and, most importantly, located in Alton, Illinois, a town with a rich abolitionist tradition. In 1950, the college had seven hundred students. The offer was tempting. Martin could live the life of a professor, teaching students about the latest theological approaches, and Coretta could be the young wife of a professor. Undoubtedly, Yolanda would have an integrated education and not grow up with the daily insults of segregation. But after careful consideration, King decided not to leave Dexter or abandon the inchoate movement in Montgomery, because he recognized that the work he wanted to do there would "take a few more years to be completed" (Carson et al. 1997, 87). Shurtleff College closed its doors two years later in 1957, the same year that King founded the Southern Christian Leadership Conference.

Having received no concessions from the Montgomery Bus Lines, the boycott continued, and King and the MIA continued to garner public attention. On Christmas Day in 1955, the Methodist Ministerial Alliance, the Baptist Ministers' Alliance, the Interdenominational Ministerial Alliance, and the MIA, collectively called the Negro Ministers of Montgomery and Their Congregations, sponsored an advertisement in the *Sunday Advertiser* and the *Alabama Journal*. The half-page advertisement detailed the many abuses African Americans had experienced on the buses for years, including but not limited to arrests, physical abuse by bus drivers, and unfair and inconsistent seating practices. The ministers reiterated the three proposals given to the Montgomery Bus Lines and concluded that the only way to seek redress was to continue the nonviolent boycott of the buses. The advertisement served several purposes. It maintained transparency with the boycotters and demonstrated that even though there were no clear victories after twenty days of the movement, boycott leaders continued to work. It also strengthened alliances among the various African American religious leaders in the city.

King and French also sought to create alliances and build support outside of Montgomery. On December 27, two days after the advertisements were published, they wrote a letter to Rev. Archibald James Carey Jr., the pastor of Chicago's Quinn Chapel AME Church, asking him to convene a committee of Chicagoans supportive of the Montgomery cause to appear before the leaders of the National City Lines at their Chicago headquarters and speak on behalf of the MIA and boycotting blacks in Montgomery. The committee comprised Bishop William Jacob Walls, senior bishop of the AME Zion Church; Joseph Harrison Jackson, president of the National Baptist Convention; James William Eichelberger Jr., secretary of the Department of Christian Education for the AME Zion Church; Congressman William Dawson, from Illinois's first district; and Earl Burrus Dickerson, president of Supreme Liberty Life Insurance, one of the first African American insurance companies in Chicago. Individually and collectively, the members of the Chicago committee had a great deal of political and economic clout, but National City Lines was not ready to bargain.

The year 1956 began with little movement by Montgomery city officials. On January 9, King and MIA leaders met again with city commissioners to reiterate their position and address unfair treatment on buses. In a resolution presented by attorney Fred Gray, they urged the bus company and commissioners to accept their initial seating proposal but dropped their demand for the hiring of African American bus drivers. Once again, city fathers rejected their offer. This time however, to break the boycott, commissioners and bus company officials met with Rev. Benjamin F. Moseley, the pastor at First Presbyterian Church; Bishop D. C. Rice, pastor of the Oak Street Holiness Church; and Rev. William K. Kinds, pastor at Jackson Street Baptist Church on January 21. None of the three ministers was affiliated with the MIA. After the meeting, Commissioner Clyde Sellers released a statement to the press that an agreement over bus seating had been reached. King was tipped off about these developments by Carl T. Rowan, a black reporter at the *Minneapolis Tribune* who wrote about southern desegregation. King and the MIA immediately issued a press statement letting black Montgomerians know of Sellers's ploy and that the boycott had not ended.

Two days later, on January 23, Mayor Gayle announced that he would no longer hold meetings with black leaders about segregated seating on buses unless the MIA ended the protest. The Montgomery bus line was losing money. Bus fares had increased for the white riders who continued to use the buses, and with the MIA's carpool providing twenty thousand daily rides, an end to the boycott was nowhere in sight. Unable to persuade or trick blacks back to the buses, city fathers sought to force them back. Police harassed carpool drivers and handed out hundreds of traffic tickets for real or imagined violations. Jo Anne Robinson, a dedicated driver in the carpool, received close to twenty tickets in a two-month period. On January 26, King was stopped by an officer and charged with "operat[ing] an automobile upon the streets of the City of Montgomery, Alabama, at an excessive speed" in violation of chapter 18, section 52, of the Code of the City of Montgomery, Alabama (Carson et al. 1997, 106). He was accused of driving thirty miles per hour in a twenty-five-miles-per-hour zone and was arrested and taken to Montgomery City Jail. It would be the first time in his ministry that he was jailed. At the Montgomery City Jail, King was processed as a common criminal and was photographed and fingerprinted. Several hours after his incarceration, Rev. Abernathy posted his bail. Two days later, at his next court appearance, he would be fined $14.

At the same time that the city officials sought to force blacks back to the buses through police harassment, white Montgomery residents sought to scare them back. One day after his return home from jail, on January 27, King received threatening phone calls. "[W]e've taken all we want from you. Before next week you'll be sorry you ever came to Montgomery," the caller warned (Branch 1998, 162). On the evening of January 30, while he was speaking at a mass meeting at First Baptist Church and Coretta and Yolanda were at home, the King house was bombed. When King arrived home, he was met by a growing angry crowd, Mayor Gayle, and Commissioner Sellers. As Gayle and Sellers offered to hear their concerns, the crowd armed themselves and accused the two men of being complicit in creating the atmosphere for such a bombing to occur. The police, who were unable to disperse the crowd, feared a riot.

Knowing that his family was safe, King's concerns turned toward the crowd outside. Some in the crowd feared that Coretta had been hurt. Others were armed and tired of violence against blacks that appeared to be sanctioned by the police. They were not convinced of King's stance on nonviolent, peaceful protest and wanted to retaliate. King left the interior wreckage and emerged on the porch to address the crowd. With raised hands and as if addressing congregants at Dexter, he told them that he and his family were all right. When they wanted proof that Coretta was uninjured, she joined him on the porch. He urged them not to "do anything panicky." He reminded them of the importance of the protest and that God was with the boycott despite the anger and violence of whites. King's talk calmed the crowd, and Mayor Gayle and Commissioner Sellers promised a full investigation, police protection for the King family, and a reward of $500 for any information leading to the arrest of the culprit. The bombing had made King more steadfast in his resolve to lead the bus boycott, and when his parents and siblings arrived the next day and begged him to return to Atlanta, he refused.

In the weeks after the bombings, King continued his MIA duties and tended to his work as a pastor. At the February 2 MIA meeting, over which he presided, the group strategized ways to protect mass meetings and boycott leaders. Eventually, it was decided that church patrols were needed and that MIA headquarters should be moved to Rev. Abernathy's First Baptist Church. On February 6, King preached his sermon "It's Hard to Be a Christian," in which he used as his text the parable of the Good Samaritan. Found in Luke 10:25–37, Jesus tells the story of a man who was attacked and robbed on a road between Jerusalem and Jericho. Both a priest and a Levite walked past the man without helping, but the Samaritan bandaged the man, put the man on his donkey, delivered him to a nearby inn to recuperate, and paid for his lodging. The parable teaches us, he reminded his audience, that fighting against injustice "is the voluntary or deliberate choice of putting ourselves without reservation at the service of Christ" (Carson et al. 2007, 252).

He received well-wishes, emotional support, and prayers from friends and colleagues from all over the country. Frank Stanley, the editor of the *Louisville Defender* and president of Alpha Phi Alpha, King's fraternity, reached out to him and informed him that his fraternity brothers were proud of his work with the boycott. Milton Britton, a deacon at Twelfth Baptist Church in Roxbury, Massachusetts, reminded King to hold fast in his fight against segregation by pointing to Matthew 5: 44. "But I say unto you, Love your enemies, bless them that curse you, do good to them that hate you, and pray for them which despitefully use you, and persecute you" (KJV). A letter from Marcus Garvey Wood, the pastor of Wainwright Baptist Church, in Charles Town, West Virginia, likened King to a "prophet of this day and age." George W. Davis, a faculty member at Crozer Seminary and one of King's mentors, prayed "that the day of our equality before men as before God may not be far away" (Carson et al. 1997, 129, 131).

King spent the latter part of February traveling throughout the Midwest to complete several speaking engagements. On February 12, he spoke at Shiloh Baptist Church in the Englewood section of Chicago, one of the city's predominantly black neighborhoods. There he discussed the virtues of the boycott during a press conference. From Chicago, he went to Tennessee on a speaking tour of historically black colleges and universities. He delivered his sermon "What Is Man?" in Nashville on February 19, during Fisk University's Religious Emphasis Week. Named after Clinton B. Fisk, a Union general and assistant director of the Freedmen's Bureau in Tennessee, the private university was founded in 1865 and by the mid-twentieth century had been home to some of the nation's leading intellectuals, including the sociologist W. E. B. Du Bois, the antilynching activist Ida B. Wells, and the writer James Weldon Johnson. The next day he spoke at Meharry Medical College, the first medical school for African Americans in the South, about the "Three Dimensions of a Complete Life." King's Tennessee speaking tour ended on February 21 at Tennessee State University. Tennessee State University was founded as the Tennessee Agricultural and Industrial Normal School for Negroes in 1912 and went on to become Nashville's premier public historically black university. King delivered a sermon titled "Going Forward by Going Backward" and like many of his sermons, he had been working on "Going Forward by Going Backward" for some time. The arguments were quite similar to those made in "Rediscovering Lost Values," a homily he delivered at Dexter Avenue Baptist Church in 1954. King contends that mid-twentieth century Americans in their quest for material goods and wealth had forgotten and ignored God. "We must," he argues, "go back and find God" (Carson et al. 2007, 163).

Back in Montgomery, city officials were attempting to destroy the bus boycott by jailing its leaders. King, along with eighty-eight others, was indicted by an all-white jury for violating an antiquated and obscure antiboycott law from 1921. He returned to Montgomery on February 23 and turned himself into the authorities at the county jail. Blacks in Montgomery and the South had feared going to jail because they did not know if they would come out. E. D. Nixon and others had turned themselves in days before King's arrest, and their eventual release on bond-galvanized boycotters who saw courage in their actions.

It was around this time that King met Bayard Rustin, a committed pacifist who had worked with the Fellowship of Reconciliation (FOR) and the Congress of Racial Equality (CORE) in the early 1940s. FOR was founded by a group of pacifists, including Rev. A. J. Muste and social worker and Nobel laureate Jane Addams, in opposition to the United States entering World War I. Throughout the early twentieth century, the organization supported the union movement, resisted the internment of Japanese Americans during World War II, and sponsored the first freedom rides to challenge segregation in interstate travel. In 1957, they published *Martin Luther King and the Montgomery Story*, a ten-cent, sixteen-page comic book that retold the story of the Montgomery bus boycott. Many of CORE's black and white founders began their work with FOR and were pacifists inspired by Gandhi's nonviolent work in India. They created the Chicago-based civil rights organization in 1942 to challenge inequality throughout the nation with a special focus on desegregation. Several CORE members participated in the freedom rides in 1947.

Rustin's pacifist philosophy led him to serve a prison sentence in the mid-1940s for refusing to participate in World War II as a conscientious objector. He arrived in Montgomery just as the indictments for boycott leaders were given. It was Rustin who suggested that boycott leaders turn themselves in. Such a strategy, he argued, would change the narrative from one wherein leaders were hunted down by the police to one where leaders were crusading heroes who voluntarily faced up to an unjust system. For weeks, he was in the background of the boycott, raising funds to post bond for those arrested, teaching Gandhian techniques, and publicizing the movement to northern supporters. At the King's home, King, Coretta, and Rustin discussed Gandhi's approaches and how they would be useful to the boycott. Before leaving town, Rustin introduced King to Glenn Smiley. By the time King met him, Smiley had been a Methodist minister in the Southwest, a field worker for FOR, and an imprisoned conscientious objector. As an adviser, he helped the MIA strategize its nonviolent movement until the boycotts ended in December.

King's four-day trial began on March 19 before Judge Eugene Carter. The prosecuting attorney for the state was Circuit Solicitor William H. Thetford. King's defense counsel consisted of Fred D. Gray, Rosa Parks's attorney; Charles D. Langford, the MIA's attorney and Gray's associate; and NAACP lawyers Arthur D. Shores, Orzell Billingsley Jr., Peter Hall, and Robert L. Carter. Langford earned his law degree from Catholic University. He was admitted to the Alabama State Bar in 1953 and opened his own practice in Montgomery shortly thereafter. Shores had been practicing law for almost twenty years by the time he met King and was one of the first African American attorneys in Alabama to represent black clients in court. Billingsley earned his law degree from Howard University in 1950 and opened a law firm in Birmingham. Hall became known in Alabama for challenging the exclusion of African Americans from juries throughout the state. Carter had worked on several landmark desegregation cases, including the 1954 *Brown* case with Thurgood Marshall. King was being defended by some of the best legal minds the state of Alabama had to offer.

Thetford presented his case and called over two dozen witnesses during a two-day period to establish that King was the primary organizer and energy behind the Montgomery bus boycott. King's defense refuted Thetford's claims, but to no avail. On March 22, Judge Carter found King guilty and sentenced him to pay a $500 fine or serve 386 days in the Montgomery County Jail performing hard labor. King's team appealed the verdict to the Alabama Court of Appeals, and Carter suspended the sentence. Again, King was released but this time on a $1,000 bond. That night he delivered an address before thousands at a MIA mass meeting at Holt Street Baptist

Church where he reiterated the righteousness of their struggle even as they broke unjust laws and vowed to continue the boycott.

Throughout the spring of 1956, a chink in the armor of bus segregation appeared. The U.S. Supreme Court ruled that segregated seating on buses in Columbia, South Carolina, was unconstitutional in *Fleming v. South Carolina Electric and Gas Company* (1956). Seeing this as a case that applied to them, officials at Montgomery City Lines unveiled a plan to desegregate buses and their drivers to begin to allow passengers to sit where they wish. Incensed, Mayor Gayle and Commissioner Sellers appeared before circuit court Judge Walter B. Jones to halt the company from instituting a desegregation plan and threatened to arrest any driver who did not follow Montgomery's segregation statutes. Jones ruled that segregation laws were constitutional and halted the bus company's desegregation plan. Gayle and Seller's unwavering stance on bus segregation continued even after the U.S. District Court ruled that segregation on intrastate buses was illegal in *Browder v. Gayle* (1956). They appealed the decision to the U.S. Supreme Court and without a clear resolution, black Montgomerians continued to walk or carpool to work and around town until the court took up the case in the fall.

King also continued to speak out against segregation and to counter claims that black political protest in general and the boycott were disturbing peaceful race relations throughout the South. In a sermon delivered in Tuscaloosa, Alabama, titled "When Peace Becomes Obnoxious," he urged African Americans not to accept the status quo of race relations and to fight a "spiritual war" to bring about a "positive peace" that created a system of justice for everyone in the South. "If peace means a willingness to be exploited economically, dominated politically, humiliated and segregated," he declared, "we must revolt against this peace" (Carson et al. 2007, 259). In May, he was the principal speaker at a service sponsored by the Greater New York Committee for a National Day of Prayer and Thanksgiving at the Cathedral of St. John the Divine in New York City, the mother church of the Episcopal Diocese of New York.

He stood before an interracial and interdenominational crowd of close to twelve thousand, the largest he had appeared before to that point, and delivered his sermon "The Death of Evil upon the Seashore." The sermon uses Exodus 14:30 as its scriptural text. "Thus the Lord saved Israel that day out of the hand of the Egyptians; and Israel saw the Egyptians dead upon the seashore" (KJV). King was inspired by Phillips Brooks's sermon "The Egyptians Dead upon the Seashore." Brooks was a nineteenth-century Episcopalian minister, bishop of Boston, and an impassioned preacher. King used biblical and contemporary political developments to link the African American freedom struggle with the ancient Israelites' captivity in and flight from Egypt. Egypt of the Old Testament, he noted, was representative of evils in the world during the mid-twentieth century, including racism, colonialism, and political and economic domination. He contended that evil would never prevail and evildoers would never prosper, because God has a plan for the world. God "is seeking at every moment . . . to lift men from the bondage of some evil Egypt, carrying them . . . to the promised land of personal and social integration" (Carson et al. 1997, 262).

During June 1956, Martin and Coretta King and Ralph and Juanita Abernathy took a much-needed three-week vacation. They drove over two thousand miles throughout the South and Southwest visiting towns on the Mexican-American border until they arrived in California. When they arrived on the West Coast, they first stopped in Los Angeles, where King preached at Second Baptist Church, the oldest and largest African American Baptist church in Los Angeles, at the invitation of Rev. Dr. J. Raymond Henderson, the pastor and friend of King Sr. He returned to Montgomery briefly during his vacation to take care of MIA business but quickly returned to the sunny California climate. The Abernathys and Kings ambled northward to the San Francisco Bay Area to the NAACP annual meeting.

On June 27, NAACP delegates from around the country gathered in a public session at the San Francisco Civic Auditorium. King shared the podium with A. Philip Randolph and Rosa Parks to discuss the origins, tactics, and larger meaning of the Montgomery bus boycott. He asserted that the boycott was a nonviolent political act by southern African Americans who had an unrelenting desire for equal rights. Only by working together in a nonviolent way, could the "cancer" of segregation "be removed [so] our democratic health can be realized" (Carson et al. 1997, 308).

By now, King's activism had gained him national attention and accolades. In May, he visited the University of California, Berkeley, where he was recognized for his work at the local YMCA. Since 1892, the Stiles Hall University YMCA had been committed to social justice and progressive causes. Honoring King's work in Alabama was one of the ways that it connected its local social service work with the burgeoning national civil rights movement. The Unitarian Fellowship for Social Justice awarded King the Holmes-Weatherly Prize. The award was established in 1951 in honor of Rev. John Haynes Holmes and Rev. Arthur Weatherly. It recognizes an individual or organization "whose life-long commitment to faith-based social justice is reflected in societal transformation," reflecting the commitment of the award's founders (https://www.uua.org). Holmes was a Unitarian minister, pacifist, and cofounder of the NAACP and the American Civil Liberties Union. Weatherly was also a Unitarian minister, served as president of the Lincoln Maternal Health Association, and worked in the suffrage movement. In Nashville, at Fisk University's eighty-second commencement on May 28, King received the University's first Distinguished Service Award.

Throughout the summer, the awards kept coming. In July, the Detroit-based Diggs Enterprises presented King with the Honorable Merit Award at the Panorama of Progress, a celebration of African American social and political progress, which took place at the Michigan State Fair Grounds. King's work in Montgomery prevented him from attending the event, and he missed appearances by jazz trumpeter Dizzy Gillespie, composer and pianist Duke Ellington, pianist Phillipa Schuyler, and one of his favorite gospel singers, Mahalia Jackson. He was able to attend a July 3 event in Birmingham, Alabama, sponsored by the National Fraternity Council of Churches, U.S.A., Inc., where he was awarded Distinguished Christian Service recognition. Alpha Phi Alpha presented him with the Award of Honor at a Buffalo, New York, meeting. King was back in Los Angeles in late August, where he spoke to the Improved Benevolent Protective Order of Elks, an African American fraternal order, and received an award named for Elijah P. Lovejoy, the nineteenth-century abolitionist and journalist.

After his vacation, King spent the remainder of the summer and early autumn crisscrossing the country and speaking to predominantly white liberal religious communities, black Baptists, and civil rights groups to gain and maintain support for the movement. H. Edward Whitaker, his friend and colleague from Crozer Seminary, had invited King to speak at New Hope Baptist Church several times. After graduating from Crozer in 1951, Whitaker and his wife moved to Niagara Falls to be the found the pastorate of New Hope and build a sanctuary there. During the winter of 1956, King accepted his invitation to speak at the congregation's annual Men's Day, and on July 22, he stood in the brand-new church before a large and enthusiastic audience. He had graced the cover of *Jet* magazine with Coretta in April and been dubbed "Alabama's Modern Moses" by the magazine, so blacks and whites in the Cataract City and its environs wanted to get a glimpse of a celebrity. The crowd was not disappointed. King, with his usual rhetorical flourish, reminded them that God was on the side of those who struggle for freedom. His appearance in Niagara Falls was remembered decades later.

King and boycott organizers knew that support of white religious liberals was crucial to changing race relations in the South and furthering the cause and blacks' demands for civil rights. They also knew that he, with his oratorical skills, was the ideal person to convince whites to support the Montgomery cause morally and economically. On July 23 and October 16, he spoke to two predominantly white religious bodies, the American Baptist Home Missions Societies (ABHMS) Conference in Green

Lake, Wisconsin, and the New York State Convention of Universalists, in Cortland, New York, respectively. The ABHMS was organized in 1824 and throughout the early nineteenth century opposed slavery. After the Civil War, it supported historically black colleges well into the twentieth century. The New York State Convention of Universalists was established in 1825 and up to 1961 was the primary organizational authority over Universalist congregations in the state. Tracing their roots to early New England Protestants, Universalists called for a separation of church and state in the eighteenth century, opposed slavery and championed women's rights in the nineteenth century, and opposed segregation in the early twentieth century. In the early 1960s, they joined with Unitarians to create the Unitarian Universalist Association. King delivered the same address to both groups, "Non-Aggression Procedures to Interracial Harmony," to advocate for nonviolent resistance because it was "nonaggressive physically" but "aggressive spiritually. It is passive physically, but it is active mentally and spiritually" (Carson et al. 1997, 325).

In September, the boycott entered its ninth month. No one had expected it to last so long. Boycotters were tired but steadfast in their protest, as was the leadership. To aid bus riders, the MIA had purchased a fleet of station wagons to replace cars that had been removed from the carpool. The bus company was losing money, cutting service, and laying off workers. While they appealed the federal court decision to the U.S. Supreme Court, Mayor Gayle and Commissioner Sellers tried one last legal maneuver to halt the boycott without desegregating the buses. In November, the eleventh month of the boycott, they appeared before Judge Eugene Carter of the Montgomery Circuit Court seeking an order to force the MIA to stop its carpool, arguing that the carpool was a violation of the Montgomery City Lines' license. To counter this move, MIA leaders appeared before the U.S. district court to block any order that Judge Carter could produce, but they were refused. On November 13, King and MIA leaders appeared before Judge Carter, who issued an injunction banning the MIA carpool. It was a foregone conclusion for King. Carter was a staunch segregationist, and the day's proceedings were largely a show to give the illusion of fair play and justice.

Miraculously, and quite by coincidence, the U.S. Supreme Court issued its ruling on November 13 and declared intrastate bus segregation to be unconstitutional, thereby upholding the *Browder v. Gayle* decision by the lower court. It took over a month for the Court's desegregation mandate to take effect, and during that time, black Montgomerians celebrated their victory over racism and discrimination. The carpool was dissolved, but they stayed off the buses. On the evening of November 14, one day after the decision, King presided over two mass meetings, one at Hutchinson Street Baptist Church and the other at Holt Street Baptist Church, wherein boycotters decided to end their protest when the court decision was received. Over a year after the boycott began, on December 21, 1956, the Montgomery City Lines resumed its service on a nonsegregated basis. The boycott proved that nonviolent protest could break down segregation and that African Americans did not have to resort to violence to effect change. For King, the boycott catapulted him into the national civil rights struggle.

# 3

## Challenging the Nation

King's leadership in the Montgomery boycott made him a nationally known leader. He sought to use the momentum of the boycott to challenge racism and segregation throughout the South and opened 1957 at an Emancipation Proclamation celebration sponsored by the National Association for the Advancement of Colored People (NAACP) in Atlanta, Georgia, at Big Bethel AME Church. The event commemorated the day Abraham Lincoln made a presidential proclamation and executive order to free African American slaves in the rebellious Confederate states in 1863. There he delivered "Facing the Challenge of a New Age" to an engaged audience who were glad that their native son had returned. As per his other sermons, King drew from many sources to demonstrate his point. Quoting the Baptist minister and teacher Benjamin Mays; the poets William Cowper, Isaac Watts, John Donne, Douglass Malloch, and James Russell Lowell; novelist and poet James Gilbert Holland; comedian Bob Hope; the transcendentalist Ralph Waldo Emerson; the English historian Arnold Toynbee; William Shakespeare; Scottish philosopher Thomas Carlyle; and passages from the Old and New Testament, King argued that God was ushering in a new era, a "new order" as he termed it, of racial justice all over the world, including the United States.

God's new order required something of all those who benefited from it, whites and blacks. The first was to pressure President Eisenhower's administration to enforce civil rights statutes that were being ignored and flouted by local and state governments throughout the South. The second was to register to vote. Through voting, King declared, African Americans could obtain and exercise political power. The third action necessary to bring about God's new order was to use the growing economic power of the national African American community to support civil rights organizations. King urged the crowd to reach into their pockets and bank accounts and "give big money for the cause of freedom." Lastly, to help God, African Americans and whites must create and support "courageous, intelligent, and dedicated leadership" (Carson et al. 2000, 85–86).

While buses had been integrated throughout cities and towns, hate crimes continued and were on the rise throughout southern municipalities. In Montgomery alone since the integration of buses, the Kings' home had been shot at, Rev. Ralph Abernathy's church, First Baptist, was bombed, and cross burnings were reported throughout the city. In Birmingham, Rev. Fred Shuttlesworth's Bethel Baptist Church parsonage was dynamited. To show strength amid violence and expand the civil rights movement, the Montgomery Improvement Association (MIA) called for a Southern Negro Leaders Conference on Transportation and Nonviolent Integration.

King was elected chairman of the conference, held at Ebenezer Baptist Church in Atlanta, Georgia, on January 10 and January 11, 1957. Conferees largely grappled with several ideas presented by Bayard Rustin regarding how the movement should proceed organizationally and tactically to challenge racism in all its forms throughout the South. After two days of enthusiastic debate about the future of the movement, participants held a press conference, sent telegrams to President Eisenhower and Vice President Nixon, and released "A Statement to the South and the Nation."

In the telegram to Eisenhower, signed by King, Rev. C. K. Steele, president of the Inter-Civic Council, Rev. Shuttlesworth, and Rev. Theodore Jemison, the ministers asked the president to broadly use his office and moral authority to help end racial violence in the South and protect the constitutional rights of black southerners. More specifically, they asked him to journey to a "major southern city" and "make a major speech" to encourage southern leaders to abide by recent Supreme Court decisions (Carson et al. 2000, 100). The ministers called on Nixon to visit the South and perform a fact-finding trip like the one he had done for the Hungarian people in late 1956, during which he concluded that Hungarian refugees needed federal aid. Such a trip to the South, they concluded, would allow Nixon to propose an effective federal plan to deal with domestic racial oppression. Their "Statement to the South and the Nation" reviewed their telegrams to the executive branch, reminded the nation of their commitment to social change through nonviolence, and called on African

Americans throughout the South to reject segregation and injustice in all its forms.

By early 1957, the Eisenhower administration had a spotted record on civil rights. Eisenhower appointed Earl Warren to be the fourteenth chief justice of the U.S. Supreme Court in 1953. Under Warren's leadership, the court struck down segregation laws throughout the South and ushered in a new era of race relations with the 1954 *Brown* decision. Eisenhower also used his authority to desegregate the federal government and the military. However, despite black discontent with segregation and southern states refusal to implement *Brown*, Eisenhower hesitated to offer a legislative path to end segregation in the South believing that "we [could not] cure all the evils in men's hearts by law" (Hitchcock 2018, 215). A. Philip Randolph wrote to Eisenhower in May and December 1956 requesting a meeting with the president to discuss civil rights. The administration's excuse was that time and previous engagements prevented such a meeting from happening. Randolph renewed his efforts to convene a conference with the president in 1957 but this time with a committee of African American leaders, and he wanted King to participate. In a January 4 letter, Randolph asked King if he was "disposed to join with such a committee" (Carson et al. 2000, 92). King agreed.

The Southern Negro Leaders Conference group met again on February 14 at New Zion Baptist Church in New Orleans, Louisiana. Led by Rev. Abraham L. Davis Jr., the church was the center of political action in the Crescent City. Participants agreed to change the name of the organization to the Southern Leaders Conference (SLC) and elected King as its president. Later, at their August convention, they would agree to call the organization the Southern Christian Leadership Conference (SCLC).

Eisenhower continually refused to publicly denounce racial violence from a southern podium, so the ministers sent him another telegram asking him to reconsider his position and to convene a White House conference on the maintenance of law and order (Carson et al. 2000, 133). If Eisenhower was not moved to act, the telegram promised, they would lead a Pilgrimage of Prayer to Washington, DC, to show the nation the extent of violence and terror meted out to blacks in the South by white legal and extralegal authorities. The group also sent another telegram to Vice President Nixon lamenting his refusal or inability to respond to their January 11 telegram and, again, asked him to journey south and complete a fact-finding mission about African Americans there. King would not meet with Eisenhower until June 1958, and even then, Eisenhower made no promises to use his authority to enforce the *Brown* decision.

King received many words of congratulations and accolades during the early months of 1957. *Jet* magazine awarded him the Man of the Year award

> **CULTURAL CONNECTION: *JET* MAGAZINE**
>
> *Jet* first appeared on November 1, 1951, at a cost of 15 cents. The magazine served as a black version of the largely white *Quick*, a small publication founded in 1949 by Gardner Cowles, the creator of *Look* magazine. *Jet*, like its white counterpart, was approximately four inches by six inches and featured brief encapsulations of the pertinent news of the day. In 1970, its dimensions broadened to approximately five inches by eight inches. According to John H. Johnson, its creator, *Jet* was designed to summarize the week's news about African Americans.
>
> Johnson created *Jet* in Chicago, Illinois, the third publication of his Johnson Publishing Company (after the *Negro Digest* and *Ebony*). The magazine's scope was broad and its news coverage brief and readable, allowing it to give a sweeping portrait of the state of the national African American community. The magazine's reputation only grew with *Jet*'s coverage of the events of 1955. In the September 15, 1955, issue of *Jet*, pictures of Emmett Till's corpse appeared. The issue sold out. Johnson Publication Company reporters covered the resulting trial of Till's accused murderers, and *Jet*'s photos and subsequent coverage alerted the African American public and the national news media of the poor state of race relations in the South. As the civil rights movements grew, *Jet* maintained its coverage, offering descriptions of the Montgomery bus boycott and resulting civil rights activism without editorial comment.
>
> Source: Thomas Aiello, "Jet Magazine," in Leslie Alexander and Walter Rucker, ed., *Encyclopedia of African American History*, vol. 3 (Santa Barbara, CA: ABC-CLIO, 2010), 827–828.

and *Time*, the American weekly news magazine, featured him on the cover of their February 18, 1957, issue. These awards, however, palled in comparison to an invitation he received from Kwame Nkrumah to celebrate Ghana's independence from March 2 to March 10, 1957. Nkrumah was an activist and intellectual who earned his bachelor's degree in economics from Lincoln University, a historically black college in Pennsylvania, in 1939. After he completed his master's degree in education at the University of Pennsylvania in 1942, he studied at the London School of Economics. In London, he became active in the West African Student Union (WASU) and began his work to end European colonialism in Africa. Upon his return to the British-ruled Gold Coast Colony, he became the general secretary of the United Gold Coast Convention (UGCC) and created a mass movement throughout the colony opposing colonialism. Nkrumah formed the Convention People's Party in 1949 and called for immediate self-government for the colony when the UGCC split. After years of working with Sir Charles Arden Clarke, the British governor of the Gold Coast,

Nkrumah brokered a deal that brought about African self-government with him serving as prime minister. In that role, Nkrumah continued to push for the creation of an independent republic. On March 6, 1957, the world witnessed the transfer of power from England to the newly formed nation of Ghana, sub-Saharan Africa's first independent nation.

In a January 22, 1957, letter, Nkrumah invited King to attend the historic event. His government could not provide for King's transportation but would provide lodging. To support King and provide him a much-needed respite from his ministry and activism, the Dexter congregation and the MIA raised $2,500 to subsidize his and Coretta's transportation. They departed Atlanta for New York on March 2, where they met other members of the African American delegation, among them, Adam Clayton Powell Jr., the fiery and controversial congressman and preacher from Harlem; elder statesmen Randolph; Ralph Bunche, the diplomat and political scientist; and Mordecai Johnson, the educator and president of Howard University. After making stops in Lisbon, Portugal; Dakar, Senegal; and Monrovia, Liberia, they landed in Accra, Ghana, the nation's capital. In Accra, the Kings participated in jubilant celebrations, attended receptions, luncheoned with Nkrumah and key Ghanaian officials, and briefly spoke with Vice President Richard Nixon, who led an American delegation in Accra. In fact, Nixon invited King to the White House to discuss the civil rights struggle in the South. Ghana's flag was officially raised at midnight on March 6 and was witnessed by hundreds of thousands of Ghanaians while King witnessed a nation being born. The Kings remained in Accra until March 12 and then set off to visit Rome, Geneva, Paris, and London, where they visited tourist sites and met with activists and intellectuals, including the Trinidadian-born historian, C. L. R. James, Barbadian writer George Lamming, and David Pitt, the Grenadian-born British Labor Party politician.

When King returned to Montgomery on March 27, he was so moved by what he had witnessed in Ghana that he shared his experiences to anyone who would listen at a MIA mass meeting on April 1 and at Dexter on April 17. He reflected upon his trip in a sermon entitled "The Birth of a Nation." He provides a brief history of the Gold Coast and draws parallels between the ancient Israelites in the biblical story of Exodus. Led by Moses, they fled slavery and oppression in Egypt, wandered in the wilderness, and then moved to Canaan. Similarly, the Ghanaian people led by Kwame Nkrumah fled British oppression and exploitation and would have to find their way into a new political wilderness of uncertainty before they could stabilize and become a strong, vibrant nation: their Canaan. Ghana's struggle for independence, King reminds his audience, offers a clear example that freedom can be won through nonviolent struggle and provides evidence that "the forces of the universe are on the side of justice" (Carson et al. 2000, 164).

Throughout April and May, King and the SLC worked to make good on their promise to hold a Prayer Pilgrimage in Washington, DC, on May 17. King wanted the event to protest Eisenhower's silence on the issue of school desegregation and his unwillingness to enforce the 1954 *Brown v. Board of Education* decision. Fearing that the Pilgrimage would put the president in a precarious situation, domestically and internationally, the Eisenhower administration worked to change the tone of the event at an April 5 planning meeting in Washington, DC. There Eisenhower's aides, along with the NAACP organizers, Congressman Adam Clayton Powell, and other black leaders successfully changed the purpose of the event from a protest to an anniversary observance of the landmark decision. King was disappointed with the shift in approach, but after the meeting, he, Roy Wilkins, and Randolph issued a joint statement. The brief statement is a political and religious appeal that details the systemic racism that African Americans endured over decades since *Plessy v. Ferguson* (1896) that allowed for "separate but equal," racially based public accommodations. It also explained how, despite the Court's 1954 *Brown* decision, eight southern states openly defied the ruling, refused to create and implement desegregation policies, and openly tried to ban the NAACP from their states. On the federal level, the three note, civil rights legislation had been slow to appear, and when it did, it proved to be limited in scope and lacked methods of enforcement. The statement ended with an appeal and invitation to all Americans who loved their nation to participate in the Pilgrimage.

During the weeks leading up to the Pilgrimage, King publicized the event. He appealed to his congregation, the MIA, and the Montgomery community with hopes of organizing and sending a sizable contingent to attend the Pilgrimage. In early May, he wrote to Frank J. Gregory, president of the Shirt Workers Union, Local 490, and asked for a monetary contribution to help with organizing costs and assistance in forming a Montgomery "delegation of five hundred to a thousand persons" (Carson et al. 2000, 198). On May 3, King promoted the pilgrimage at Abyssinian Baptist Church, Powell's congregation. The church had deep roots in New York City. Sixteen African Americans refused to accept segregation in the predominantly white First Baptist Church in 1808 and, with the aid of Rev. Thomas Paul, formed Abyssinian Baptist Church on the Lower East Side of Manhattan. The church moved to midtown Manhattan in 1902, and eighteen years later, during the height of the Great Migration, Abyssinian moved to the heart of Harlem, at 138th Street between Lenox and Seventh Avenues. When King addressed the audience, the church had a membership of close to ten thousand. To involve members of different faiths, King appeared before congregants at the Stephen Wise Free Synagogue and spoke about "The Future of Integration." Stephen Wise was a founding member of the NAACP and established the Free Synagogue in 1907 to be a socially and politically progressive Jewish voice in New York City. "The Future of Integration" was a talk that King often delivered to predominantly white and integrated audiences. With an eye toward contemporary psychology and its concerns with social maladjustments, King says that he is maladjusted to a society wherein discrimination, racism, violence, militarism, and economic inequality are the norm and calls on his listeners to be maladjusted as well, as the prophet Amos and Jesus were. He ended his visit to New York City speaking to a supportive crowd at the Hotel Theresa, a premier lodging uptown that also doubled as political organizing space for progressive causes.

Approximately twenty-five thousand people attended the three-hour May 17 Prayer Pilgrimage for Freedom at the Lincoln Memorial in Washington, DC, and heard addresses from Howard University president Mordecai Johnson, Adam Clayton Powell, Roy Wilkins of the NAACP, and others. The gospel great Mahalia Jackson recited biblical scripture and graced the audience with a song. King was the closing speaker at the rally, and his message was emphatic: the president and Congress must ensure the voting rights of African Americans. "Give us the ballot," he demanded, and African Americans would be able to use their voting power to transform race relations in the South. With the ballot, black people would be able to elect officials to local, state, and national offices that would enforce the Supreme Court's decision. African Americans would also be able to "place judges on the benches of the South who will do justly and love mercy." His "Give Us the Ballot" speech was also critical of national leadership and maintained that Democrats and Republicans "betrayed the cause of justice" (Carson et al. 2000, 210–211). He ended his speech with words of encouragement to the audience and called for them to keep fighting nonviolently for freedom and justice. The Prayer Pilgrimage did not attract the fifty thousand attendees that the organizers wanted; however, it was successful in keeping the issue of African American civil rights in the media and therefore an issue that President Eisenhower would have to address.

With the Pilgrimage behind him, King spent the spring and summer of 1957 attending commencement ceremonies, consulting with political leaders, and speaking to civil rights and religious groups. During commencement season, he attended exercises at Morehouse College, where he received an honorary doctor of humane letters, and Kentucky State University in Frankfort, Kentucky. Chicago Theological Seminary, a liberal seminary with faculty committed to and active in the civil rights movement, was the first seminary to give King an honorary doctor of divinity. Howard University in Washington, DC, awarded King an honorary doctor of laws at its commencement. In his quiet moments alone, he was mulling over the idea of accepting a job as dean of Howard University's school of religion, an invitation extended by Howard's president Johnson. After much thought and prayer, however, King decided to decline Johnson's generous offer because his work in the South was not finished.

On June 13, he and Ralph Abernathy met with Nixon and labor secretary James P. Mitchell for two hours to discuss racial violence throughout the South and the need for federal intervention there. At the meeting, King suggested that Nixon visit cities throughout the South to show that the Eisenhower administration was committed to African American civil rights, that Nixon publicly and unequivocally press southern leaders to stop suppressing the black vote and assemble Republican congressmen and senators to urge them to support federal civil rights legislation. Nixon was reluctant to commit to any of King's suggestions but agreed in principle that more needed to be done to protect African Americans. In a June 15, 1957, letter Nixon wrote to King, he remarked that he had enjoyed meeting with him and provided King with several speeches wherein he had spoken favorably about African American civil rights.

Two weeks later, on June 28, King was in Detroit, Michigan, accepting the forty-second Spingarn Medal at the NAACP's annual convention. Since 1914, the Spingarn Award has been given annually through generous contributions and a later bequest by Joel E. Spingarn, an early chairman of the board of directors at the NAACP, "for the highest or noblest achievement by an American Negro during the preceding year or years" (naacp.org/find-resources/scholarships-awards-internships/awards). When he stood on the podium to accept the award from Richard Emrich, Protestant Episcopal bishop of Michigan, King did so on behalf of his family and the tens of thousands of women and men in Montgomery, Alabama—the "salt of the earth," he called them. They, unlike him, would not be remembered for their contributions to Alabama's history or to the movement for racial justice in the nation despite boycotting the city buses for over a year, sometimes at the cost of their livelihood and personal safety. As he continued his speech, he argued that with regard to race relations, the United States had been through at least three unique periods. The first period, 1619 to 1863, began with the arrival of the first African slaves to North America and ended with the Emancipation Proclamation. During this era, African Americans were not considered humans or citizens. In the second period, 1863 to 1954, an era King refers to as the "period of segregation," blacks are second-class citizens. *Brown v. Board of Education* (1954) marked the start of the third period in race relations that was beginning to unfold. While the first and second periods were marked by white supremacy and discrimination against blacks, the third period, through black political agitation and protest, African American voting, and legislation would be the age of "complete and constructive integration" (Carson et al. 2000, 229–231).

King appreciated all the accolades he had received and reveled in his busy speaking schedule, engagements that often took him away from his pastoral duties at Dexter, but he wanted to expand his influence, share the tactics of nonviolent direct action, and further the cause for African American civil rights throughout the South. To do so meant that he would need new platforms from which to speak, and he spent the closing months of 1957 pursuing new avenues of expression with varying degrees of success.

In July, King flirted with the idea of pursuing a partnership with Billy Graham, the fiery white southern Baptist evangelist. Throughout the opening years of the 1950s, Graham, along with his well-trained staff, had successfully organized many religious revivals, called crusades, that attracted tens of thousands of white and black participants in major cities throughout the United States and Europe. By 1957, Graham was one of the most well-known white preachers in the United States, so for King, a Graham-King Crusade was appealing. On July 18, two months into his sixteen-week crusade in New York City at the famed Madison Square Garden, Graham invited King to the pulpit to offer a prayer. As he stood with his head bowed before the thousands of hungry souls, he asked God to offer them strength to let go of their own fears and fight against injustice. After several private meetings between the two while he was in New York, a professional partnership between Graham and King appeared promising. King profusely thanked Graham in a letter one month later and urged Graham to visit the Deep South and hold an integrated crusade to continue the budding relationship.

Within a year, however, it was clear that there would be no Graham-and-King crusade. Graham, unlike King, was unwilling to use his position to openly reject and oppose segregation throughout the South. King, unlike Graham, was unwilling to compromise with it. A year after King's prayer at the Madison Square Garden crusade, he sent another message to Graham, but this time he was far from ingratiating. Graham had been invited to share the stage with recently elected and staunch segregationist governor Price Daniel at a San Antonio, Texas, rally in late July. Daniel, along with other southern politicians, opposed the implementation of the *Brown v. Board of Education* decision. For Graham to appear with Daniel, King maintained, gave the impression that he supported Daniel's segregationist agenda and racial discrimination throughout Texas and the South, a stance in opposition to Graham's Christian teachings of brotherhood. He urged Graham to rescind the invitation and clarify his position on racial segregation.

King also shared his ethical, personal, and religious ideas with the black reading public in "Advice for Living," a column in *Ebony*, a monthly magazine that highlighted African Americans' achievements, which were largely ignored in white mainstream media. "Advice for Living" began publication in September 1957 and ran for a little over a year, and like the popular "Dear Abby" column, readers posed questions and King proffered responses. Most of the questions dealt with marital issues, and King usually advised individuals to be introspective, see what mistakes and missteps they may have made before placing blame on others, and seek counseling from a therapist or minister. King discouraged individuals from ending their marriage and saw divorce as a major problem that the church had to help solve. Sometimes, however, King's marital advice missed the mark. When one woman explained that her husband was having an affair with another woman and wanted ideas on what she should do, he, per usual, suggested that she and her husband see a marriage counselor but then suggested she "study" her husband's mistress to "see what she does for your husband that you might not do." He hinted that she may be the cause for her husband's infidelities because of her potential nagging, poor grooming habits, and failure to make her husband feel special. In another instance, a woman revealed that her alcoholic husband was physically abusive. King acknowledged that her suffering was "quite miserable" but urged her to remain with her husband to assist in his recovery.

Throughout the column, King emerges as product of his time: a socially conservative black minister on issues of gender politics, family life, music, and sex. He opposes premarital sex, one of the "contributing factors to the present breakdown of the family," believes gambling leads to the "breakdown in the structure of social life," abhors the consumption of alcohol, and holds that the "primary obligations of the woman is that of motherhood" (Carson et al. 2000, 268, 280, 306, 326, 504, 520). King did not call rock and roll music the devil's music, as so many other black preachers did, when a teenager asked him if it was a sin to be a rock and roll musician. However, he did maintain that rock and roll music "plunges men's minds into degrading and immoral depths" (Carson et al. 2000, 392). In the January 1958 issue of *Ebony*, a young black homosexual came out to King. "I am a boy," he writes, "but I feel about boys the way I ought to feel about girls." Fearful that his parents would find out his secret, he wrote to King asking him for information about a place that he could go to apparently cure himself. King maintained that the boy's "habit" was not an "innate tendency" but something he learned from his environment and could be resolved by consulting a "good psychiatrist" (Carson et al. 2000, 348–349).

The columns were also a platform for King to voice his opposition to segregation, racism, and war and to highlight a developing prophetic voice regarding race relations and social change. On several occasions, he discussed interracial marriage. One African American woman was in love with a white man and asked King if they should marry despite the

## Cultural Connection: Rock and Roll

Black spirituals and African American Protestant songs of the mid- to late nineteenth century were the foundation upon which African American blues music was created. Blues music, black secular music that used the musical structure of spirituals to tell stories of African Americans' everyday life during the early twentieth century, was the precursor to rhythm and blues. Rhythm and blues gave birth to rock and roll in the early 1950s, and the first rock and roll performers were African American and included Chuck Berry and Little Richard, who initially performed and recorded for predominantly black audiences. By the late 1950s, however, with the baby boom, new developments in recording technology, and the growth of independent and more established record companies, record executives found and cultivated new markets for the music and new musicians who played it. Both were predominantly white.

During the first week of April 1958, when King attempted to dissuade a young man from playing rock and roll music, three of the top ten most popular songs in the country, "Tequila," "Sweet Little Sixteen," and "Breathless," were rock and roll hits. "Tequila," recorded for the Challenge label by the Champs, is a rock instrumental influenced by Mexican music and reached the number one position on the popular and rhythm and blues charts. In 1959, the Champs won a Grammy Award for best rhythm and blues performance. "Sweet Little Sixteen," by rock legend Chuck Berry, was a Chess Records recording and celebrates young people who challenged social mores and embraced rock and roll. The Beach Boys, the California rock band, used the tune for the 1962 hit, "Surfin' U.S.A." Jerry Lee Lewis's "Breathless," recorded for Sun Records, offers a glimpse of desperate teenage love. When he played piano and sang, "You leave me ooh breathless ah ooh baby ooh crazy, honey you're much too much you know I can't love you enough," teenage girls went wild. "Breathless" tied with Elvis Presley's "Don't" to be the seventh most popular song and reached number three on the rhythm and blues chart.

Top Ten Most Popular Songs, April 7, 1958

1. "Tequila," The Champs
2. "Sweet Little Sixteen," Chuck Berry
3. "Lollipop," The Chordettes
4. "He's Got the Whole World (In His Hands)," Laurie London
5. "Who's Sorry Now," Connie Francis
6. "Sugartime," The McGuire Sisters
7. "Don't," Elvis Presley
8. "Breathless," Jerry Lee Lewis
9. "Sail Along Silvery Moon," Billy Vaughn and His Orchestra
10. "Are You Sincere," Andy Williams

objections of their parents. A white boy was in love with a black girl and wanted King to explain whether there were biblical prohibitions against interracial marriage. Another reader was troubled that famous African American men and women "always marry white." King did not promote interracial marriage, knowing that to do so would be political suicide, but he did not condemn it; instead, he reminded his audience that individuals, not races, marry, that interracial marriages were not immoral, and that marriage was a "cooperative enterprise" and "mutual agreement" regardless of the racial group to which one belonged (Carson et al. 2000, 269, 357, 417).

Whenever possible, King continued to promote his idea of nonviolent, passive resistance. When a man was hit over the head with a lead pipe but walked away from his attacker, King declared that a person who "accepts violence without returning it is much stronger than he who inflicts it." His position on interpersonal nonviolence and passive resistance as a method for societal change also applied to international politics. In his December 1957 and September 1958 columns, King opposed the testing of nuclear bombs and called for a complete ban on the development of nuclear weapons and the international elimination of war. If war was not abolished, he argued, humankind would "be plunged into the abyss of annihilation" (Carson et al. 2000, 327, 471).

"Advice for Living" was a moderate success, but its audience was primarily black, and King wanted a wider national appeal. With the Billy Graham-Martin Luther King Crusade out of the question, he turned to publishing his first book, *Stride toward Freedom*. In October 1957, he enlisted the services of Marie Rodell and Joan Daves, Inc., a literary agency in New York City, to negotiate publishing contracts for him. Rodell was a mystery novel editor and author of three mystery novels who established her own literary agency in 1948. Joan Daves started working as an editor at Harper and Brothers before she started the Joan Daves Agency in early 1953. During the mid-1950s, when white middle-class women were expected to stay home and take care of their husbands and children, Rodell and Daves were challenging boundaries in the literary world. In October 1957, they secured a contract for King to write a memoir about the Montgomery bus boycott for Harper and Brothers publishing company with a publication date in late summer 1958.

King expected to have a draft of *Stride toward Freedom* completed by early December, but that proved difficult for several reasons. He was occupied with pastoral duties at Dexter. In fact, when Martin Luther King III was born on October 23, King was attending a business meeting at Dexter and had to see Coretta and his new son after visiting hours had ended. King also maintained a busy work schedule with the SCLC. From late October to mid-December, he traveled to Fairmont (North Carolina),

Memphis, Atlanta, Washington, DC, Jamaica (New York), Chicago, and St. Louis. Traveling made it impossible to set aside time for the writing process to unfold. By late December, King had written almost nothing and informed Marie Rodell that "unexpected and unforeseeable circumstances . . . prevented [him] from doing any real work on the book" (Carson et al. 2000, 346). Most important, King was a talented minister, not a writer, historian, or chronicler of contemporary events.

To overcome these challenges, King sought the wise counsel and ideas of trusted confidantes, mentors, and editors. He consulted with Stanley Levison when writing "Pilgrimage to Nonviolence," chapter six of *Stride toward Freedom*, and sought his help in explaining nonviolence to lay readers. Levison, a white attorney based in New York City, helped King formulate his "Give Us the Ballot" speech, raised money for the MIA, negotiated the contract with Harper and Brothers, and served as a liaison between King, Rodell, and Daves. After reading draft chapters, George D. Kelsey, one of King's professors at Morehouse, urged King to emphasize the role that religion, specifically African American Christianity, played in the bus boycott. Rodell assigned the writer, editor, and critic Hermine Popper to work with King "to simplify, to sharpen, to pare away . . . so that your truly great story will speak for itself" (Carson et al. 2000, 387–388). Throughout the winter of 1958, Popper and King communicated through the mail to improve the narrative arc of King's manuscript and to complete what she called the framework of the book. Melvin Arnold, another Harper and Brothers editor, helped King clarify his thoughts to be sure that white critics could not purposefully misinterpret the bus boycott or King's work for their own political gain.

King also drew upon the works of other contemporaries. His chapter "Where Do We Go from Here?" features ideas Harris Wofford presented in his November 1957 Howard University address "Nonviolence and the Law" about how and why one disobeys and breaks unjust laws. Wofford studied Gandhi's philosophy in India, where he became committed to nonviolent direct action and was one of the first white students to enroll at Howard University's Law School. The chapter also includes material from Theodore E. Brown's "The American Negro and the American Trade Union Movement." By 1957, Brown had been a steadfast member of the Brotherhood of Sleeping Car Porters, mentee of A. Philip Randolph, and assistant director of the civil rights department of the American Federation of Labor and Congress of Industrial Organizations (AFL-CIO). King asked Brown for insight about the blacks' experiences with trade unionism. Brown responded with a piercing discussion about the exploitation of the African American working class, which King used. In the winter and spring of 1958, Bayard Rustin was involved in nuclear disarmament work and traveled to Europe to participate in on-the-ground campaigns but took time to read, comment, and add to the first draft of the book, helping King clarify the sources of nonviolent doctrines in the Bible.

After submitting his manuscript to Harper and Brothers in late spring 1958, King spent the college commencement season, from mid-May to early June, speaking to graduating seniors at historically black colleges. He started in Houston, Texas, at Erma Hughes Business College, moved to Daytona Beach, Florida, to speak at Bethune-Cookman College, continued on to Arkansas Agricultural, Mechanical and Normal College in Pine Bluff, Arkansas, then traveled to Morgan State College in Baltimore, Maryland, and ended at Central State College in Wilberforce, Ohio, where he received an honorary doctoral degree.

King also spent the summer writing and delivering one of his most influential sermons, "A Knock at Midnight." He first delivered the sermon at the Alabama State University on July 31, expanded upon it for his 1963 publication *Strength to Love*, and revisited it many times for close to a decade. The homily uses Luke 11:5–6 as its point of departure. "And he said unto them, Which of you shall have a friend, and shall go unto him at midnight, and say unto him, Friend, lend me three loaves; For a friend of mine in his journey is come to me, and I have nothing to set before him?" (King James Version). King uses the midnight hour, the darkest time of the day, as a metaphor for life in the mid-twentieth century. "It is . . . midnight in our world," he writes, "and the darkness is so deep that we can hardly see which way to turn" (Carson et al. 2000, 65). Throughout the sermon he argues that the darkness and gloom present in the American political, psychological, and moral order leave individuals hungry for the bread of hope, love, peace, economic justice, forgiveness, and faith that only religious institutions can and must provide. King places great importance on the role and function of the church, whose prophetic voice is not only the moral conscience and compass of the nation but also the sole force that will lead it out of darkness into the light of dawn.

*Stride toward Freedom* was published in September 1958 and tells the story of "50,000 Negroes who took to heart the principles of nonviolence, who learned to fight for their rights with the weapon of love, and who in the process, acquired a new estimate of their own human worth" (King, *Stride*, 2010, xxix). The book accomplished what he set out to do: it bolstered his following among African Americans and helped him gain a larger white audience. The black press, from the Baltimore *Afro-American* to the *Pittsburgh Courier*, praised *Stride toward Freedom* and King's leadership. Abel Plenn of the *New York Times* said that his "story bears on our own moral responsibility as a people and our future as a nation" (Plenn 1958). Writing for the *Saturday Review*, Lillian Smith said that "this is the most interesting book that has come out of the current racial situation in the South: important as documentary, full of accurate facts that historians will value; exciting as one dramatic scene after another unfolds; wise and compassionate in its point of view" (Smith 1958). Perry Miller at *The Reporter* maintained that "Dr. King's style has a factual simplicity that suits his restraint as easily as John Woolman's prose conveyed the Quaker serenity. By any standards, Northern or Southern, Christian or secular, he has written a major tract for our times" (Miller 1958). Harold Isaacs of the *New Republic* observes that "King throws down a rigorous challenge to American white society and to Negroes" (Isaacs 1958).

To promote the book, he embarked on a four-day publicity tour in New York City. King arrived in the city on September 15 and stayed at the Statler Hotel, a popular midtown establishment known for staging elaborate conventions. The following day, he spent time at Rockefeller Center to promote *Stride toward Freedom* on NBC's *Today Show* with David Garroway, one of the show's founders and its anchor. King spent the next two days autographing his book and attending a fundraiser for SCLC at Williams Institutional Christian Methodist Episcopal Church in Harlem, speaking at St. Augustine Presbyterian Church in the Bronx, and appearing on local radio programs, including *The World Tonight* on CBS radio. King also attended a political rally in the center of Harlem on 125th Street and Lenox Avenue and shared the stage with A. Philip Randolph; baseball legend Jackie Robinson; Hulan Jack, the Manhattan Borough president; New York governor W. Averell Harriman; and Harriman's rival, gubernatorial hopeful Nelson Rockefeller. Saturday, September 20, was to be a typical book signing; King had developed a rapport with his admirers and seems to have enjoyed the attention. He arrived at Blumenstein's Department Store in Harlem to a long line of supporters who wanted to see their hero in person and encounter greatness. At about 3:30 p.m., Izola Curry approached King and stabbed him in the chest with a letter opener.

King recounts the harrowing events in his *Autobiography*. "And while sitting there, a demented black woman came up. The only question I heard from her was, 'Are you Martin Luther King?'" After replying in the affirmative, "the next minute, I felt something sharp plunge forcefully into my chest. Before I knew it, I had been stabbed . . . by a woman who would later be judged insane" (Carson 1998, 117–118). King was rushed to Harlem Hospital.

Harlem Hospital opened in 1887, under the aegis of the New York City Department of Charities. Originally, it was a small treatment center for patients with minor health matters and a receiving center for patients with serious and/or contagious illnesses that required treatment at Bellevue Hospital or larger hospitals on Randall's and Wards Islands. In 1905, Harlem Hospital was placed under the jurisdiction of the Trustees of Bellevue and Allied Hospitals. Two years later, the hospital moved from East 120th Street to Lenox Avenue between 136th and 137th Streets, where it expanded its capacity from 54 to 150 beds and established an ambulance service. As one of the municipally funded hospitals in the Bellevue and Allied Hospitals system, Harlem Hospital provided care for the poorer citizens of the community who could not afford private care.

King was under the care of a group of well-trained physicians who performed surgery on him to remove the blade. Aubré Maynard received his medical education at New York University School of Medicine and joined Harlem Hospital as an intern in 1926. In 1958, he was the chief of surgery. John Cordice also trained at the New York University School of Medicine, and after being honorably discharged from the Army in 1947, he worked in the hospital's emergency room and earned a resident position on the surgical staff. Helen Mayer was an anesthesiologist who trained at the University of Chicago and Columbia-Presbyterian Hospital and joined Harlem Hospital in the early 1950s along with Emil Naclerio, a thoracic surgeon who trained at Marquette Medical School at the Overholt Clinic, in Boston, Massachusetts. Leo Maitland, the chief resident of surgery, was a graduate of City College and Meharry College. Before joining Harlem Hospital, he was associate director of surgery at Sydenham Hospital. After taking X-rays and opening King's chest on the right side, the surgeons removed the blade, which had pierced the breastbone and was millimeters away from King's aorta, the main artery that carries blood from the heart.

Curry was arrested, taken to the local police precinct for processing, and charged with felonious assault. She was later transferred to the East Sixty-Seventh Street station house and then to Bellevue Psychiatric Hospital, where she was examined and put under constant observation. There, psychiatrists Theodore Weiss and John Cassity diagnosed her with paranoid schizophrenia. On October 17, a grand jury indicted her on first-degree attempted murder, but her mental illness made her unfit to stand trial. She was committed to the Matteawan State Hospital for the Criminally Insane, spent the remainder of her life in and out of mental health facilities, and died in 2015 at age ninety-eight.

King recovered for several days under the watchful eyes of the hospital's physicians and was joined by Coretta Scott King and his family. It was determined that he was not well enough to fly or be driven back to Alabama, so King continued his recuperation in Rev. Sandy Ray's parsonage for several weeks. Ray attended Morehouse with King Sr. in the late 1920s and was a close family friend and pastor at Cornerstone Baptist Church in Brooklyn, New York. King returned to Montgomery on October 24 to the welcoming arms of his congregation and supporters. Upon arriving, he gave a prepared statement thanking everyone for their concern and support during his convalescence in New York City and told them that his brush with death renewed his conviction in the nonviolent struggle for freedom. "I have come back to rejoin the ranks of you who are working ceaselessly for the realization of the ideal of Freedom and Justice for all men," he said (Carson et al. 2000, 513).

King's physicians warned him not to overextend himself at least until early December, and for the most part, King listened to their instructions. He slowly regained his strength and engaged in his pastoral duties, spending most of November and December in and around Montgomery. He spent only several days out of the city for the remainder of the year. His short trip took him first to Atlanta, where he met with SCLC staff and spoke at Wheat Street Baptist Church, a church founded shortly after the Civil War and tended by Rev. Williams Holmes Borders Sr. From Atlanta, he flew to Indianapolis, Indiana, where he addressed the Senate Avenue YMCA at Cadle Tabernacle. For decades, the YMCA sponsored events and speakers that celebrated African American history and culture and advocated for racial equality. They even sponsored speakers including the activist W. E. B. Du Bois, scientist George Washington Carver, and former first lady Eleanor Roosevelt.

On Sunday, December 21, several days before Christmas, King stood before the Dexter congregation and delivered a timely address for the season. Unlike most Christmas season sermons, his does not celebrate the birth of Jesus and does not reference the story as told in the books of Matthew and Luke. Instead, King looks to the opening verses of the book of Revelations. "The Revelation of Jesus Christ, which God gave unto him, to shew unto his servants things which must shortly come to pass; and he sent and signified it by his angel unto his servant John who bare record of the world of God, and of the testimony of Jesus Christ, and of all things that he saw. Blessed is he that readeth, and they that hear the words of this prophecy, and keep those things which are written therein: for time is at hand" (Revelations 1:1–3, KJV). As Jesus' birth was the starting point for Christianity, Jesus must also be the point of departure or starting point for humanity. Starting with Jesus, King says, creates hope within the believer, engenders courage to fight against injustice, encourages mutual aid, and nourishes love for one's enemies. King ends his sermon quoting from a song written by the early nineteenth-century English Baptist minister Edward Mote: "My Hope Is Built on Nothing Less." "My hope is built on nothing less than Jesus' blood and righteousness; I dare not trust the sweetest frame, but wholly lean on Jesus's name." The refrain says, "On Christ, the solid rock, I stand; all other ground is sinking sand, all other ground is sinking sand." The song was often sung at Dexter and by African American congregations, despite denominational affiliation, throughout the South. Black freedom, exhorts King, must stand on the solid foundation of God.

He ended 1958 making plans to visit India. In his *Autobiography*, he notes that ever since he was a child, he "wanted to take a trip to India" and since Gandhi's nonviolent techniques were so influential to the Montgomery bus boycott, he decided to follow friends and colleagues' advice and visit the subcontinent. In letters to associates, he asked for ideas of people and places to visit while there. C. Ramachandran, one of Gandhi's followers, secretary of the Gandhi National Memorial Fund and founder of a college based on Gandhi's ideas, formally invited King to India to "share with the Indian people your own experiences and ... study how Mahatma Gandhi evolved the techniques of peaceful action to solve innumerable social and national problems " (Carson et al. 2000, 553). Not wanting to travel alone, he decided that Coretta and his friend, writer L. D. Reddick, would be his traveling companions for the two-month journey.

As he looked toward 1959, King was hoping for spiritual enrichment and a path to be more politically effective in the growing civil rights movement.

# 4

## Embracing a Larger Movement

In the opening weeks of January 1959, King continued convalescing from Izola Curry's stab wound. He would not receive a clean bill of health from his doctors until late January, so he continued to follow their orders and maintained a modified work schedule. He stayed close to home, preparing, and modifying sermons he delivered at Dexter, maintaining correspondence, and traveling a relatively short distance once to Atlanta, Georgia, to attend a Southern Christian Leadership Conference (SCLC) meeting and to Hot Springs, Arkansas, to participate in the board of directors meeting of the National Baptist Convention. His most extensive trip that month was to New Haven, Connecticut, where he was invited by Whitney Griswold, Yale University's president, to speak. He delivered two lectures at Yale during his visit, one on January 14 titled "The Future of Integration" and the other on January 15, his birthday, titled "Problems of the South." In Ivy League style, his northern white liberal supporters welcomed him and even surprised him with a cake adorned with candles in honor of his thirtieth birthday when his second talk concluded.

As January came to a close, King received a clean bill of health, and he and Coretta prepared for their journey to India. They had a lot of well-wishers. The Montgomery Improvement Association (MIA) threw them a goodbye party, congregants welcomed the Kings into their homes, and the Women's Council at Dexter Avenue Baptist Church organized a farewell event. At every event, prayers were offered for their safe travel. He would not leave the country for several days, and in the interim, honored commitments he had made to supporters and friends. He and Walter Reuther, the head of the United Auto Workers (UAW) met in Detroit on January 31 to talk about the intersection of race, economics, and civil rights in the country. In the late 1950s, the UAW was one of the most powerful unions in the nation and had become committed to the civil rights struggle. The following day, Sunday, with little rest, King stood before congregants at Bright Hope Baptist Church in the predominantly black section of North Philadelphia, Pennsylvania, where Rev. William H. Gray Jr., the past president of Florida Agricultural and Mechanical University, was pastor. King visited Vine Memorial Baptist Church that afternoon to address the congregation, as he had several years before when he was still a graduate student. The next day, Monday, February 2, King set out for New York City and delivered an address to the War Resisters League (WRL) annual dinner.

The WRL was a secular, pacifist, anti-war organization founded in 1923, and its early members had opposed the United States' entry into World War I. During the 1940s and 1950s, the organization opposed the United States' entry into World War II, the Korean War, and the Vietnam War. King discussed the features and value of nonviolence in the fight against segregation as he had done in other settings, but the significance of the speech was the connection he made between the fight against racism domestically and the need for global peace. To work for racial justice at home, he notes, one must "simultaneously resist war" and adhere to the principles and practices of nonviolence at home and "in international relations" (Carson et al. 2005, 122). He ended his talk by pointing to the importance of people of color in the international peace movement, noting that the "spiritual power" they possess had the potential to save Western civilization (125).

The Kings and their traveling companion, Lawrence Reddick, departed from Idlewild Airport (renamed John F. Kennedy International Airport) and began their international journey on February 3. They spent several days in Paris and were entertained by Richard Wright, author, social critic, and African American expatriate who had made the City of Light his home. On February 10, they landed in Delhi, India's capital, and upon disembarking, King participated in a press conference with over two dozen reporters. He offered brief prepared remarks wherein he expressed his hopes and enthusiasm for the trip, talked briefly about the Montgomery bus boycott, and answered reporters' questions.

King spent several days in Delhi meeting with cabinet ministers, members of parliament, and other elected officials, including prime minister Jawaharlal Nehru, with whom he dined at the prime minister's residence. They discussed India's domestic economy and its relationship to Gandhi's philosophy, the appeal of communism to newly independent nations, and ways to forge a stronger relationship between African Americans and Indians. From Delhi, they traveled by air to the state of Bihar in northeast India and toured the ancient city of Patna. Traveling by car, a short distance from Patna, King visited a Buddhist and Hindu monastery in Bodha Gaya. The cultural center of east India, Calcutta, in West Bengal state followed, where King met with young Indians and dined with leaders from the area. After Calcutta, they traveled on to Madras state, and King was welcomed by the governor, Bishnuram Medhi. In Trivandrum, the capital of the southern Indian state of Kerala, the Kings and Reddick meet E. M. S. Namboodiripad, India's leading communist, for lunch. Two days were spent in Bangalore in Mysore state, giving King the opportunity to meet with the governor there. During the last days of February to the opening days of March 1959, the weary travelers toured India's west coast and the subcontinent's northeast region, including Bombay, India's largest city, as well as Ahmadabad and Kishangarh. Before returning to Delhi on March 4, King visited the Taj Mahal, the famous seventeenth-century, white marble mausoleum in Agra. The last several days of their Indian tour was spent in Delhi, where King held meetings with followers and associates of Gandhi and was honored at a reception. On his last day in India, he recorded a "Farewell Statement" for All India Radio. In it, he acknowledged the importance of Gandhi's vision in India's social and political life. He also maintained that India could be a beacon of hope on the international stage by being the first nation to eliminate weapons of destruction (Carson et al. 2005, 136). For thirty days, the Kings and Reddick traveled throughout India, meeting elected and appointed officials, spiritual leaders, nonviolent activists, and students. In his *Autobiography*, King said his trip to India was "one of the most concentrated and eye-opening experiences" of his life (Carson 1998, 122).

Reminiscent of his trip to Ghana in 1957, King took every opportunity to share his experiences upon his return to the United States. Almost immediately after landing in New York City, he held a press conference and argued that the United States should offer aid to India to prevent the Indian government and people from turning to the Soviet Union and communism. On March 22, Palm Sunday, the Christian feast day celebrated the Sunday before Easter, King delivered a homily that discussed Gandhi's political and spiritual contributions to India and the West. He uses verses from the Gospel of John as his text: John 10:16 and John 14:12. John 10:16 reads, "And Other sheep I have which are not of this fold; them also I must bring, and they shall hear my voice; and there shall be one fold, and one shepherd" (King James Version). John 14:12 reads, "Verily, verily, I say unto you, He that believeth on me, the works that I do shall he do also; and greater works than these shall he do, because I go unto my Father." In expounding upon these verses and retelling the life of Gandhi, King tells his listeners the verses apply to Gandhi himself, who was not of the Christian "fold" but took Jesus' teachings "and was able to do even greater works than Jesus did in his lifetime" (Carson et al. 2005, 148).

In a March 23 letter to Reuben Nelson, the general secretary of the American Baptist Convention, and an April 7 letter to William Stuart Nelson, dean at Howard University, King said that the trip offered him "meaningful insights" and help him "deepen" his understanding and commitment to nonviolence (Carson et al. 2005, 158, 181). At Dexter, the Kings told stories of their travels to congregants and friends. King traveled to Toronto on April 28 and appeared on *Front Page Challenge*, a Canadian television show, where he spoke about his trip and the importance of Gandhi's approach to nonviolence. During his commencement address at Morehouse College in early June, he told the graduating young men at his alma mater about his trip to India and connected the economic plight of poor Indians and peoples in developing countries with the plight of the United States and black America. *Ebony* magazine published an article about King's journey, "My Trip to the Land of Gandhi," in July. He concluded the account by informing *Ebony's* readers that the United States should help India "preserve her soul and thus help us save our own" (Carson et al. 2005, 238).

By late spring 1959, with the glow of his India visit all but extinguished, King fell into a routine. As he had done in prior years, he delivered addresses at commencements, convocations, and graduations at colleges and universities. The 1959 commencement season took him to four historically black colleges—Bishop College in Marshall, Texas; Maryland State College in Princess Anne, Maryland; Dillard University, in New Orleans; and Talladega College in Talladega, Alabama—as well as his alma mater, Boston University, where he received an honorary degree. Bishop College was founded in 1881 by the Baptist Home Mission Society to serve black students in East Texas. Maryland State College, now the University of Maryland, Eastern Shore, was established by the Methodist Episcopal Church in the mid-1880s. Affiliated with the United Methodist Church and the United Church of Christ, Dillard College, now Dillard University, was founded in 1869. Founded in the late 1860s by freedmen with the aid of the Freedman's Bureau and the American Missionary Association, Talladega College graduated its first baccalaureate class in 1895.

King spent the remainder of 1959 preaching at Dexter once or twice per month and speaking around the nation delivering messages on nonviolence and racial integration. In mid-July, he spoke about nonviolence at the NAACP fiftieth annual convention, in New York City. At the annual National Bar Association Conference in Milwaukee in August, he delivered a speech about the history of race relations in the United States and implored the lawyers in attendance to love and not fall victim to hate.

> **CULTURAL CONNECTION: *EBONY***
>
> *Ebony* magazine was first published on November 1, 1945, and served as a "black" counterpart to the largely "white" photographic magazines *Life,* founded in 1936, and *Look,* founded in 1937. From its inception, it depicted the accomplishments of African Americans in business and their celebrity in the entertainment industry. John Harold Johnson created *Ebony* in Chicago, Illinois, the second publication of his Johnson Publishing Company. Johnson saw black achievement in business and in entertainment in returning African American veterans after the close of World War II. Perhaps more important, he saw such achievement underrepresented by mainstream "white" periodicals. The growth of photojournalism in the late 1930s and early 1940s prompted Johnson to create *Ebony,* a publication saturated with photographs to portray the successes of African Americans and their contributions to American culture.
>
> *Ebony* early avoided "the race question," choosing instead to present a portrait of black success that others in the community could strive toward. Hard work would breed success, argued the Johnson Publishing Company, and the success of some would breed the success of others. *Ebony* revived the Booker T. Washington model of social progress. By using a white middle-class model for success, Johnson and *Ebony* alienated some, but the tone of the magazine changed as the civil rights movement's militancy increased. *Ebony* included news on the fight for integration, often praising the activism of African American college students. As the movement's issues changed, so did *Ebony's* coverage, moving in the 1960s to cover impoverished inner-city living conditions, the racial inequity in educational and hiring practices, and the misapplication of drug laws to entrap African Americans.
>
> *Ebony* featured the writing of many leading African Americans from the liberal intellectual community. Carl T. Rowan and Kenneth Clark contributed articles. Martin Luther King Jr. wrote a column for the periodical called "Advice for Living." Through the close of the civil rights movement proper and its continuing reverberations in the 1980s, 1990s, and 2000s, *Ebony* maintained its attempt to represent the black middle class and the successes its lifestyle creates.
>
> Source: Thomas Aiello, *"Ebony,"* in Leslie Alexander and Walter Rucker, ed., *Encyclopedia of African American History,* vol. 3 (Santa Barbara, CA: ABC-CLIO, 2010), 749–750.

At Dexter King delivered the sermon "A Tough Mind and a Tender Heart" which he would further develop and publish in *Strength to Love.* Matthew 10:16 is his text for this sermon. Jesus is speaking to his disciples, who are about to leave him to spread his teachings. Before they go, Jesus says, "Behold, I send you forth as sheep in the midst of wolves: be ye therefore wise as serpents and harmless as doves." King interprets the verse in the context of the African American quest for social justice and racial equity. Like Jesus's disciples, blacks must be "tough-minded," like serpents. They must possess discipline and keenness of insight to move beyond myth and irrationality to find and embrace social and political facts. It is only through tough-mindedness that America could "break loose from the shackles of prejudice" and the threat of "spiritual death" (King, *Strength*, 2010, 5). A tough mind must be developed in conjunction with a tender heart, a characteristic commonly attributed to a dove. Such dove-like qualities allow one to love their enemies, see themselves as part of an interrelated whole, and not fall victim to individualism and materialism. In the civil rights struggle, a tender heart and tough mind work together in nonviolent resistance to "avoid the complacency . . . of the softminded and the violence . . . of the hardhearted" (8).

In late September he was back in the Deep South, in Jackson, Mississippi, offering advice to African American ministers in their fight against segregation. By then, King was looking to become more active in the struggle for black civil rights, but his SCLC had not become an effective political force, especially with the organization's failed voter registration drives and lack of meaningful campaigns against discrimination. King needed a change, and he and his confidantes pondered his next move. They acknowledged that King was barely at Dexter as it was and that he felt guilty because of his absenteeism. If he wanted to be more active in the civil rights struggle with the SCLC, such work would take him away from his duties as a local church pastor and place him even more on a stage beyond Montgomery. All agreed that King needed to spend more of his time working for the organization. To do that, he would have to move to Atlanta, where the SCLC was headquartered. Not coincidentally, King's father, Daddy King, wanted his son by his side in the pulpit at Ebenezer Baptist Church, one of Atlanta's most influential black churches with a membership of over four thousand.

On November 16, Ebenezer Baptist Church unanimously voted and offered King the copastorship at the church. King met with the trustee board of Ebenezer in late November and tenured his resignation to Dexter. Weeping, he announced his departure at Dexter after the morning service on November 29. On December 1, the SCLC released a statement, "Dr. King Leaves Montgomery for Atlanta," making the case that his new position would give the "American Gandhi more time and a much better location" to develop and implement the SCLC's new political campaigns throughout the South (Carson et al. 2005, 323–324; 328–329). *Jet* magazine printed an article about King's decision to leave Dexter and go to Atlanta in the December 17, 1959, issue, titled "Why M.L. King Is Leaving Montgomery: Leader Says Time Is Ripe to Extend Work in Dixie." Talking with the reporter, King said that one of his reasons for leaving Dexter was that he "for almost four years [had] been faced with the responsibility of trying to do as one man what five or six ought to be doing" and he had been "giving, giving, giving." Now, he concluded, it was time to "reorganize my personality and re-orient my life" ("Why M.L. King Is Leaving Montgomery" 1959).

As per the terms of his resignation, King continued his role as pastor at Dexter until January 31, 1960, and when not speaking to various groups and congregations around the country, he spent the month of December and early January tying up loose ends, attending farewell gatherings, preaching at Dexter, and concluding his work with the MIA. On December 3, before a supportive crowd of close to one thousand, he delivered his final address as president of the MIA, a position he had held since the group's founding in 1955. He discussed the bus boycott's success and influence on other protests throughout the South. The boycott not only ended segregation on city buses, he noted, but also gave African Americans a "new sense of dignity and destiny" throughout the nation (Carson et al. 2005, 333). Contemporary challenges were also noted, including continued white resistance to school integration five years after the *Brown* decision and politicians' threats to close public schools in Montgomery to avoid desegregation. Despite his leaving Montgomery and the continued recalcitrance of white segregationists, he declared to his listeners, it was necessary for the MIA to continue to fight against segregation creatively and nonviolently. King closed his address by providing reasons for his move to Atlanta. As he moved to his conclusion, King reminded the audience that "the freedom struggle in Montgomery was not started by one man, and it will not end when one man leaves" (342). King, Coretta, and their children moved to the heart of black Atlanta in the opening days of February, where they were welcomed with open arms.

While the Kings were getting settled, a student sit-in movement was gaining momentum in Greensboro, North Carolina, when on February 1, 1960, four black students from North Carolina Agricultural and Technical College walked into a local Woolworth's department store. After buying sundries, they sat down at a white-only lunch counter and asked to be served but were refused service. Despite the refusal, Clarence Henderson, Franklin McCain, Joseph McNeil, and Billy Smith continued to sit at the counter quietly studying. After the police were called but no arrests made, the counter was closed. Undaunted, the students returned the next day and again were refused service. Day after day, they continued to return for the remainder of the week and each day their numbers increased. The initial four demonstrators swelled into hundreds of students, and sit-ins spread to other local department stores in Greensboro that refused to serve African Americans at lunch counters. Within weeks, sit-ins were taking place in large and small cities throughout the South, and by the end of the year, students had organized sit-ins in seventy-five southern cities and towns.

## Cultural Connection: Historically Black Colleges and Universities (HBCUs)

A few black colleges appeared immediately before the Civil War, such as Lincoln and Cheyney Universities in Pennsylvania and Wilberforce in Ohio. With the end of the Civil War, the daunting task of providing education to more than four million formerly enslaved people was shouldered by both the federal government, through the Freedman's Bureau, and many northern church missionaries. During the postbellum period, most black colleges were so in name only; these institutions generally provided primary and secondary education, a feature that was true of most historically white colleges—starting with Harvard—during the first decades of their existence.

With the passage of the Second Morrill Act in 1890, the federal government again took an interest in black education, establishing black colleges. This act stipulated that those states practicing segregation in their public colleges and universities would forfeit federal funding unless they established agricultural and mechanical institutions for the black population. Despite the wording of the Second Morrill Act, which called for the equitable division of federal funds, these newly founded institutions received less funding than their white counterparts did and thus had inferior facilities. Among the seventeen new "land grant" college were institutions such as Florida Agricultural and Technical University and Alabama Agricultural and Mechanical University.

Until the 1954 *Brown v. Board of Education* decision, both public and private black colleges in the South remained segregated by law and were the only educational option for African Americans. After the *Brown* decision, private black colleges, which have always been willing to accept students from all backgrounds if the law would allow, struggled to defend issues of quality in an atmosphere that labeled anything all black as inferior. During the 1960s, the federal government took a greater interest in black colleges. To provide clarity, the 1965 Higher Education Act defined a black college as an institution whose primary mission was the education of African Americans.

Black colleges in the twenty-first century are remarkably diverse and serve varied populations. Although most of these institutions maintain their historically black traditions, on average, 13 percent of their students are white. Just as predominantly white institutions are varied in their mission and quality, so are the nation's black colleges. Today, the leading black colleges cater to those students who could excel at any top-tier institution regardless of racial makeup. Other institutions operate with the needs of blacks in the surrounding region in mind.

Source: Marybeth Gasman, "Historically Black Colleges and Universities," in Leslie Alexander and Walter Rucker, ed., *Encyclopedia of African American History*, vol. 3 (Santa Barbara, CA: ABC-CLIO, 2010), 806–809.

When King learned of the student movement developing throughout the South, he became an ardent supporter and saw it as "one of the most significant developments in the whole civil rights struggle" (Carson 1998, 139). By the time he visited North Carolina during the second week of February, the sit-in movement had spread beyond Greensboro into neighboring towns and cities, including Durham. At the request of Reverend Douglass Moore, a Methodist minister, adviser to the student activists and one of King's former classmates, King visited Durham to see the effects of the sit-ins: lunch counters were closed because store managers did not want to serve black students. At Moore's behest, King delivered "A Creative Protest" at White Rock Baptist Church, one of the oldest black churches in Durham, on February 16, in which he offers his and the SCLC's full support and compares the energetic young protesters to stars radiating and injecting their "heat and light" in the civil rights struggles. He calls their sit-in movement "fresh," "marvelous," and "significant" for the "whole of America" (Carson et al. 2005, 369). He told the students that in their struggle against segregation, there would be confusion, doubt, debates, and hesitation, as he and black residents of Montgomery had during the Montgomery bus boycott, and that white North Carolinians may see them as agitators. Despite all this, it was critical that the students continue their dignified, nonviolent struggle, because God was on their side and justice would inevitably prevail.

During the winter and early spring of 1960, King tried to balance his support of the burgeoning student movement and his fight against a state of Alabama perjury indictment against him for allegedly lying on his income taxes in 1956 and 1958. He was arrested at Ebenezer by two local deputies on February 17, when he returned from North Carolina, was formally charged, and was released on a $2,000 bond. Less than two weeks later, he was in a Montgomery, Alabama, court, where he was arraigned again and eventually released after paying $4,000 bail. King knew of discrepancies in his income taxes and remitted a payment of $1,600 to Alabama tax collectors to resolve the matter years before. However, to punish him for his activism in the state, Alabama governor John Patterson sought to prosecute King and threatened him with ten years in prison.

King's arrest and indictment were virtually ignored by the mainstream white press, but black newspapers and King's supporters saw the indictment and upcoming trial as a witch hunt and offered their support. Writing from Detroit, where she moved shortly after the Montgomery bus boycott, Rosa Parks called King's tax troubles "segregationists' attempts to intimidate and embarrass you" (Carson et al. 2005, 389). E. D. Nixon, the former treasurer of the MIA wrote to King and told him that he had "complete faith in you with reference to any money matters" (373). Cynthia and

Julius Alexander, congregants at Dexter, called the state's arrest and indictment of King a "new low" and told King to "faint not" because the Montgomery community was behind him and had every faith in his innocence and integrity (374–375). Despite the outpouring of support and his innocence, Coretta recalled that she "had never seen Martin affected so deeply. My husband's sense of morality was so offended . . . that he agonized to the point of feeling guilty" (King 1993, 169–170).

Within days of his release on bail, King's supporters formed the Committee to Defend Martin Luther King and the Struggle for Freedom in the South with the goal of raising $200,000 to support King's legal defense and the SCLC's political work. The committee was an assemblage of some of the most important contemporary activists and artists. A. Philip Randolph, the founder of the Brotherhood of Sleeping Car Porters, and Dr. Gardner Taylor, pastor of Concord Baptist Church in Bedford-Stuyvesant, Brooklyn, served as the chairmen of the committee. Stage and screen actors Harry Belafonte and Sidney Poitier served as chairmen of the cultural division. Grammy award–winning singer, songwriter, and pianist Nat King Cole served as the treasurer. Bayard Rustin served as the executive director. On March 29, the committee took out a full-page advertisement in the *New York Times* urging people to support the fund. Over sixty leading intellectuals, activists, and artists endorsed the appeal, including but not limited to singer and actress Eartha Kitt, former first lady Eleanor Roosevelt, and writer Langston Hughes. The committee also retained the services of noted black attorneys Hubert Delaney, William Ming, Fred Gray, Charles Langford, Arthur Shores, and S. S. Seay Jr. to represent King in court.

His trial did not begin until late May, and despite fears that the public had lost faith in him, King returned to the lecture circuit to raise money for the SCLC and support the student sit-in movement. By April 1960, there had been scores of student demonstrations throughout the South, but there was no coordinating body to direct student protest. King hoped that the SCLC would provide the student sit-in movement with organizational support and help the students channel the sit-in movement so that it could achieve maximum effectiveness. In March, he and Ella Baker, the executive director of the SCLC, put out a call to student leaders to meet at Shaw University in Raleigh, North Carolina, from April 15 to April 17 to discuss the impact and future of the sit-in movement. Between 150 and 200 students attended the Youth Leadership Conference, and King addressed the press on the opening day. Students, he maintained, "revealed to the nation . . . their determination and courage" by taking "the struggle for justice into their own hands" (Carson et al. 2005, 427). King's and the SCLC's support was critical, and the three-day conference allowed students to adopt a number of resolutions and lay the foundation for a new, student-centered, student-directed, and student-led organization, the Student Nonviolent Coordinating Committee (SNCC).

On the last day of the youth conference, King appeared on *Meet the Press*, where he explained the importance of the student sit-in movement. Sitting around the "press table," King responded to questions posed by Frank van der Linden, a correspondent for the *Nashville Banner*, a daily newspaper in Tennessee; May Craig, perhaps the most popular newswoman of the era and correspondent for the *Portland Press Herald*; Anthony Lewis, a reporter for the *New York Times* who often covered the Supreme Court; and Lawrence Spivak, the longtime *Meet the Press* moderator. In response to Spivak, who asked if the "sit-in strikes are doing . . . the Negro race more harm than good," King responded that rather than harming black people, the sit-in movement had an "educational value" by forcing southern whites to "reevaluate the stereotypes that they have developed concerning Negroes" (Carson et al. 2005, 429). In another exchange, Spivak asked King if breaking local segregation laws and risking imprisonment by participating in sit-ins was a "good method of procedure." King answered that in breaking local laws, students were obeying the 1954 *Brown* decision, so they were "breaking local laws . . . to affirm the real and positive meaning of the law of the land" (430). Later in the interview, he declared that "sit-ins . . . dramatize the indignities and injustices which Negro people are facing" (434).

In an article published in *The Progressive* in May, King again defended the student sit-in movement and opposed those who suggested that it was communist inspired or started by communist groups. Student activists were simultaneously part of the longer American tradition started by the founding fathers, who rejected tyranny, and part of a contemporary worldwide movement of oppressed people demanding dignity, respect, and equality before the law. Using nonviolent direct action, they were part of a "revolution . . . in both the social order and human mind" (451).

King returned to Montgomery with his wife and parents to stand trial in late May. The four-day trial began on May 25 with a white judge, a white prosecutor, and an all-white jury. In the history of the South and Alabama, such an all-white arrangement rarely saw justice for black defendants, and King and his defense team were not optimistic. There were three days of testimony and cross-examination, during which time King and Scott King testified. On the fourth day, the prosecution and defense rested their case and then turned the matter over to the jury for their verdict. The twelve men deliberated for close to four hours, four agonizing hours for King, and returned with a not guilty verdict. Moments after the verdict, King spoke with reporters and praised Judge James Carter, the presiding judge, and the "brilliant array of lawyers" who defended him (Carson et al. 2005, 462). According to Coretta, King's acquittal "foreshadowed the lesson Martin's enemies were to learn more than once: his integrity was too powerful to be besmirched by direct assault" (King 1993, 171).

Exonerated, a heavy burden was lifted from King's shoulders, and with renewed vigor, he resumed his work supporting student protesters and ministers who participated in the sit-in movement, forging coalition with other civil rights organizations, and attempting to influence the civil rights platforms of presidential candidates John F. Kennedy and Richard M. Nixon.

Multitudes of students joined the growing sit-in movement as it expanded throughout the South in the late spring and summer of 1960. Encouraged by SNCC, scores of students were arrested, and while there were those who refused bail, opting to serve their prison time, many who were arrested wanted to post bail but had no resources to do so. With nowhere to turn, students reached out to the SCLC. King soon realized that an inability to pay legal fees would discourage student participation and lead to a loss of momentum for the sit-in movement. To keep the movement going, King continued his fundraising speaking tours. He spoke at various events throughout the nation, such as the Tulsa Ministerial Alliance in Tulsa, Oklahoma. On July 29, King and the SCLC organized a "Friend of Freedom" national appeal. In a letter to potential donors, he spoke of "recent developments" in the African American freedom struggle. Of foremost importance was the student sit-in movement, where college students had selflessly challenged unjust and immoral segregation laws and were met with expulsions, arrests, and violence. He reminded the reader that "funds are desperately needed for legal defense . . . for the student movement" (488). A pledge card and a stamped envelope were included for contributors to return to keep SCLC's work "going on a substantial basis" (489). The campaign was a success with individuals and organizations supporting it, including the Retail, Wholesale and Department Store Union (RWDSU), from New York City, which donated $3,000 and the Harlem Labor Union, which gave $1,250.

With black and white students using nonviolent direct action to fight racism and segregation and the SCLC becoming an important civil rights organization, there were ruptures between the civil rights groups. Some young people argued that the NAACP's litigation strategy in fighting racism was outmoded, and NAACP leaders questioned young people's immature hubris. Some NAACP leaders questioned King's motivations and saw him as a calculating upstart. Jackie Robinson, the African American baseball player who integrated American baseball, was a businessman and member of the NAACP board of directors from the late 1950s to the early 1960s. In a May 5, 1960, letter to King, shortly after students created SNCC, Robinson reported that he heard reports that SCLC members were "knocking" the NAACP and expressed his concern that the two organizations were falling victim to outside agitators trying to "divide and conquer" the movement (Carson et al. 2005, 454). Seeing the fight against racism to be more important than organizational wrangling, King tried to mend fissures. He replied to Robinson and assured him that the NAACP continued to be an important civil rights organization and was held in high regard by the SCLC leadership, who saw their work as supplementing his organization's work. He reiterated this message from lecterns and pulpits throughout the summer and fall.

In an address before the National Urban League on September 6, King told his audience that the major civil rights organizations—CORE, the NAACP, and the SCLC—must begin to understand and implement a "division of labor in organizational work" and "accept the [each] other as a necessary partner in the . . . struggle to free the Negro" (Carson et al. 2005, 506–507). A couple of weeks later, King was in Charlotte, North Carolina, addressing close to three thousand NAACP members, reminding them they must be unwavering in their fight for freedom, justice, and equality and use every nonviolent method at their disposal. He also told them, in a conciliatory manner, that everyone who was "working courageously to break down barriers of segregation and discrimination are the real saviors of democracy" (509).

Both American political parties had ignored, betrayed, and taken African Americans for granted for generations. President Eisenhower refused to enforce the 1954 *Brown* decision. Civil rights activists and leaders wanted to change that with the upcoming 1960 presidential election between Massachusetts Democratic senator John F. Kennedy and Republican vice president Richard Nixon. King met Nixon during his trip to Ghana and had subsequent correspondence with him when he returned home. He saw Kennedy during a trip to New York City in late June 1960. Both men wanted King's endorsement and knew that the support of one of the most trusted black activists and public intellectuals would translate into thousands of African American votes. However, King refused to publicly support either candidate and chose a different strategy.

Together with his trusted advisers Bayard Rustin, A. Philip Randolph, and SCLC leadership, King lobbied the Democratic and Republican parties to convince them to insert a civil rights agenda into their party platforms. Though they characterized their proposals as "minimal," their ten suggestions were robust and carefully considered; they included but were not limited to a presidential executive order prohibiting discrimination throughout the federal government and those businesses and companies receiving contracts from the federal government, an African American member of the presidential cabinet, the expulsion of "segregationist, white supremacists, [and] racists . . . in your ranks," and a clear adherence to federal law and constitutional amendments that prohibited discrimination on the basis of race (Carson et al. 2005, 484). To publicize their demands, the SCLC held rallies at the Democratic National Convention in Los Angeles, California, on July 10, and at the Republican National Convention in Chicago, Illinois, on July 25, 1960. At both conventions, King addressed crowds of thousands and told them that black people could not wait "because for 100 years successive Republican and Democratic national administrations have failed to enforce our Constitutional liberties" (487). Neither party included bold civil rights agendas in their party platform and even after John F. Kennedy won the presidential election, he dragged his feet on the issue of civil rights for fear that he would lose the support of the exact same white segregationists that SCLC wanted to be removed from the Democratic Party.

Roslyn Pope, a student at Spelman College, and Julian Bond, a student at Morehouse College, were the leaders of a sit-in movement in Atlanta on March 15 with close to two hundred black students participating. According to historian Taylor Branch, the early March sit-in movement "lasted only one day before being smothered under the combined influence of the [African American] and white power structures" (Branch 1988, 286). King was focused on his upcoming tax trial and was settling into his copastor position at Ebenezer at the time and did not participate. In October, however, the Atlanta student sit-in movement resumed, this time with fresh SNCC activists ready to demonstrate at Rich's Department Store, a sprawling retail complex in downtown Atlanta. Students had listened to King's statements about filling jails and refusing bail and were ready to heed his call. On the morning of October 19, he joined close to three dozen students at Rich's who requested to be served at a snack bar but were denied service. When they refused to leave, they were arrested and charged with trespassing and sent to the Fulton County jail.

Later that day, King stood before Judge James E. Webb, who set his bail bond at $500. In refusing bail, he told the judge that he was willing to spend time in jail because "segregation debilitates the white man as well as the Negro" (Carson et al. 2005, 522). Many of the students followed his lead and refused to post bail, demanding that the charges against them be dropped. The city of Atlanta was on edge, and white elected officials, led by Mayor William Hartsfield, met with the city's black leadership to work out a compromise to secure the protester's release. Negotiations were intense, but the participants hammered out an agreement: the city and department stores would drop their charges, Hartsfield would serve as a liaison between the city's stores and student protesters, sit-ins would be postponed for thirty days to allow for a cool-down period, and all protesters would be released—except King.

The previous May, King had been given a citation for driving with an out-of-state license. In late September, he appeared in court before Judge J.

Oscar Mitchell, pleaded guilty to driving without a proper driving permit, paid a small fine, and was given a suspended sentence. His arrest at the sit-in, authorities maintained, was in violation of his suspended sentence. To determine the validity of this legal argument, King was cuffed, shackled, and transferred to De Kalb County to stand before Judge Oscar Mitchell again. On October 25, six days after King's initial arrest at the sit-in, Judge Mitchell determined that King had violated the terms of his suspended sentence and sentenced him to four months hard labor at the Georgia State Prison in Reidsville. King would begin his sentence the next day and was taken to Reidsville in the early morning hours.

The Georgia State Prison in Reidsville opened in 1937 and is close to two hundred miles from downtown Atlanta. Able-bodied prisoners often worked on projects in and outside of the prison facility, including the maintenance and cleaning of public buildings, construction, and road-work details. King had preached that suffering was redemptive and told his audiences that he was prepared to go to jail, so when he arrived at the rural prison, shocked and bemused, he was preparing himself to complete his sentence.

The thirty-one-year-old would not serve out his sentence, however, because King had friends in high places. After his initial arrest on October 19, the Kennedy presidential campaign failed to gain his release. On the morning of Thursday, October 27, Senator Kennedy's campaign manager, brother, and soon-to-be U.S. attorney general, Robert Kennedy, called Judge Mitchell expressing dismay at his decision. The next morning, Mitchell held another hearing and set King's bail at $2,000. Released from prison, King was interviewed by an NBC reporter who asked him to explain the supposed contradiction in breaking laws by participating in sit-ins while arguing that Supreme Court laws should be obeyed. He responded that "if a particular law is not in line with the moral laws of the universe . . . a righteous and just person has no alternative but to protest against that unjust law" (Carson et al. 2005, 535). After his release and interview, he quickly left Reidsville and flew back to Atlanta.

His imprisonment had shaken him, but it did not weaken his support for the sit-in movement. Participating in another demonstration would have certainly landed him in jail again, making him useless to the movement except as a martyr, so he strategically worked behind the scenes advising students and working with community leaders, including the presidents of black colleges in Atlanta. He also returned to the lecture circuit, raising funds for SCLC by speaking to community groups and universities.

November and December 1960 were marked by three significant events. First, King visited West Africa again, this time at the invitation of Nnamdi Azikewe of Nigeria. Nigeria was one of seventeen former European colonies that obtained its independence in 1960, and Azikewe was sworn in as its first governor-general on November 16. King visited the new nation for several days in mid-November, participated in independence celebrations, and spoke with Nigerian leaders as well as activists and political leaders from new and emerging African nations about American racism. He had already understood the connection between the fight against racism at home and the independence struggles of African and Asian nations and always maintained that the principles of nonviolence needed to be fundamental in all these struggles. His presence in Nigeria and his communication with new, independent African leadership underscored these connections and led him to conclude that if the United States wanted to maintain and extend its influence among emerging nations abroad, then it would have to give and preserve black people's constitutional and civil rights at home.

The second key event in the closing months of 1960 was King's appearance on *The Nation's Future*. The show aired on Saturday nights on NBC from November 1960 to September 1961 and featured academics, activists, and public figures who discussed and debated contemporary societal issues. On November 26, two days after Thanksgiving, King appeared on the show and debated James J. Kilpatrick before a live studio audience. Kilpatrick, the editor of the *Richmond News Leader*, was a staunch defender of southern segregation and used his Virginia newspaper to excoriate the civil rights movement, especially sit-ins. After the 1954 *Brown* decision, he helped organize white resistance to school integration, which led to the closure of some public schools in the state. John McCaffery, the radio and television personality, moderated the debate. King and Kilpatrick sparred over his question: "Are sit-in strikes justifiable?" King provided an opening statement, followed by Kilpatrick's, and then, according to McCaffery, the men had "an opportunity for discussion, for cross-examination . . . for rebuttal" (Carson et al. 2005, 560). King argued that the sit-ins were justified because their "ends were humanitarian, constructive, and moral" (557). Kilpatrick, on the other hand, saw the sit-in movement as an attempt to undermine Western civilization and erase important ethnic and racial lines that white southerners held dear. King characterized the sit-ins as peaceful and nonviolent. Kilpatrick said that they were marked by "restrained violence and hostility" (559). Unsurprisingly, the two disagreed on just about everything. King saw the sit-in movement as necessary, because segregation statutes were in direct violation of federal law, while Kilpatrick saw the sit-in movement as a nuisance that challenged personal property rights and the South's racial hierarchy. Neither won the debate, but it was an opportunity for King to have a nationwide audience.

The third significant event came in December, when the Young Women's Christian Association (YWCA) published an abridged version of King's "The Rising Tide of Racial Consciousness" in the *YWCA Magazine*.

Founded in 1855, the YWCA was created to empower women. In 1946, the organization adopted its "Interracial Charter" that declared that "wherever there is injustice on the basis of race, whether in the community, the nation, or the world, our protest must be clear and our labor for its removal vigorous and steady" (YWCA n.d.). By the late 1950s, the YWCA supported the civil rights movement on national and local levels. The Great Migration, educational achievement, upward economic mobility, the 1954 Brown decision that prohibited racial segregation in public education, and the anticolonial and independence movements among developing nations caused the "Rising Tide of Racial Consciousness" among black people in the late 1950s and early 1960s, which in turn led black people to demand and fight for racial equality and justice.

To eliminate racism, to live up to the nation's democratic values and extend constitutional rights to every citizen regardless of race, King argued that all branches of the federal government must put forward and implement bold initiatives instead of playing politics for their representatives' own personal gain. However, when the federal government fails to act, black people must implement a two-pronged strategy: nonviolent direct action and self-improvement. Nonviolent direct action such as the sit-in movement must continue and be expanded, because segregation laws were immoral and should never be accepted or followed. To overcome the seemingly insurmountable challenges of poverty, crime, cynicism, and disillusionment in black communities nationwide, King said it was imperative that black people create "a constructive action program" to solve their own problems (Carson et al. 2005, 506).

In having such an approach, King weaves together major tenets of twentieth-century black political thought. One tenet called for strong government intervention to improve the lives of black people and end racism. Randolph advocated for such an approach and pressured presidents Franklin Roosevelt and Harry Truman to use their authority to ban racial discrimination in the military and among military contractors. The other major tenet called for self-help. This approach urged black people to create their own businesses and institutions to uplift their community. Such a line of thinking harkened back to Marcus Garvey, the founder of the Universal Negro Improvement Association, and Booker T. Washington, the prominent black political leader of the late nineteenth and early twentieth centuries and founder of the Tuskegee Institute in Alabama. A quote commonly attributed to Washington is, "The individual who can do something that the world wants done will, in the end, make his way regardless of his race." Perhaps King had that in mind when he said, "We must do our life's work so well that nobody could do it better" (506).

From the time he departed for India in early February 1959 until December 1960, King's life was in transition. He maintained his commitment to nonviolence and became more convinced of its power, but as time unfolded, he became less wedded to his calling to be a congregational leader. He simply could not have done the important work necessary for Dexter to thrive or given his flock the necessary spiritual guidance and be a national leader and spokesperson for the growing civil rights movement. His move back home to Atlanta as copastor at Ebenezer gave him the time and space to reenergize the SCLC and make it into a militant civil rights organization. He had survived Izola Curry's stabbing, endured Alabama's attempt to sully his reputation with tax evasion charges, and walked out of a Georgia State Prison, all the while spreading his nonviolent ideas and being a major participant in a growing movement for racial justice. The sit-in movement proved that nonviolent direct action was an important and effective tool for challenging and changing segregation laws and could led by students. In the coming years, King and the SCLC would use nonviolent direct protests of their own in southern cities, and his influence would continue to grow.

# 5

## The Nation and the World Are Listening

King was busy in 1961, and for most of the year, he traveled the nation speaking to a variety of audiences at churches, schools, universities, and labor union halls in almost every major American city. He gave a lot of speeches and sermons, but he had a repertoire that he delivered frequently and could improvise with. Two speeches he often used and were well received by audiences were "The American Dream" and "The Future of Integration," and two of his most popular sermons were "The Man Who Was a Fool" and "Paul's Letter to American Christians." Between speaking engagements and fundraising for the SCLC, King carved out time to write articles for publication in the *New York Times* and *The Nation* and to be copastor at Ebenezer Baptist Church with his father. Though he would not participate in the Congress of Racial Equality's (CORE's) freedom rides during the spring and summer, King became an ardent supporter. In fact, he would not participate in any direct nonviolent actions until late 1961, when he led a march in Albany, Georgia.

"The American Dream" was a popular speech in 1961, but it is not the same as King's "I Have a Dream" speech delivered at the August 1963 March on Washington. He delivered the speech to mostly black and multiracial audiences several times throughout the year. In June, the 1961 graduating class at Lincoln University near Oxford, Pennsylvania, heard the lecture at their commencement ceremony. Central New York residents heard his eloquence in mid-July at Syracuse University. During a series of speaking engagements in the Pacific Northwest in early November, King visited Garfield High School on November 10 and spoke to the students in the school gymnasium. Carver Gayton was a young black teacher at the school during King's visit and recalls that he "had never heard an orator in my life that sounded like him" (Jenks 2018).

King begins by referencing the Declaration of Independence and declares that the United States of America is an unfolding dream wherein blacks and whites are citizens with God-given rights and are destined to live together in peace and equality. The American dream, he notes, continues to endure lasting moral injury because of American slavery and its legacy of segregation. Black communities all over the country bear and battle white supremacy, where white vigilantism, police, and politicians refuse to accept Supreme Court rulings and use legal and extralegal methods to deny them their constitutional rights.

To make the American dream a reality for everyone, King suggests several interconnected strategies. The first is that black people must see their fight for civil rights within a larger worldwide context of anticolonial movements in Africa and Asia. Having spoken to African and Asian leaders during his trips to Ghana, Nigeria, and India, he reminds his audience that new nations were watching the United States to see how it would handle its nationwide discrimination against black people. However, he did not stop with black people or other oppressed people of color in the United States; instead, King urged his listeners to commit to a twentieth-century cosmopolitanism in which all humans, despite race, nation, and religion, were part of a single, universal, world community. The second strategy he suggests is the complete eradication of the ideology of white supremacy in which white Americans and white Europeans are understood to be superior to every other racial group in the nation and on the planet. Finally, King recommends that those of goodwill who want to end the immoral practices of segregation recommit to nonviolence and engage in direct, nonviolent mass action.

With these nonviolent weapons in their arsenal, he advises those involved in the civil rights struggle to dismiss arguments made by whites who preferred a gradual end to segregation. Such gradualists often insisted that an end to segregation must be achieved slowly through the education of white segregationists, not through the legislative process, presidential decree, or nonviolent direct action. He admits that the social education of white segregationists is important and through such education, white southerners may learn to turn from their bigoted ways. However, such an approach, King concludes, is myopic and limiting because education, legislation, and protests must be used together to end the humiliating and demoralizing system of segregation and discrimination in employment, housing, and other sectors of American life, not education alone.

"The American Dream" ends on a hopeful note with King reminding the audience that with Christian love and the weapon of nonviolent resistance, racial justice would be achieved, because the civil rights struggle was a righteous one and God was on their side.

"The Future of Integration" was often reserved for predominantly white college audiences, and throughout the year, King delivered the address at the University of Utah, New York University, Cornell University, Lewis and Clark College, Portland State College, Wisconsin State College, Los Angeles Valley College, Linton High School in Schenectady, New York, and Canoga Park High School in the San Fernando Valley of Los Angeles County. After his visit to New York University, a student reporter wrote in the university newspaper that "no recent visitor to the Heights received the tumultuous reception we gave Dr. King. No one stirred our conscience, penetrated our lethargy, and fired our idealism as much as he" (Monjeau 2021). At Portland State University, a student recalled that "at 11 a.m. classes were dismissed so students could attend the convocation, and the auditorium was filled to overflowing. King received an enthusiastic reception from the students, who gave him a standing ovation at the conclusion of his speech" (Wettland 1961).

In "The Future of Integration," King situates African Americans in three periods of black–white relations in U.S. history. During the first period, which begins with the arrival of West African slaves and ends with the 1863 Emancipation Proclamation, he notes that Africans and their descendants are only seen as chattel and tools used by whites on plantations with no political rights. The second era, from the Emancipation Proclamation to the 1954 *Brown* decision, was a period of limited freedom wherein racial slavery was abolished and black people were legally free but not recognized as full citizens of the United States. It was during this period that the promises of Reconstruction went unfulfilled and Jim Crow laws were passed to reestablish white supremacy and relegate most of the black population in the South to servitude. King and his contemporaries were experiencing the third period of black–white relations, which began when the U.S. Supreme Court declared that racial segregation in schools was unconstitutional in the *Brown v. Board of Education* decision in 1954. King calls the time an era of constructive integration where, with the backing of the Supreme Court decision, the South had the opportunity to move toward positive interactive and relational living unimpeded by Jim Crow.

He cautions his audience that during this third period in race relations, integration was not a foregone conclusion. The Ku Klux Klan, White Citizens' Councils, and white segregationist politicians continued to oppose integration through violent threats, economic reprisals, and their bully pulpit to thwart desegregation efforts. Integration would occur through bold and direct leadership from federal, state, and local governments as well as meaningful efforts by community-based and religious institutions whose work could counterbalance segregationist forces and support those organizations and individuals who suffer under their opposition.

"The Man Who Was a Fool" was broadcast on a local radio station when King was in Chicago in late January. He delivered it again in Detroit in early March 1961, in a special service ushering in the Easter season. He uses Luke 12:16–21 (King James Version) as his text for the sermon:

> And he spake a parable unto them saying, The ground of a certain rich man brought forth plentifully: And he thought within himself, saying, What shall I do, because I have no room where to bestow my fruits? And he said, This will I do: I will pull down my barns and build greater; and there will I bestow all my fruit and my goods. And I will say to my soul, Soul, thou has much good laid up for many years; take thine ease, eat, drink, and be merry. But God said unto him, Thou fool, this night thy soul shall be required of thee: then whose shall those things be, which thou hast provided? So is he that layeth up treasure for himself, and is not rich toward God.

King uses Jesus's parable to discuss contemporary individual, interpersonal, and international relationships.

With regard to the individual, the man in the parable was a fool because he was too concerned with the accumulation of goods. His primary relationship was to his goods and fruit, which he did not create or grow by himself. This unbalanced relationship led to a compromised spiritual and intellectual life. King maintains that the parable is a warning. It is not telling the individual to avoid material prosperity, give away their wealth, or become lazy; instead, Jesus's teaching tells his followers to create a humane existence that balances one's livelihood with cultural, intellectual, and spiritual pursuits, and their connections to others.

In the area of interpersonal relations, specifically black–white relations, King says the parable has significance. The man was a fool because he subscribed to the false belief that his life was not inextricably linked to the lives of others. With all his creature comforts and materials, he believed he was somehow independent and inherently better than others. Similarly, many whites in the contemporary South were fools because they subscribed to the foolish notion of white supremacy and failed to see how their lives were inseparable from the lives of black southerners. Equally important is the foolishness of black supremacy, because neither black nor white supremacy would bring about equality for all.

Jesus's parable resonates in international relations, King thought. The United States, like the man in the parable, had surplus materials. Like the man in the parable, the nation spent large sums of money erecting and fortifying its barns to store its surplus. As the man failed to wisely share his wealth, so did the United States. King referenced his recent trips to

West Africa and India, where he saw homelessness and poverty and connected it to U.S. foreign policy. Rather than subscribing to the foolish policy of keeping surplus materials for one's nation or oneself, like the fool, the United States should store its surplus in the bellies of poor, starving people around the world. Personally, interpersonally, and internationally to bring about a brotherhood, one must move from "a worship of things" to a worship of God.

During the late summer and throughout autumn, King delivered "Paul's Letter to American Christians," first at Flipper Temple African Methodist Episcopal Church on July 5 and then one month later at Ebenezer on August 6. Two weeks after the Ebenezer sermon, he gave the address at Riverside Church in New York City. On October 8, the audience and participants at Detroit's New Calvary's Men's Day celebration heard the homily, followed by the members of Philadelphia's White Rock Baptist Church during their anniversary celebration on October 22. King first delivered a version of the sermon in 1956 and had performed it many times in the years preceding 1961. Paul was a disciple of Jesus and one of the earliest Christian missionaries. Throughout his missionary work, he wrote a series of important letters, or epistles, to various Christian communities to explain Jesus's teachings, support Christian converts, and guide nascent Christian communities in Asia Minor. Many of his writings became part of the New Testament.

King did not liken himself to Paul but was clearly inspired by him when he wrote and delivered "Paul's Letter to American Christians." At the beginning of his remarks, he says the letter is "imaginary" and was an attempt to channel the Apostle Paul's energy, insight, and commitment to bringing about a just, beloved community. The sermon comments on several aspects of American life. First, King/Paul says that American technological advancements were made at the expense of moral advancements because rather than anchoring the nation's moral foundations on the age-old, universal teachings of Jesus, the nation's political and religious leaders put their faith in transitory, human-made institutions. In its constant search for innovation, the nation and its leaders failed to search for and achieve a caring and harmonious brotherhood. King/Paul appreciates scientific advances and does not want the nation to lose sight of their importance; however, he encourages the American people to align their moral and technological advancement.

In the economic realm, King/Paul notes that capitalism has allowed the United States to become the most affluent society in history while creating gross economic inequalities where a small minority possesses and controls most of the nation's wealth. Because God has "left in the universe enough," he "intends for all of his children to have the basic necessities of life" (Carson et al. 2007, 340). To eradicate poverty, he warns the congregation not to fall under the influence of communism because communism was inherently un-Christian, as it was based on an "ethical relativism and metaphysical materialism" (341). The fair and just redistribution of wealth in the nation must be accomplished through democratic means.

He continues with an observation of the Christian church in the United States. There were hundreds of Protestant denominations in the country claiming to possess and espouse the ultimate and infallible truth. Segregation existed in the church, making the Sunday morning service "the most segregated hour in Christian America" (Carson et al. 2007, 342). Churches must unify to avoid sectarianism and end segregation in the American Christian church and throughout society to live together in harmony with God's law and the "heartbeat of the moral cosmos" (346).

Furthering his struggle for racial justice, King participated in two high-profile interviews in 1961 and used the medium of television to continue his fight against racism and segregation. On February 7 and 8, he sat down again with journalist Mike Wallace. During the late 1950s and early 1960s, Wallace was one of the few popular white journalists sympathetic to the black people's movement for justice and equality. He first interviewed King in 1958 for his popular televised show *Night Beat*. One year later, with the black journalist Louis Lomax, Wallace produced *The Hate That Hate Produced*, an exposé about the Nation of Islam. In the late 1960s, Wallace joined *60 Minutes*, a nationally televised, weekly investigative journalism program and soon became the anchor journalist, a position he held until his retirement in 2006 at the age of eighty-eight.

In 1961, King appeared on Wallace's *The Mike Wallace Interviews*, and Wallace published the transcript of the interview in the *New York Post*. King clarified the relationship between the NAACP and the SCLC and said that the SCLC supplemented the NAACP's work. He went on to explain his position and reason for disobeying unjust laws and declared that he would "openly disobey the unjust law and willingly accept the penalty in order to arouse the conscience of the community" (Carson et al. 2007, 159). In response to Wallace's question about whether white southerners had the right to protest school integration, King said that white southerners should follow their conscience and use peaceful and nonviolent action. When speaking about the role of the federal government in dismantling segregation throughout the South, King argued that President Eisenhower's leadership in the civil rights struggle had been weak and failed to bring about positive results for African Americans. Consequently, it was imperative that President Kennedy use his executive powers to end racial discrimination in federally funded housing, airport construction, hospital expansion, and in any business that received government contracts.

## Cultural Connection: The Motown Sound

The northern soul aesthetic was defined by Motown in the late 1950s and early 1960s. Started by Berry Gordy Jr., the label created a sound that made use of southern-based gospel vocals and rhythm and blues but in a more polished and stylistic manner. Gordy, born and raised in Detroit, expressed an interest in music at an early age. Before making his start in the music business, he dropped out of high school and was a professional boxer, an assembly-line worker with the Ford Motor Company, and a soldier in the U.S. Army, serving in Korea. In 1959, Gordy founded Tamla Records and in 1960 incorporated the company into the Motown Record Corporation. Gordy's Motown, which began in a single dwelling, soon burgeoned into nine buildings on its block. With Motown's first multimillion-dollar hit, "Shop Around" (1960), cowritten by Gordy and Smokey Robinson, the company began to develop the signature Motown Sound. This sound, broadly defined, was a lighter soul rendition with simple arrangements, tight orchestrations, driving rhythms, bass lines, and a generally refined quality, and it appealed to R&B and pop markets.

The Motown Sound was defined by a collective of musicians known as the Funk Brothers and a stable of songwriters that included Holland, Dozier, and Holland (Eddie and Bryan Holland and Lamont Dozier), Smokey Robinson, and Stevie Wonder. The Funk Brothers were a versatile band of solid musicians capable of executing grooves as varied as hard funk and lush ballads. Advances in technology were also paramount in the development of this sound, as the use of eight-track recording enabled producers to isolate certain parts of the rhythm section. Multitracking afforded greater control and flexibility for recording drums and percussion, as many Motown songs featured two drummers performing simultaneously or on overdubbed tracks. These musicians rarely worked directly with the vocalists because the instrumental tracks were created first and the vocals were added later and because they were a studio band and rarely toured.

The company's use of pop elements as well as diligent packaging and marketing of its early artists such as the Supremes, Martha and the Vandellas, and the Miracles attracted a large white audience. During the early years of Motown's history, song lyrics were light in content, steering away from political or social contexts. During the late 1960s, the label began to produce harder-edged songs featuring lyrics that addressed more than just the different scenarios of love relationships. Instead, they pressed on to widen the discussion of quality-of-life issues, including the topics of inner-city life and the ever-widening gap between economic classes. Motown's roster was diverse, consisting of a number of girl groups (the Marvelettes, Martha and the Vandellas), solo artists (Mary Wells, Tammi Terrell, Marvin Gaye, Stevie Wonder), and male groups (the Four Tops, the Miracles). However, two groups, in particular, were key to their popularity with mainstream audiences—the Supremes and the Temptations.

Source: Tammy Kernodle, Katherine Gould, and Amanda de la Garza, "The Birth of Soul: Stax and Motown Records, 1957–1967," in Jamie Wilson, ed., *50 Events That Shaped African American History*, vol. 2 (Santa Barbara, CA: ABC-CLIO, 2019), 476–477.

After King spoke about growing up in segregated Atlanta, Georgia, and the resentment and discontent he felt being a second-class citizen, Wallace asked him how he felt about being the figurehead of the growing civil rights movement. King responded that he was learning to be more comfortable with the idea of being a symbol of the movement for justice and equality, although it required constant meditation and introspection and often took time away from his family. He admitted that while he was often compared to Gandhi, Jesus, and Henry David Thoreau, he did not "want anybody to feel that I'm Christ, or that I'm a Gandhi or . . . a Thoreau," because as a mortal, fallible man who was not omniscient, he had "no pretense to absolute goodness" (Carson et al. 2007, 166). Instead, he was deeply influenced and inspired by Jesus, Gandhi, and Thoreau, as were others who came before him.

From October 28 to October 30, King was in London, England, where he delivered a sermon at Bloomsbury Central Baptist Church and spoke to Christian activists at the iconic Central Hall. On October 29, journalist John Freeman interviewed him on *Face to Face*, a popular discussion and talk show in the United Kingdom. *Face to Face* ran from 1959 to 1962 and featured some of the leading intellectuals and public personalities of the era, including the psychiatrist Carl Jung, philosopher Bertrand Russell, and poet Edith Sitwell. Throughout the thirty-minute interview, Freeman's questions were not particularly incisive, and King's responses were measured and thoughtful. King retold how his leadership began with the Montgomery bus boycott and explained how throughout the years that followed, the cost of being a leader included receiving threatening letters and phone calls with inadequate police protection from white mobs and vigilantism or hate crimes such as cross burnings. Being a leader and symbol of the civil rights movement has moments of fear, loneliness, and feelings of inadequacy. His deep faith in God and his commitment to the efficacy of nonviolent direct action buoyed his spirit and offered him strength to continue in the struggle in times of self-doubt. The *Face to Face* interview offered King a new, international audience.

Television was still a new medium of expression in 1961, and King deftly used it along with the radio to further the black struggle for freedom. While *The Mike Wallace Interviews* and *Face to Face* provided King with his largest multimedia audiences, he did not shy away from regional television or radio interviews. In March, when he was in Worcester, Massachusetts, his lecture and answers to public questions were broadcast on WTAG, a radio station in central Massachusetts. Later that month, in Kansas City, Missouri, he was interviewed on WDAF-TV, a station that served the Kansas City metropolitan area. The *Los Angeles Report* aired an interview with King on a local CBS affiliate when he visited the City of Angels in June. Syracuse University's radio station, WAER, aired King's address on the campus in July. WERD in Atlanta, the first African American–owned radio station in the United States, transmitted King's talk at the Butler Street YMCA in October. During his trip to the Pacific Northwest, KOAP-TV, an affiliate of the Oregon Public Broadcasting system, aired a panel discussion with King and interested followers. On the Sunday following Thanksgiving, November 26, he was interviewed again and responded to audience members' questions on *Open Circuit*, a local Cleveland, Ohio, television show.

King also used the press to rally support for the civil rights movement and published three articles, one in *The Nation*, titled "Equality Now: The President Has the Power," and two in the *New York Times Magazine*, titled "What Is the World's Greatest Need?" and "The Time for Freedom Has Come." His February 4 article in *The Nation* provides prescriptions for how President Kennedy—he calls Kennedy's term a "well-meaning Administration" and "an Administration with goodwill"—could use his "Presidential prestige" and executive authority to help end racial discrimination against black Americans. By presidential prestige, King suggested that "as the embodiment of the democratic personality of the nation," what the president does and how he is seen is important. If President Kennedy through his actions and behaviors does not condone racism by participating in segregated events, then he would set an example for other Americans, especially white southerners. Kennedy's most effective weapon to end racial discrimination, King argued, was through executive orders. Abraham Lincoln issued the Emancipation Proclamation. Franklin Roosevelt issued executive orders to stabilize the country during the Great Depression. Harry Truman desegregated the military with Executive Order 9981. King urges President Kennedy to use these former presidents as examples and fully use his executive power to end racial discrimination in federal employment and in all industries and sectors receiving federal funding, including housing, the Department of Agriculture, health care, and education. He goes on to offer several concrete suggestions:

> Executive orders could prohibit any contractor dealing with any federal agency from practicing discrimination in employment by requiring (a) cancellation of existing contracts, (b) and/or barring violators from bidding, (c) and/or calling in of government loans of federal funds extended to violators, (d) and/or requiring renegotiation of payment to exact penalties where violations appear after performance of a contract. (King, "Equality," 1961)

Finally, to implement an effective, rigorous, and all-encompassing federal program to combat racial discrimination, King called on the president to appoint a secretary of integration who would be above petty partisan politics to "complete a process of democratization which our nation has taken far too long to develop" (King, "Equality," 1961).

"What Is the World's Greatest Need?" was published on April 2 and is an ethical entreaty. King warns that "unless we can reestablish the moral end for living in personal character and social justice, our civilization will destroy itself by the misuse of its own instruments" (King, "What Is the World's Greatest Need?," 1961). As he argued in his sermon "Paul's Letter to Christian America," the nation needed to align its moral advancement with its technological advancement to avoid self-destruction.

In King's article "The Time for Freedom Has Come," published on September 10, he defends and supports black college students' nonviolent direct actions against Jim Crow and all forms of racial discrimination in the United States. The article explains the origins, motivations, and strategies of black college students' sit-ins and freedom rides. He calls African American students pioneers in the struggle against social injustice who were motivated by anticolonial struggles throughout Africa and Asia and wanted more than token integration where a few black people are welcomed into white institutions. Using nonviolent direct action, civil disobedience, and satire as their weapons, they sought to eliminate Jim Crow peacefully and completely throughout the whole United States, not just for black people, but for the well-being of the nation, and were willing to fill jails throughout the South for disobeying unjust Jim Crow laws. King urged white northern liberals to support the student movement and use their political power to press the Kennedy administration for quick and decisive actions to end racial discrimination. He also challenged them to "mobilize their forces behind a real honest to goodness 'End Jim Crow Now' campaign" (King, "The Time," 1961).

Throughout the South in the late 1950s and early 1960s, African Americans endured segregation and discrimination in interstate transit, despite Supreme Court rulings banning the practice. To encourage President Kennedy to enforce the court's rulings in the South, CORE began the freedom rides during the first week of May. The original plan was to enlist an interracial group of CORE volunteers who would board two Greyhound buses in Washington, DC, bound for New Orleans, Louisiana. During their journey throughout the South, they would challenge segregation laws: the white passengers would sit in the back of the bus where blacks were supposed to sit, and blacks would sit in the front of the bus in seats reserved for whites. At rest stops, the white passengers would use facilities reserved for blacks, and blacks would use facilities reserved for whites. After leaving the nation's capital, for close to two weeks, they planned to stop in Greensboro, North Carolina; Rock Hill, South Carolina; and Atlanta, Georgia. From there they would make three stops in Alabama: Anniston, Birmingham, and Montgomery. After leaving Alabama, they intended to travel to Jackson, Mississippi, and end their journey in New Orleans. Outside Anniston, Alabama, one bus was bombed. In Birmingham, the Ku Klux

Klan brutalized freedom riders. On May 20 in Montgomery, a white mob assembled and beat several of the freedom riders and federal agents attempting to protect them.

King arrived in Montgomery on May 21 to lead a rally at Reverend Ralph Abernathy's First Baptist Church to support the freedom rides. The mass meeting began at 8:00 p.m. with over 1,500 congregants, including the freedom riders. Outside the church, federal U.S. marshals were guarding the church as a rowdy white mob grew. Shortly before the meeting began, King and several other clergymen stepped out of the church to check the perimeter of the building and were met with racial epithets and flying projectiles. They saw that the marshals had set up a perimeter several yards across from the church and were trying to control the crowd with their nightsticks. As the evening progressed, the white mob, advancing closer to the church, overturned and burned a car. King made a phone call to Robert Kennedy, asking for immediate assistance. Kennedy responded that more marshals were en route from the local air force base on the outskirts of town.

As the marshals arrived, "the attackers battered against the front doors, and some of the marshals, hearing cries from within that the doors had been breached, gained entry through the back door of the basement. They ran through the clogged corridors in time to push the rioters back outside with nightsticks and shoulders" (Branch 1988, 460). Outside they used tear gas to disperse the crowd, and the plume of gas engulfed the church, choking the anxious and nervous congregation. King called for calm: "The first thing that we must do here tonight is to decide that we aren't going to become panicky. And we're going to be calm. And that we are going to continue to stand up for what we know is right. And that Alabama will have to face the fact that we are determined to be free" ("Ain't Scared of Your Jails" 1987). Late into the night, when Alabama's national guard reinforced federal marshals, King was told that the 1,500 congregants, who included children and the elderly, would have to remain in the church until the next morning. Again, he called Robert Kennedy, seeking further assistance, but with no success. It was not the time for speeches and eloquence. The only thing left to do was to roll up his sleeves, deliver much-needed pastoral care and reassurance to those trapped in the church, and make the best of a bad situation until sunrise when the white mob had dispersed, and the guardsmen could provide them safe passage home.

After the May 21–22, 1961, siege on First Baptist Church, King spent several days in Montgomery advocating for and supporting freedom riders. Given the violence meted out to the riders and the clear lack of local protection against white vigilantism and mobocracy, King, the SCLC, and local black leaders were concerned for the freedom riders' safety. Some thought it unwise for them to continue and called for a cooling-off period, to allow angry white locals to calm down and media attention to cease. However, the young and undeterred freedom riders were adamant that they should continue to Jackson, Mississippi, as soon as possible. To stop the freedom rides or wait meant a loss of momentum. King prayed and strategized with the college students during prayer meetings and planning sessions. At times, the meetings were contentious, and the riders questioned King's convictions. During one meeting, Diane Nash, one of the freedom riders from Fisk University in Nashville, Tennessee, asked King to join them and go to Jackson to be true to his pronouncements about how civil rights activists should fill the jails and face death if they must. The freedom riders continued the next leg of their dangerous journey at the Montgomery bus station late Wednesday morning on May 24. King was present, shook hands, and wished them well but did not get on the bus.

Why King refused to participate in freedom rides from Montgomery, Alabama, to Jackson, Mississippi, is unclear. Perhaps it was the state itself. Mississippi was nationally known for its antipathy toward blacks' constitutional rights and its violence toward them. For decades, white mob lynching of African American men and women was commonplace. Further, most freedom riders were teenagers or in their early twenties. King, on the other hand, was a father, husband, and a successful copastor of Ebenezer Baptist Church. Having been to jail on questionable charges and still on probation for a not-so-routine traffic stop, it appears that he was reluctant to go back to jail. He decided he could do better spreading the word of nonviolence and raising money for the SCLC out of jail rather than being an imprisoned martyr.

King traveled the nation and the world speaking about the philosophy of nonviolence and nonviolent massive resistance, made appearances on radio and television supporting the student sit-in movement and freedom rides, and was the figurehead of a movement for justice, but King still had spiritual commitments to the members of Ebenezer Baptist Church. As a copastor of the church, he was concerned with and had an obligation to his congregation's spiritual development. Throughout the year, King offered several sermons to the congregation about a variety of issues, including marriage and family life, the nature of God's love, anxiety and fear, and Christian ethics. In a sermon titled "What Then Are Some of the Secrets of a Happy Marriage?," King tells his congregation that marriage "sanctifies the privilege of sharing in creative life" and reminds them that people should be cautious when entering wedlock because happy marriages require those being married to know their personal expectations and be able to compromise (Carson et al. 2007, 433). His homily "The Secret of Adjustment" builds from Philippians 4:11: "Not that I speak in respect of want: for I have learned, in whatsoever state I am, therewith to be content" (KJV). Here Jesus's apostle Paul is writing to the people in the city of

## CULTURAL CONNECTION: KU KLUX KLAN

During Reconstruction (1866–1877), agents of the Democratic Party revived the tradition of pre–Civil War regulators and slave patrols to create paramilitary vigilante groups. These secretive ritual fraternities, quickly subsumed under the label Ku Klux Klan, endeavored to counter the Freedman's Bureau, destroy the Republican Party infrastructure, reestablish control over black labor, and restore racial subordination in all aspects of southern political, economic, and social life.

Conflating sexual fear and partisan politics, Klansmen posed as chivalrous avengers of victimized white womanhood, their chosen symbol of the white South. By the mid-1920s, the Second Klan had become a predominantly urban, mainstream social movement of four million members that represented a cross section of white Protestant denominations and social classes. In the context of the time, these Klansmen were not more reactionary, racist, ethnocentric, religiously bigoted, or socially alienated than the general white Protestant population. World War II provided a new context, as black veterans spearheaded the Double Victory campaign. Despite the tireless efforts of anti-Klan activists such as Stetson Kennedy to mobilize the Justice Department against them, Klan terrorists responded to African American activism with arson and dynamite, targeting black businesses, homes, and churches in the 1940s and early 1950s.

Implementation of the 1954 Supreme Court decision in *Brown v. Board of Education* in border states led to the first organization of Citizens' Councils by middle-class whites throughout the South. The ultimate failure of massive resistance, however, turned people toward the Klan. Alabama Klansmen bombed homes and churches in Montgomery and abducted and castrated black handyman Edward Aaron near Birmingham. During a fifteen-month period in 1957–1958, forty-six bombs exploded at black and Jewish institutions in Miami, Jacksonville, Nashville, and Atlanta. Klan violence also grew more lethal in the 1960s. In September 1963, Klansmen planted a massive bomb beneath the 16th Street Baptist Church in Birmingham, Alabama. It exploded during the Sunday church service, killing three little girls. In 1964, Georgia Klansmen killed serviceman Lemuel Penn. In Mississippi, thirty-five shootings, thirty bombings, thirty-five church burnings, eighty beatings, and at least six racially motivated murders took place during the first eight months of 1964. Between 1964 and 1971, media exposure, selective enforcement of local law, tax audits, and an FBI covert action program finally neutralized Klan violence. Klan membership declined to a few thousand as white supremacy slowly changed from being an integral part of southern life into an extremist ideology. Klans revived in the rural South during the late 1970s and attacked civil rights activists with weapons on a number of occasions. In general, however, as society changed around them, white supremacists lost touch with the mainstream.

Source: John Drabble, "Ku Klux Klan," in Leslie Alexander and Walter Rucker, ed., *Encyclopedia of African American History*, vol. 3 (Santa Barbara, CA: ABC-CLIO, 2010), 853–856.

Philippi, an affluent Roman colony. King argues that like Paul, it is necessary for members of his congregation to move beyond belief, know "that over against changeableness [of life] . . . there is a changeless structure of goodness," and therefore learn to be more content and at peace with themselves (435).

He also led the Ebenezer congregation and the nation to think about the nature of hell. In January 1961, *Ebony* magazine asked ministers around the nation to give a brief statement about their beliefs and understanding of hell. Among those asked were two of King's mentors, Dr. Howard Thurman and Benjamin Mays. In response to the question "What Happened to Hell?," King, who had trained at two northern liberal Christian theological schools, Crozer Seminary and Boston University, departed from more traditional African American Christian teachings about hell, where an individual's soul is given over to eternal damnation. Unlike Reverend Marmaduke Carter of Chicago's Saint Philip Lutheran Church, who responded that "hell is real, not symbolism" with "eternal hell-fire," King suggested that hell "is man's refusal to accept the Grace of God [and] the state in which the individual continues to experience the frustrations, contradictions and agonies of earthly life" ("What Happened to Hell" 1961).

King avoided the jail time that freedom riders endured after they continued their freedom rides to Jackson and New Orleans, but only for a short while. Seven months after the freedom rides, he was arrested and jailed in Albany, Georgia. The city of Albany is in rural southwest Georgia along the Flint River, and in 1960, over half of its population of about fifty thousand were African American. Unlike other areas in the Georgia and the South that had started the process of desegregation, whites in Albany were resistant to any change in the city's racial hierarchy and white supremacy. Despite the federal government prohibiting segregation in interstate travel, Albany was out of compliance with the Interstate Commerce Committee's orders to desegregate and continued to maintain white- and black-only public facilities. Members of the Student Nonviolent Coordinating Committee, led by Charles Sherrod and Cordell Reagon, arrived in Albany in the fall of 1961 to assist black residents' challenges to segregation. Local black Albany's efforts were coordinated by the Albany Movement, an organization that helped direct, manage, and assist local civil rights groups, led by Dr. William G. Anderson. Sit-ins occurred at local schools and city hall. Read-ins took place in the city library. Blacks also demonstrated in movie theaters and parks. In addition, young people ignored segregation laws in bus terminals and train stations and refused to use separate and inferior accommodations in the blacks-only section.

By early December, hundreds of housewives, students, and working-class blacks were arrested for following federal law but violating local customs. Feeling overwhelmed and needing help because of the mass arrests,

Dr. Anderson and his team contacted the Southern Christian Leadership Conference (SCLC), asking them to come to Albany to help raise funds to bail out the imprisoned activists. King drove the 190 miles from Atlanta to Albany on Friday, December 15. With him was the inner circle of SCLC: the Reverends Ralph Abernathy, Wyatt T. Walker, and Andrew Young. The plan was for King to arrive, deliver a speech, use his national and international stature to attract a large crowd and raise money for the Albany Movement, and then return home late that evening so he could use Saturday to prepare his sermon for Sunday services at Ebenezer.

The plans changed, however, when Anderson publicly asked King to lead a demonstration with him to city hall the next day to pray on the steps of the city government. Despite other obligations, King reluctantly agreed. On Saturday morning, he addressed hundreds of protesters at Shiloh Baptist Church, and after speeches were given and prayers were said, King, Abernathy, and Anderson led a procession of close to three hundred marchers to Albany City Hall. City Hall was approximately a half mile away from the church, and the demonstrators began their march in silence. They had only walked a short time when they were met by police chief Laurie Pritchett and his officers.

In an interview, Pritchett remembered the Albany Movement and his approach to black demonstrators:

> I had information from another law enforcement agency.... And they had informed me that Dr. King's intentions were to come into Albany and join the Albany Movement. Upon learning this, I did research. I found his method was non-violence. That his method was to fill the jail.... And once he filled the jails, we'd have no capacity to arrest and then we'd have to give in to his demands. After learning this and studying this research, I started orientation of the police department into non-violent movement: no violence, no dogs, no show of force.... We're going to out non-violent [them] and this is what the police department and the other people did. (Pritchett 1985)

Pritchett told the marchers that they were parading without a proper permit, blocking traffic, and illegally assembling on the sidewalk, and he ordered them to disperse. When they refused, Pritchett and his men arrested everyone, including King. Bail was set for the protesters, but King refused to be bailed out. Abernathy made bail and returned to Atlanta, hoping to garner national support for the imprisoned King. Fearing that white vigilantes would bring more chaos to Albany by harming King, Pritchett transferred him and Anderson to the Sumter County jail in Americus, Georgia, forty miles away.

In Sumter County jail, King had a restless night's sleep but was adamant that he would remain in jail for several weeks. Unbeknownst to him, local black Albany Movement leaders were at work working with white Albany officials on a settlement. The *New York Times* reported that "[i]n Albany, Georgia, Negro and white leaders agreed on a plan to end troubles" ("Dr. King Is Freed" 1961). On Monday, December 18, King and Anderson were returned to Albany and, while awaiting their trial, were told that as part of the deal, all demonstrators, including King and Anderson, were to be set free. In the late afternoon, King and Anderson stood before Judge Abner Israel and made bail. Despite asking for his assistance, the majority of black Albany Movement leadership did not need King as a political prisoner to further their cause, and white Albany elected officials did not want him bringing more national attention to their small, segregated city. King left Albany and returned to Atlanta that evening, but he would return to Albany in the summer of 1962 to face charges associated with his December 1961 arrest.

The deal struck between movement leaders and city officials was in name only. Segregation continued unabated, and Chief Pritchett was praised for his professionalism, ostensibly for keeping the peace but truly for maintaining segregation without brutalizing black demonstrators in the process. For some, Pritchett and Albany exposed the limits of nonviolent direct action. For it to be effective, whites must resort to violence, but when opponents of integration do not show violence, all that was left were shallow promises, incarcerated protesters, and the status quo. The situation in Albany taught King and the SCLC lessons they would apply as they challenged racism and discrimination in Birmingham in 1962.

During 1961, King continued to spread the word of nonviolence around the nation and around the world and would continue to do so with the same energy and zeal in 1962. In a December 1961 interview with a *New York Amsterdam News* reporter, he said that in 1962, the SCLC would "concentrate on the states of Alabama, South Carolina, and Mississippi because there has not been any desegregation activity in those states at all" and that they would "fight to the death" ("Rev. King Says" 1961).

# 6

## People to People and People in Action

In January 1962, *Look* magazine published a special issue celebrating its twenty-fifth anniversary and asked prominent Americans in a variety of fields and an assortment of expertise to predict what might occur in the next twenty-five years. President Kennedy hoped that "tranquility will have replaced terror in the intercourse" and that the nation would "make progress in protecting the natural charm of America." Billy Graham, the evangelist, said that "there will be a period of history when Satanic forces will be unleashed upon the world on a scale without parallel in human history." King was more optimistic than Graham, the man he had once admired and considered working with, and said that between 1962 and 1987, he expected that the Christian era would have begun and hoped that "militarism and mass ignorance will have become ugly relics of a vain quasi-civilization" ("The Next 25 Years" 1962).

In early 1962, King was the father of three young children. Yolanda turned seven, Martin III turned five, and Dexter turned one that year. Having been married to Coretta since 1953, the two celebrated their ninth wedding anniversary, the willow anniversary. It had been six years since the Montgomery bus boycott, and despite some reluctance on his part, King appeared more comfortable in being a national leader in the fight for integration. As with his 1957 *Ebony* magazine column "Advice for Living," King sought to use the black press to express and disseminate his views on civil rights issues and was hired by the *New York Amsterdam News* to contribute biweekly to their "People in Action" column. He also published two high-profile articles, one in the *New York Times* and the other in *The Nation*. Throughout the year, he continued to be copastor at Ebenezer Baptist Church with his father and tended to the spiritual development of the congregation through sermons and pastoral care. He also continued to be president of the Southern Christian Leadership Conference (SCLC) and as such, toured the nation lecturing to raise money for the organization. Having reflected on failed integration attempts in Albany in 1961, King and the SCLC sought to use new tactics and approaches to bring about racial justice for tens of thousands of African Americans there in 1962 and was arrested and jailed again.

The *New York Amsterdam News* began circulation in 1909 when its founder, James H. Anderson, began selling the paper from his Amsterdam Avenue home. By the early 1960s, the *Amsterdam News* was one of the most important African American weekly newspapers in the country, reaching tens of thousands of readers. King shared the "People in Action" column with other black leaders, including Roy Wilkins, the executive secretary of the National Association for the Advancement of Colored People. Every two weeks, King offered his comments about the struggle for racial justice.

In his February 3 column, "Turning Point of Civil Rights," he argued that the 1954 *Brown* decision was a "psychological turning point" for black people's struggle for racial equality in the United States because it made "indisputably clear" and "irrevocably permanent" that African Americans were equal to whites and any other racial group despite centuries of state-sanctioned discrimination against them. Emboldened by the decision, he argues, working-class and working-poor African Americans challenged segregation in Montgomery with the bus boycott, college students used nonviolent direct protest during their sit-ins, and young white and black people challenged segregation in interstate transit with freedom rides. In closing his column, he declares that black people would continue to use the courts and nonviolent protest to enact change in every southern state.

King commented on President Kennedy's track record in the field of civil rights in "The President's Record," his February 17 installment. The Kennedy administration had been friendly to King in the past and had come to his aid when Birmingham's First Baptist Church was under siege by angry white mobs in May 1961 and when King was arrested and jailed in Georgia. Before he was elected president, Kennedy sought King's endorsement, and after he was elected, he invited King to his inauguration, though King did not attend. So when responding to questions about Kennedy's position on civil rights, he had to be as diplomatic as possible to not upset the president. He praised the appointment of African Americans in government positions as well as Kennedy's Executive Order 10925. The order established the President's Committee on Equal Employment Opportunity. It also prohibited discrimination against any employee or applicant for employment in the federal government or companies contracting with the federal government because of race, color, religion, or national origin. However, in his final evaluation of President Kennedy's work on black civil rights, King declared that the president's work in the field was lacking in vision, commitment, and strong leadership. Kennedy's New Frontier, his proposals for improvements in American infrastructure, health care, education, and race relations, was not fresh or new for black people.

In late February, the SCLC began its "People to People" tours, visits to black communities throughout the nation to enlist volunteers in voter registration drives and speak to everyday African Americans about issues facing their communities. "Pathos and Hope," the March 3 column, discusses King's "People to People" tour visit to Mississippi. *Pathos* is a Greek word meaning "suffering." King uses *pathos* to mean something that induces pity or sadness. In black communities in Mississippi, pathos and hope existed simultaneously. The desperate gut-wrenching poverty that many functionally illiterate black Mississippians experienced evoked pathos. Their commitment to and struggles for an end to racial inequality and discrimination, despite economic reprisals by white planters and threats of violence by white vigilantes, was a reason to be hopeful. Cause for hope was also to be found in Theodore Trammell's campaign for a seat in the U.S. House of Representatives. Trammell was a black Mississippi native, Methodist minister, teacher, and activist whose bid for Congress galvanized the local black population and encouraged many to try to register to vote.

"Most Abused Man in the Nation," published on March 31, was a tribute to Rev. Fred Shuttlesworth, the pastor at Bethel Baptist Church in Birmingham, Alabama, and a founding member of the SCLC and the Alabama Christian Movement for Human Rights (ACMHR). King informs his readers of Shuttlesworth's fight against Jim Crow in Alabama and the price he had to pay for that fight for justice. His church and home were bombed, and he and his wife were victims of white mob violence. On January 25, 1962, he was arrested for violating unjust segregation laws in Birmingham, denied bail, and sentenced to serve sixty to ninety days in prison performing menial labor. He served thirty-six days of his sentence. To celebrate his release and activism, Birmingham residents gathered to welcome him home, and King wrote that future generations would benefit from Shuttlesworth's activism because he was a "guiding star . . . for freedom for us all."

King, Wyatt T. Walker, Ralph Abernathy, Fred Shuttlesworth, and Dorothy Cotton, the educational consultant for SCLC, constituted the

SCLC Task Force and conducted a "People to People" tour in Virginia from March 27 to March 29. During their tour, they visited and talked with black residents in Dinwiddie County, Prince George County, and Chesterfield County, and Prince Edward County, the area commonly called Virginia's Black Belt, because of the large number of African American residents residing in the area. The area was a bastion of segregation in the Old Dominion. Only a small minority of black eligible voters were registered to vote because of poll taxes, economic reprisals, and African Americans' fear of attempting to register. During the tour, he delivered "The American Dream" at Edward Christian Glass High School in Lynchburg. He told them that "the motor is cranked up and we are moving up the highway of freedom toward the city of equality" ("Dr. King's Speech" 1962).

During the rally, Ralph Abernathy asked the audience for volunteers to help the SCLC fight against racial discrimination in Virginia. An eleven-year-old white boy named Chuck Moran of Charlottesville, Virginia, offered his assistance. Remembering the event in 2017, Moran recalls:

> Something inside is calling me, pushing me. Excited, I lean forward and, looking across my sister, I ask my parents if it's okay if I go down there. They nod. I climb over my family's legs and step out into the aisle. Unafraid, I walk toward this man, this warm, smiling man. No one is in line in front of me. . . . Dr. King leans toward me and takes my hand in his. His hand is big, soft and strong. He clasps my shoulder and looks me right in the eye. I feel so welcome, cared for, appreciated. (Moran 2017)

In his April 14 column, "Virginia's Black Belt," King recalled that Moran's "tender spirit" encouraged others to volunteer so that a total of 118 volunteers were recruited to assist in their voter registration drive in the area. Later, in Petersburg at First Baptist Church, 158 people joined the effort.

On March 15, President Kennedy signed the Manpower Development and Training Act of 1962 to train "hundreds of thousands of workers who are denied employment because they do not possess the skills required by our constantly changing economy" (Kennedy, "Statement," 1962). The law would provide monetary allowances and job training for up to fifty-two weeks for those eligible. In "Nothing Changes Unless," King's "People in Action" column from April 28, he maintains that the act is a step in the right direction but has its limitations. First, he notes, the law did not provide adequate funding to reach the largest number of people possible in 1962. Second, the act did not consider the larger number of individuals forecasted to lose their jobs in the future due to automation. Finally, the act did not consider historical discrimination against African American workers that kept them out of jobs and jobs training programs and failed to address contemporary racial discrimination in hiring practices throughout the nation. For King, the Manpower Development and Training Act was "too little, too late" for black people.

South Carolina was the site of the third "People to People" tour for the SCLC Task Force. While there, King addressed several thousand people at Mother Emanuel African Methodist Episcopal Church in Charleston, South Carolina, and encouraged his listeners to register to vote. Fifty-three years later, on June 17, 2015, nine black worshippers at Mother Emanuel were shot and killed by an avowed white supremacist during a worship service. He also visited William Fleming's home. Fleming was a local undertaker who suffered economic reprisals from the local White Citizens Council. Bobby Fleming was five years old when King visited his father's home and remembered King. "I just remember being picked up, placed on his knee and rocked and he said one day you're going to be a great man" (Miskewicz 2006).

King used his May 12 "People in Action" column to talk about his South Carolina trip and Esau Jenkins, one of South Carolina's unknown black civil rights heroes. Jenkins was a native of John's Island, South Carolina, a sea island close to Charleston. In the late 1940s, he and his wife Janie began a bus service and transported the island's children and their parents to the city of Charleston for school and work. During the journey, they taught some of the adults basic literacy skills and helped others read portions of the state constitution so they could pass the literacy test and register to vote. His work on the buses helping blacks register to vote in the early 1950s was the foundation of the SCLC's citizen school program in the early 1960s. By 1962, nine southern states were homes to citizenship schools that taught African Americans basic literacy and political education. Jenkins was also a successful businessman who cofounded the C.O. Credit Union, which provided low-interest loans to the sea islands' black residents. In the 1970s, he helped create Rural Mission Inc., which provided social services to residents and migrants.

One major obstacle to African American's voting was literacy tests. Ostensibly, literacy tests were used to determine whether a potential voter had a fundamental understanding of written and spoken English. In practice throughout the South, they were used to disenfranchise larger portions of the electorate to maintain white political power. In early May 1962, the U.S. Senate defeated a literacy bill that would have made the completion of the sixth grade the basic literacy standard for voting nationwide. King lamented its defeat in "Literacy Bill Dies," his May 26 column. The bill's failure, he noted, revealed lessons to learn. The first was that Senate debating rules required change. White southern segregationist used their power to close debate on meaningful civil rights legislation and disenfranchise Americans. The second lesson was that the president needed to use his power to inform the electorate of the importance of civil rights

### Cultural Connection: White Citizens' Council

The White Citizens' Council was the southern white reaction to the Supreme Court's landmark 1954 *Brown v. Board of Education* decision, which mandated the end of racially segregated public schools. Groups such as the Ku Klux Klan sought to resist segregation through violence and terror, and "high-minded" southern politicians hoped to forestall the demise of Jim Crow with a revival of archaic constitutional theories, such as nullification and interposition. The White Citizens' Council, a segregationist organization that would eventually draw in thousands of anxious members across the South, appealed to the more "respectable" elements of society in its quest to undermine *Brown* and sustain the racial caste. Eschewing the predatory tactics of the Klan, the Councils instead relied on political pressure, economic intimidation, and legal maneuvering to achieve its goals. Before petering out in the 1960s, the Citizens' Council became one of the most powerful and effective instruments in rallying white public opinion against desegregation.

Residents in Indianola, Mississippi, organized the first chapter of the White Citizen's Council in July 1954. Within a matter of months, the council movement had spilled over into Alabama, Georgia, Virginia, and eventually all the former states of the Confederacy. By 1956, arguably the Council's peak year, organizers claimed more than 250,000 dues-paying members, making it, in the vaunted words of one official, one of the greatest mass movements of public opinion in American history.

The council movement found its most fertile ground in the Black Belt regions of the South, where African Americans composed a substantial portion of the population and, for the most part, continued to earn their living as sharecroppers and tenant farmers. The ranks of the early councils were filled with middle and upper classes of southern white society—planters, lawyers, bankers, doctors, businesspeople, and politicians—who foresaw an erosion of their political hegemony with the implementation of *Brown* and who shuddered at the thoughts of their children attending class alongside the offspring of their employees and clients. To counter such a threat, thousands of prominent lowland whites readily adopted the council philosophy, which demanded a rigorous defense of the social order, strict conformity to the ideals of white supremacy, and a veritable holy war against the evils of "miscegenation" and "mongrelization."

African Americans were not the sole targets of the council's wrath. White racial moderates and others who appeared "soft" on integration also found themselves at the mercy of the expanding movement. By the early 1960s, after enjoying years of unbridled political and social influence, the Citizens' Council movement began to decline. Random acts of violence by council members, petty infighting, and most important, its failure to uphold segregation destroyed the organization. After the passage of the Civil Rights Act of 1964 and the Voting Rights Act of 1965, all that remained were the diehards and "bitter-enders" who refused to accept the inevitable tide of history.

Source: Gary S. Sprayberry, "White Citizens' Council," in Leslie Alexander and Walter Rucker, ed., *Encyclopedia of African American History,* vol. 3 (Santa Barbara, CA: ABC-CLIO, 2010), 1097–1098.

legislation, such as the literacy bill. When the literacy billed died, King proclaimed, "a bit of the American Dream died" with it.

In "Can We Ever Repay Them?" and "New Harassment," King's columns from June 9 and June 23, respectively, he discussed the old and new methods southern white racists used in their attempts to thwart the civil rights movement. One of the old techniques used was house bombings. In Shreveport, Louisiana, a city in northwest Louisiana, bombs destroyed the primary and summer homes of Cuthbert O. Simpkins, a black dentist and leader of the United Christian Movement, the local affiliate of the SCLC. When visiting Shreveport in June, a bastion of the White Citizens' Council, SCLC staff members Bernard Lee and Wyatt T. Walker were arrested for allegedly loitering and were held without bail pending a coroner's commitment, a new method of harassment. A coroner's commitment was a full examination by the state coroner to determine whether the detained was mentally competent to be released. Despite old and new forms of harassment, the freedom struggle would continue, King declared, because black people "realize [America's] democratic potential" and because the futile attempts to stop the movement toward racial equality was "as vain as trying to hold back the tides of the sea."

On July 10, King and Abernathy returned to Albany, Georgia, to receive their sentence stemming from their December 1961 arrest. They were given a choice: pay a $178 fine or spend forty-five days in jail. Writing from the Albany jail in his July 21 "Message from Jail" column, he explained why he chose to go to jail. Having preached about how civil rights activists must be ready to fill the jails for their activism, King and Abernathy chose to go to jail to "change it into a haven of liberty." They were released on July 12, less than forty-eight hours later, after an anonymous person posted bail for them.

After his release from jail on July 12, King and SCLC remained active in Albany. He and other local leaders met with police chief Laurie Pritchett and city leaders several times. When a judge from the U.S. District Court of Columbus issued a restraining order preventing the SCLC from participating in nonviolent mass actions in Albany, they successfully petitioned to have it overturned in the Fifth Circuit Court of Appeals. King also addressed several mass meetings at Shiloh Baptist Church and Mount Zion Baptist Church to encourage Albany's black community to remain committed to peaceful, nonviolent mass protests to bring about integration. He had planned mass demonstrations on July 25; however, violence erupted in predominantly black Harlem neighborhood the night before, and police arrested black demonstrators (not affiliated with the Albany Movement), so King reluctantly postponed the demonstrations to allow for a cooling-off period, a day of penance. During that time, he, Abernathy, and others walked the streets throughout the day visiting pharmacies, dry cleaners, a bar, and a billiard hall to encourage people to remain nonviolent so protests could resume.

After lunch on July 27, King went to the Albany city hall with SCLC and Albany Movement members. City fathers refused to meet with them, so they knelt on the stairs of the building to pray. Reverend Ralph Abernathy led the prayer: "We pray, oh God, that Thou would touch the hearts of the people and let them know that there will be no peace in this community until we talk over our differences" (Sitton 1962). Chief Pritchett and his officers gave several warnings to disperse, but the small group continued to pray and were arrested and charged with disorderly conduct, congregating on the sidewalk, and disobeying the commands of an officer.

Rather than post bail, King decided to serve the forty-five-day sentence and remained in jail from July 27 to August 10. During his incarceration, his father, Coretta, and his children, along with SCLC staff members, visited him. He also spent time with other prisoners, led devotional services in the mornings and evenings, read the Bible, listened to the radio, and kept a diary that was later published in *Jet* magazine. "The Albany jail," he wrote in his July 29 entry, "is dirty, filthy, and ill-equipped. I have been in many jails and it's really the worse I have ever seen" (King, "Rev. M.L. King's Diary in Jail" 1962). On Friday, August 10, fifteen days after their initial arrest, King and Abernathy appeared before Judge Adie Norman Durden, who fined them $200 and gave them a suspended sixty-day sentence.

King was undeterred after his release and reflected on the efficacy of using nonviolence in Albany to achieve integration in several articles he wrote for the *Chicago Daily Defender* in early August. On August 18, the *Amsterdam News* published "Why It's Albany," another column King wrote from his jail cell in Albany, Georgia. King maintained that Albany was like other southern cities that stubbornly maintained segregation and suppressed the economic, political, and educational opportunities of its black population by custom, law, and force when necessary. The student sit-ins, freedom rides, Montgomery bus boycott, and other successful civil rights protests and nonviolent resistance throughout the nation provided concrete examples of how segregation could be challenged even in the most intransigent southern cities and towns. It provided black Albany citizens with resolve that they could change their circumstances and fight for freedom. Destiny, King said, had chosen the city of Albany by chance and made it a symbol of "segregation's last stand." During the last weeks of August, he returned to Albany several times to lend his support in the ongoing voter registration drives and negotiations to end racial segregation in the city. King's jailing and black protest, however, did not immediately bring about desegregation in the city. Segregationists prevailed in Albany in the short term, and African Americans continued to endure segregation throughout 1962. When he reflected on the 1961–1962 Albany Movement in his *Autobiography*, King declared that despite its inability to break down the walls of segregation, the movement for racial justice in the city was not a total failure because the "people of Albany had straightened their backs" (Carson 1998, 168) and that they were a "powerful force in breaking down the barriers of segregation" (King, "New Negro Battling" 1962). By early 1963, black voters in Albany used their power to elect enough white moderates and an African American to the city commission, which repealed all segregation statutes in the spring of 1963.

Throughout fall 1962, the *Amsterdam News* published several more columns written by King. Among those published, two stands out as particularly important: "The Role of the Church" and "JFK's Executive Order."

In "The Role of the Church," published on September 15, King speaks directly to Protestant and Catholic denominations. For years he had commented on how Sunday mornings are the most segregated times in the United States, with whites and blacks worshipping in segregated churches either by custom or law. King proclaimed that 1962 was the year that Christians throughout the nation should say in a singular voice that segregation was wrong and a moral evil in society. He challenged church leaders to use their authority and positions to contest racist discourse and discrimination. First, he urges Christian leaders to use their religious education programs to help root out racial prejudice and teach their parishioners and congregants that "racial prejudice is . . . based on fears, suspicions, and misunderstandings." Next, church leaders must also use their position to refute the idea that there are superior and inferior races of people. In addition, the faith leaders must refute ideas that African Americans are "inherently criminal." At the same time, King notes, those who profess to follow the teachings of Jesus must be committed to opening lines of communication between blacks and whites to foster understanding and goodwill. Finally, to fight racial injustice, it was imperative for denominations to develop a political action plan and be at the forefront of social reform in all facets of American society. "The Role of the Church" reiterates King's stance that religious institutions and African American Christianity are not otherworldly places and vehicles for spiritual escape but spaces wherein participants are challenged to reconstruct their society and the world in spiritually progressive and moral political ways.

"JFK's Executive Order" was published on December 22 and discusses President Kennedy's November 20, 1962, Executive Order 11063, "Equal Opportunity in Housing." The order directed "all departments and agencies in the executive branch of the Federal Government, insofar as their functions relate to the provision, rehabilitation, or operation of housing and related facilities, to take all action necessary and appropriate to prevent discrimination because of race, color, creed, or national origin" (Kennedy, "Executive," 1962). When courting African American voters during his presidential campaign, Kennedy promised to quickly eliminate racial discrimination in federally financed and federally supported housing with an executive order. In a 1967 interview, James Farmer of the Congress of Racial Equality remembered that Kennedy "indicated that there was one huge area of racial discrimination which could be wiped out by a stroke of the pen... that he, if elected, would use that stroke of the pen and issue an executive order banning discrimination in housing" (Farmer 1967). King noted that although the executive order was significantly delayed, signed twenty-two months after Kennedy took office, it fulfilled his promise to the black community and was a "step in the right direction." However, like Kennedy's Executive Order 10925, which addressed federally funded and supported employment, King said that Executive Order 11063 did not go far enough to protect the rights and well-being of black people in the field of housing. King noted that millions of dollars of federal money had been invested in the Federal Housing Administration, the Public Housing Administration, and federally backed housing programs for decades through loans that discriminated against qualified black borrowers and supported the contemporary home financing business. One of the problems with the order was that it had no method to address past racial discrimination, so millions of African Americans who had been denied federally backed loans had no redress. While white borrowers accumulated wealth tied up in their homes and gave that wealth to future generations, all black people were left with was another federal promise to do better. Further, according to King, Executive Order 11063 did not provide safeguards for black people attempting to secure loans through private banks and other real estate lenders, who could still deny them loans solely based on race.

King looked beyond the African American press in 1962 to influence the white progressive middle class. On March 3, his article "Fumbling on the New Frontier" was published in *The Nation* and offered a year in review of civil rights developments of 1961. On August 5, the *New York Times* published his article "The Case against Tokenism" which largely repeats ideas from his *New York Amsterdam News* column but offers a fierce conclusion that black people's freedom will be won through their own efforts, not by "passively waiting for deliverance to come from others out of pity."

"Fumbling on the New Frontier," however, was more insightful. Throughout the article, his comments are measured so as to not alienate and besmirch the president but firmly state King's point. During 1961, President Kennedy and his administration had provided some direction and energy with regard to the African American struggle for equality. However, Kennedy had been too cautious and yielded to southern segregationists about black equality in southern states for fear of losing their support on other issues, such as international trade. According to King, the final piece of the Kennedy Administration's work in the field of civil rights

> **CULTURAL CONNECTION: BLACK ROCK AND ROLL: THE EARLY 1960S**
>
> The first wave of rock and roll lasted only about five years, from 1955 to 1960. The beginning of the new decade saw a commercial turn away from rhythm and blues-based and country-based sounds and a move toward the more polished sounds of pop. Chubby Checker is a pivotal performer in this context: his smash hit version of "The Twist" (Parkway Records, 1960) made twisting not just the best-known type of rock and roll dancing but in fact one of the most popular dances of the twentieth century. Dick Clark, rock impresario and host of television's *American Bandstand*, helped push "The Twist" to the top of the charts in 1960 and again in 1962. Checker continued to capitalize on the twisting craze by releasing several follow-ups, such as "Twistin' USA" and "Let's Twist Again" (both for Parkway Records, 1961). Other artists followed suit, including (among many others) Sam Cooke, with "Twistin' the Night Away" (RCA Victor Records, 1962).
>
> In 1959, Berry Gordy Jr. made his hometown in Detroit, Michigan, the headquarters of his new record company, Motown. The Motor City would soon yield some of the best black recording artists of the 1960s, with a sound that was designed to appeal to all American teenagers (regardless of race). Irrespective of whether we consider Motown artists such as Martha Reeves and the Vandellas to be rock artists (as opposed to pop artists or rhythm and blues artists or soul artists), it is a fact that Gordy's Motown Sound had an indelible effect on artists whose music is, by any measure, rock music. Homage has been paid to Berry's artists in the form of covers such as Vanilla Fudge's 1967 hard-rock version of "You Keep Me Hangin' On" (Atco Records, originally recorded by the Supremes in 1966) and also in the form of explicit lyrical tributes such as that heard in "R.O.C.K. in the U.S.A. (A Salute to '60s Rock)" by John Cougar Mellencamp (Riva Records, 1986).
>
> Source: Christopher Doll, "Rock 'n' Roll," in Emmett G. Price III, Tammy L. Kernodle, and Horace J. Maxile Jr., ed., *Encyclopedia of African American Music*, vol. 3 (Santa Barbara, CA: ABC-CLIO, 2011), 845–846.

"was characterized by inadequacy and incompleteness" because Kennedy's immediate plan on civil rights was shortsighted and the long-term plan was lacking. King deftly noted that the president had a ten-year plan to get the first human on the moon but did not have a concrete plan for black voting rights on Earth.

King's use of the word "fumbling" is important. During the late summer and throughout autumn of 1961, football was America's pastime, and the season culminated in the Green Bay Packers playing the New York Giants at the City Stadium in Green Bay, Wisconsin. Close to forty thousand people were in attendance, and millions watched on television. Throughout the year, fans saw their favorite football icons fumble, or lose possession of the ball. King used that imagery to further his point: like a football player,

Kennedy fumbled the ball on African American civil rights and gave possession to his and black people's opponents, white southern segregationists. With an uncanny foresight, King observed that black people's quest for equality and justice in America would "continue . . . [to be] a political football unless national government abandons the traditional piecemeal approach."

Writing biweekly columns in the *Amsterdam News* allowed King to connect with a larger African American audience. Throughout the year, he also continued to offer his ideas to predominantly white audiences on college campuses and other venues during fundraising tours for the SCLC. In May, King spoke to the students, faculty, and staff at Dartmouth College in Hanover, New Hampshire. He had been scheduled to address the college in 1960, but legal problems stemming from Alabama's frivolous tax evasion charges prevented him from visiting the school. In May 1961, his visit to the campus was cut short to allow him to return to the South and work with the sit-in movement, whose participants were assaulted by violent white mobs. During the third week of May 1962, King had the time to visit the campus, meet the students and faculty, and deliver an address about the history of racism in the United States and black people's contemporary challenges to the racial structure.

He made history on July 19 by being the first African American to address the National Press Club, the most exclusive association of white male reporters and journalists in the nation. Established in 1908, throughout the early to mid-twentieth century, presidents, policy makers, and other influential people addressed the exclusive club. His speech contained many elements he had presented in other forums throughout the nation: desegregation efforts in the South, the need for the Protestant church to be an agent for social change and integration throughout the nation, the effectiveness of nonviolent mass action, Gandhi's influence on the black freedom movement, and the importance of bold, federal action in the quest for equal rights. After his speech, he was asked a series of predetermined questions about politics, the news media, and the larger civil rights movement, and he demonstrated his knowledge and dexterity on a variety of subjects. When asked why he supported the sit-in movement, he declared that he supported the movement because segregation statutes were unjust, degrading, and "out of harmony with the moral laws of the universe." In response to a question about the Kennedy administration and its commitment to civil rights, he provided another restrained response wherein he praised Kennedy's enthusiasm on the subject but maintained that the president "has yet given the kind of leadership in this area that the enormity of the problem demands" (Carson and Armstrong 2014, 537).

Shortly after Labor Day on September 12, King was in New York City delivering an address to the New York State Civil War Centennial

Commission at the Sheraton Park Hotel to commemorate the one-hundredth anniversary of President Abraham Lincoln's preliminary Emancipation Proclamation, which freed slaves in southern confederate states. King told the audience, which included the wealthy SCLC patron and governor of New York, Nelson Rockefeller, that the nation had produced two of the most important documents in human civilization: the Declaration of Independence and the Emancipation Proclamation. The Declaration of Independence's importance lies in its unequivocal statement that all human beings are unmistakably and inherently equal. The Emancipation Proclamation sought to "uproot [the] social order" that denied African Americans their full constitutional rights.

Despite the grandeur and eloquence of these documents, King argues, since its organization, the federal government has failed to live up to the high ideals of these documents because of its willingness to compromise with the southern slaveholding elite in the eighteenth and nineteenth centuries and their white segregationist offspring in the twentieth century. This compromise with the South together with sustained efforts by whites in northern cities and southern states to segregate blacks created a system of structural inequality affecting all aspects of black life in America. In commemorating the Emancipation Proclamation, King noted, it was necessary "to reach back to the origins of our nation when our message of equality electrified an unfree world and reaffirm democracy by deeds as bold and daring as the issuance of the Emancipation Proclamation" (Del Signore 2014).

King visited Cornell College, a small liberal arts college affiliated with the United Methodist Church located in rural Mount Vernon, Iowa, on October 15. Since the early twentieth century, the college had been at the forefront of liberal causes, including racial integration, and graduated its first African American graduate, Frank Jeremiah Armstrong, in 1900. King reminded students, faculty, and staff that the United States had taken important and noticeable actions in eliminating racial equality, or as he put it, "extending the frontiers of civil rights" ("Dr. Martin Luther King's Visit to Cornell College" n.d.). Efforts had been made to eliminate the poll tax that prevented blacks from voting. Lynching was on the decline, black people were not tied solely to agricultural pursuits in the South, and the Supreme Court overturned *Plessy v. Ferguson*, which upheld racial discrimination, with the *Brown* decision. However, a survey of black life in the United States revealed that black people still suffered underemployment as compared to their white counterparts. Black children in many locations still attended segregated schools because of the intransigence of white elected leaders, and white election board officials continued to deny millions of blacks the right to vote throughout the South. If one compared the economic, political, and cultural status of blacks in the mid-twentieth century to the mid-nineteenth century, African Americans might have come a long way. However, the overarching lack of economic justice and continued denial of basic constitutional rights meant the nation had a "great deal of work to do" ("Dr. Martin Luther King's Visit to Cornell College" n.d.).

In assessing race relations, King calls on his audience to avoid two commonly held viewpoints. The first is the pessimistic perspective that argues that nothing meaningful has been done or can be done to bring about racial equality. The second is the optimistic perspective that suggests that racial equality and integration have already been accomplished. King maintains that a middle ground, a realistic approach, be adopted: recognition that there have been positive developments in race relations and the lives of millions of African Americans throughout the nation, but more work needed to be done by all three branches of government, white moderates in the South, religious leaders, and black people. When the federal government, white moderates, and religious leaders failed to act or move too slowly, African Americans must use nonviolent mass action to shake them out of their apathy and encourage them to act.

Throughout 1962, King continued to serve as copastor at Ebenezer Baptist Church alongside his sixty-two-year-old father and, when home in Atlanta, delivered important sermons to support and grow his congregation. Two of his sermons, "Levels of Love" and "Can a Christian Be a Communist?" are important demonstrations of King's deep and inclusive Christian faith and profound belief in God.

In "Levels of Love," King quotes from the sixteenth-century English playwright and poet William Shakespeare, the nineteenth-century writer and American poet Edgar Allen Poe, the eighteenth-century German philosopher and Enlightenment thinker Immanuel Kant, the twentieth-century Jewish philosopher Martin Buber, the nineteenth-century Russian writer Fyodor Dostoevsky, and the nineteenth-century English poet and hymnist Charlotte Elliot. He maintains that there are at least six kinds of love governing human relationships: utilitarian love, romantic love, mother's love, friendship, humanitarian love, and Christian love.

Utilitarian love is a practical love wherein one only loves another person to benefit personally. It is a conditional love motivated by selfishness where the lover objectifies the person they claim to love. Of all the levels of love, utilitarian love is the lowest and the most tragic. Above utilitarian love is romantic love. Being a product of his time and culture, King only sees romantic love in the heterosexual context between men and women; however, the basic idea of his premise is universal. Romantic love is based on attraction between lovers. It is not motivated by the objectification of one's desire or altruistic elements. However, King argues that romantic love is "basically selfish" because "you love your lover because there is something about the person that attracts you." One's motivation for loving is to please oneself. Mother's love, the love that a mother has for her child, the love immediately above romantic love, is sincere and noble in its intent; however, it is also marked by self-interest because a mother loves her child because it is *her* child.

The love between friends, friendship, is above mother's love. It is characterized by shared mutual interests between individuals and unimpeded by the whims of sexual attraction or a biological and/or familial connection, because individuals enter friendships freely. King observes that true friendships are rare and when found are beautiful relationships but are still marked by a degree of individual selfishness. One loves a friend because one likes them and gets something—support, assistance, intellectual stimulation, and joy—from associating with them.

Is it possible to love someone you don't like? Humanitarian love, the next level of love, seeks to address this question. With humanitarian love, one loves all of humankind regardless of race, color, creed, religion, or gender and begins to see that every individual is made in God's image and animated by a divine spark from the creator. It ends where Christian love, the highest form of love, begins. Christian love, King says, is "love of God operating in the human heart." It loves everybody regardless of physical and sexual attraction, mutual interests, likability, familial ties, or evil deeds. Christian love is a gift from God and is the "greatest force in . . . the world" (Carson et al. 2007, 444).

In "Can a Christian Be a Communist?" King answers in the negative. No, a follower of Jesus cannot be a communist for several reasons. First, according to King's understanding of communism, its atheist philosophical approach is grounded in a materialism that rejects the existence of God, and the Russian communist state opposed and persecuted Christians and Christianity. Second, to promote its political agenda, King argues, communist regimes use immoral and violent tactics to bring about its political programs and ends, but Christianity looks to immutable moral principles that cannot be dismissed for political ends. Lastly, a Christian cannot be a communist because communist regimes restrict and deny individual God-given freedoms and force their citizens to be cogs in the political machine rather than free individuals. Christianity and communism "are opposed to each other" for these reasons and "no Christian can be a communist" (Carson et al. 2007, 448).

However, he believed that communism and its influences cannot be completely dismissed. Communists' dreams of making the world a better place reveal "the danger of the profit motive as the sole basis for an economic system" (Carson et al. 2007, 451). In the American capitalist system, most of the nation's wealth was concentrated in the hands of a small minority, while degrading and dehumanizing poverty denied millions of children a quality education and robbed families of safe and affordable housing. Additionally, communism's commitment to social justice and racial equality challenged the American Christian church, which had openly supported segregation and racial injustice, had sat by passively and done nothing to address these issues, or had become too otherworldly in its focus on the afterlife and heaven. While rejecting communists' creed and approach, King maintains that American Christians must accept communists' concerns and develop a dynamic social gospel to meet the communist challenge and attempt to "make this old world a new world" with the same fervor and zeal of individual communists and communist regimes the world over (Carson et al. 2007, 454).

"Can a Christian Be a Communist?" shows that by late 1962, King had broadened his political horizon as well as his critique of contemporary society. While he continued to be a champion of African American civil rights, he began to see racial justice as inextricably linked to other issues, including international politics, income inequality and poverty, and American militarism abroad.

Throughout 1962, King continued to spread his message of nonviolence and love on the lecture circuit, in national publications, and in the African American press. He also used these venues and platforms to comment on contemporary political and cultural developments and discuss and critique President Kennedy's civil rights agenda. His message was consistent: the three branches of the federal government needed to use their power to guarantee African Americans' constitutional and God-given rights throughout all sections and states of the country. His work in Albany led to his arrest and two-week imprisonment. Although his and SCLC's efforts at immediately desegregating the city were not successful, he and the organization learned valuable lessons about white southern resistance and the reluctance of the Kennedy administration to involve itself in the daily struggles of the civil rights movement in the South, lessons that would be useful in their Birmingham campaign in 1963.

# 7

## Birmingham and Standing before God

In 1962, Rev. Fred Shuttlesworth, pastor at Bethel Baptist Church in Birmingham and a founding member of the Alabama Christian Movement for Human Rights and the Southern Christian Leadership Conference, convinced King and the SCLC staff that they should focus their efforts on Birmingham to desegregate that city. With a population of 340,000, of which close to 40 percent were African American, Birmingham was a stronghold of white supremacy and a rigidly segregated city in the early 1960s. King called the city a "symbol of hardcore resistance to integration" (Hudson and Houston 2011). Blacks were victims of legal and extralegal violence meted out by police and white vigilantes, and African American homes and businesses were routinely bombed in the city. In 1956, Shuttlesworth's home was bombed. According to the historian Vincent Harding, "every black person seemed to know someone who had been beaten, bombed, raped, or murdered [by whites] in Birmingham" (Harding 1980, 167). Throughout late 1962 and early 1963, King and the SCLC made plans for a large-scale, nonviolent confrontation to integrate the city in the spring of 1963. On April 3, several days after the birth of King's fourth child, Bernice Albertine King, the Birmingham campaign began.

Called Project C (for "confrontation"), the SCLC set up its headquarters at the Sixteenth Street Baptist Church and used the master suite at the Gaston Motel, an establishment owned by local black businessman A. G. Gaston, as its operations strategy center. Project C started with sit-in demonstrations at several downtown stores that continued to enforce segregation. Like other sit-in demonstrations, well-dressed black people committed to nonviolence entered an establishment, sat down at the lunch counter, and requested service. When they were denied service, they quietly remained seated until removed by police. On the first day of the campaign, twenty-one protesters were arrested. As the campaign progressed, boycotts and picketing accompanied the sit-ins, and hundreds of demonstrators lined city streets with signs reading "Don't Buy Segregation," "Birmingham Merchants Unfair," "Let Your Dollar Redeem Birmingham," and "Police Brutality Violates Fourteenth Amendment." The city was amid the busy Easter shopping season, the second-busiest shopping season of the year, and the African American boycott of downtown stores began to be felt by city merchants. In the evenings, mass meetings were held in black churches throughout the city where King and others preached about the strategies, methods, and goals of their nonviolent mass action.

Local white political and business leaders and the Kennedy Administration did not support the SCLC's campaign in the city and wanted King and his organization to wait and see how newly elected white moderates in the city government would deal with racism and segregation. When arrests and threats from white thugs did not slow the movement or weaken blacks' resolve, city officials went to court. One week after the campaign began, on April 10, Judge William A. Jenkins of the Alabama state court issued an injunction barring more protests throughout the city. King, Wyatt T. Walker, and Ralph Abernathy received the orders during breakfast on April 11 and spent the day in the living area of their Gaston Motel suite agonizing over their next move. To end the protest meant to lose momentum and the support of thousands of black Birmingham residents who put their lives on the line for freedom and justice. Hundreds were already in jail, and funds had been depleted, so they could not be bailed out. To violate the injunction and continue protesting meant going to jail and potentially losing the support of white moderates and any hope of support from the Kennedy administration, which had questioned King's timing and motives. Going to jail also meant that King would not be available to raise funds to secure bail for the hundreds in jail, but it could also galvanize the community and encourage blacks who were not committed to the movement to join.

During the early afternoon of Friday, April 12—Good Friday—King, and the SCLC stalwarts were still deliberating and making calls to determine the constitutionality of the injunction when he quietly left the sitting room and went into the bedroom to pray. Thirty minutes later, he emerged dressed in denim pants and a shirt and told his colleagues that he would lead a march and violate the immoral injunction. After attending an afternoon mass meeting at Sixteenth Street Baptist Church, King and Abernathy led a group of forty marchers toward city hall. The commissioner of public safety, Theophilus Eugene "Bull" Connor, allowed the marchers to walk for several blocks before apprehending them. King was arrested and charged with parading without a permit and violating the state injunction against demonstrations.

Processed, King was placed in solitary confinement. While there, eight white clergymen published a statement in the *Birmingham News:* Charles Carpenter, Episcopal bishop of Alabama; Joseph A. Durick, auxiliary bishop of the Catholic Diocese of Mobile-Birmingham; Rabbi Milton Grafman, Temple Emanu-El; Bishop Paul Hardin, Alabama-West Florida Conference of the Methodist Church; George M. Murray, bishop coadjutor, Episcopal Diocese of Alabama; Edward V. Ramage, Moderator, Synod of the Alabama Presbyterian Church; and Reverend Earl Stallings, pastor at First Baptist Church of Birmingham. "White Clergymen Urge Local Negroes to Withdraw from Demonstrations" never mentions King or the SCLC by name but says that the "unwise and untimely" demonstrations throughout the city were led by "outsiders" who, unlike local black leaders, lacked "knowledge and experience of the local situation." The sit-ins, boycotts, demonstrations, and marches were "extreme measures" that incited violence, stirred up racial hatred, and had not "contributed to the resolution of our local problems." They close the appeal urging the white public and the police to continue to show "restraint" and encouraged blacks to press their "cause . . . in the courts and negotiations among local leaders, and not in the streets" ("White Clergymen" 1963).

Perturbed by the article and the clergymen's position, King wrote a rebuttal to it, "Letter from Birmingham Jail," while in solitary confinement. In "Letter from Birmingham Jail," King explains why he and the SCLC were assisting black Birmingham residents in their fight against racial discrimination and refutes the idea that he was an outside agitator. He goes on to explain the purpose and strategy of nonviolent direct action and civil disobedience and compares black political activity in the city with the work of early Christians, Socrates, and the protesters at the Boston Tea Party. King also expresses his disappointment with white moderates, especially ministers who use their position to support systems of oppression instead of challenging and changing them. Copies of the letter were circulated first around Birmingham by the SCLC and local black activists. Later, it was published in a pamphlet format by the American Friends Service Committee, a Quaker organization. *Ebony, Christian Century,* the *New York Post*, and other periodicals also published "Letter." It gained further prominence when King included it in his 1964 book *Why We Can't Wait.*

While King was in jail, the movement in Birmingham stalled, and when he posted bail nine days after his arrest, on April 20, he and the SCLC were forced to reconsider their strategy in the city. King was convinced that the only way to be successful in Birmingham was to fill the jails and force the authorities to negotiate. At a mass meeting shortly after his release, he asked for volunteers to be arrested, and when no adults volunteered, young people did. King initially refused their offer. However, during strategy sessions with Rev. James Bevel, King and the other SCLC staff saw the importance of the children's involvement. Adults in Birmingham had everything to lose if they were seen openly participating in demonstrations. Their employers could fire them. Banks could revoke loans. Homes and cars could be lost. The children, however, had nothing to lose. May 2, D-Day, as it was called, began the next phase of Project C: the Children's Crusade.

Bevel recruited local black disc jockeys to help spread the word about the Children's Crusade. He also visited local high schools and enlisted the help of the football team and cheerleaders, the popular students on campus, who helped persuade other students to participate in a demonstration and eventually be arrested. On Thursday, May 2, black students throughout the greater Birmingham area went to school as usual. In the late morning, as they had planned, thousands left their classrooms and schools and went to the Sixteenth Street Baptist Church with the intention of marching in downtown Birmingham. Assembled at the church, the students sang freedom songs, recommitted themselves to nonviolence, and grappled with the likelihood that they would not return home that evening. The plan was to leave the church, walk across Kelly Ingram Park, the boundary between black and white Birmingham, and proceed to the downtown business area. The students organized themselves into groups of fifty. At noon, Bevel opened the doors of the church, and the first fifty students emerged and began to march. Bull Connor's men promptly arrested them. Students were placed into police wagons and taken to jail. Then the next group of fifty emerged and was arrested. When police wagons failed to handle the sheer number of students, Connor brought in school buses to haul off the students. Close to one thousand students had been arrested and charged with parading without a license by 3:00 p.m. At a mass meeting, King consoled worried parents whose children had been arrested and assured them that their children would be fine and that they were fighting for freedom by being arrested.

On Friday, May 3, children walked out of school again and assembled in Kelly Ingram Park. They were joined by thousands of spectators and the press. Connor's men were present with attack dogs, and the fire department was attaching high-powered water hoses to hydrants. After refusing to disperse, Connor ordered the hydrants opened, and the fire department turned the hoses on the children in the park. The pressure of the water knocked children to the ground and dispersed the crowd. When the hoses were turned off, the dogs were used. Those children who had not been arrested or hosed were bitten by the dogs. Arms and legs were pierced by the dogs' sharp teeth, and clothes were ripped to shreds. Angry black spectators threw bricks, bottles, and rocks at the officers and the firefighters. By the end of the day, close to two thousand students had been arrested. The shocking event was photographed and recorded by journalists. Americans around the country saw the images on television that evening and in the paper the next day. King and the SCLC had succeeded in gaining national attention for the Birmingham movement and forced the Kennedy administration to get involved.

On May 4, the third day of the Children's Crusade, close to 4,100 young people were arrested, and President Kennedy contacted King to discuss ways to get the children out of jail. The Children's Crusade continued for several more days. Students held sit-ins at or picketed downtown stores, and each day thousands more were arrested and met by dogs, fire hoses, and police brutality. In hopes of restoring order, white Birmingham businesspeople were forced to negotiate with King, Shuttlesworth, and other leaders of the movement. On Friday, May 10, over one month after the first sit-ins began, Birmingham business leaders and civil rights leaders came to an agreement: downtown business establishments would desegregate, racially discriminatory hiring practices would be prohibited, and a biracial committee would be created to oversee the desegregation process. The events in Birmingham also forced the Kennedy administration to openly support the civil rights movement and encourage Congress to work on civil rights legislation.

With desegregation plans in place in Birmingham, King left the city and toured the country speaking about the Birmingham campaign and raising funds to repay loans the SCLC had taken out when they posted bail for the men, women, and children who were arrested and jailed. His first stop was Cleveland, Ohio, on May 14, where he spoke to the predominantly white Episcopal Society for Christian and Racial Unity at St. Paul's Episcopal Church in Cleveland Heights. Later that day, he went to the largely African American neighborhood on Cleveland's east side, where he spoke at four African American churches: Cory Methodist Church, Greater Abyssinia Baptist Church, Greater Friendship Baptist Church, and St. Marks Presbyterian Church. At each church, he was received by thousands of eager and supportive listeners. "Nobody with any sense wants to go to jail," he told his audience. "But if they put you in jail, you transform it from a dungeon of shame to a haven of dignity and freedom" (Sams 2010). Offerings taken at the churches for the SCLC amounted to $15,000.

Two weeks later, on May 26, King addressed an integrated crowd of forty thousand at a Los Angeles freedom rally at Wrigley Field in South Los Angeles. Hollywood stars were also in attendance, including Dorothy Dandridge, Rita Moreno, Paul Newman, Sammy Davis Jr., and Dick Gregory. A singer, dancer, and actress, Dandridge was the first African

American to be nominated for an Academy Award, for Best Actress in 1954. Moreno, the Puerto Rican actress, was well known for her performance in *West Side Story*. By 1963, Newman had received critical acclaim for his performance in the films *Cat on a Hot Tin Roof*, *The Hustler*, and *Hud*. Davis was a well-known singer, dancer, and actor, popular on stage and screen, who had a prominent role in the 1961 classic *Ocean's 11*. Dick Gregory was a popular comedian and had recently been released from jail for his participation in the Children's Crusade. When it was his turn to speak, King reminded the crowd, "Birmingham or Los Angeles, the cry is always the same. We want to be free" ("Los Angeles Freedom Rally" n.d.). At a reception at Burt Lancaster's swanky Beverly Hills mansion, the actor donated $5,000 to the SCLC and encouraged his fellow artists to follow his lead. When combined with the $35,000 netted at the rally, the donations obtained at the Lancasters' home provided the SCLC with $75,000. Together, the donations collected in Cleveland and Los Angeles totaled $90,000.

After Los Angeles, King was welcomed in Chicago on May 27, where he shared a stage with Mahalia Jackson, the queen of African American gospel music; jazz singer Dinah Washington; and Aretha Franklin, the queen of soul. There the SCLC received $40,000 in donations. In late April, King and the SCLC were trying desperately to bring attention to discrimination in Birmingham. During the height of the movement in the city, his motives and tactics were questioned. Now, in late May and early June 1963, when his and the SCLC's strategy were successful, the country embraced him as they did in the aftermath of the Montgomery bus boycott.

The nation was paying attention to racial injustice through the media, and during the summer, King and other civil rights activists sought to use this ephemeral national attention to influence the Kennedy administration's civil rights agenda. Given the national attention he had received in May and June, King may have expected a private audience with the president, but he was denied; instead, on June 22, King, along with other leading religious leaders, met with President Kennedy, Vice President Lyndon B. Johnson, and Attorney General Robert F. Kennedy. Journalist Charles Hobb noted that "the public aim of the meeting was for the Kennedy administration to ensure the civil rights leaders that the White House would back a push for what would later become the Civil Rights Act of 1964; the private undertone was for Kennedy to pressure King into standing down on his planned March on Washington that was scheduled for that August" (Hobbs 2022). Defiant, King became the headliner at the March on Washington. Kennedy would be assassinated in November 1963 before his civil rights bill would come into fruition.

The day after meeting President Kennedy, on June 23, King attended the Walk to Freedom in Detroit, Michigan. The event was organized by the

Detroit Council for Human Rights (DCHR), an African American civil rights organization founded by Rev. C. L. Franklin, pastor of New Bethel Baptist Church in Detroit and father of Aretha Franklin; Rev. Albert Cleage, the fiery black nationalist, author, and founder of the Pan African Orthodox Church; and Benjamin McFall, a prominent Detroit mortician. The Walk to Freedom sought to bring attention to racial injustice, discriminatory hiring practices in the private and public sectors, and police harassment in Detroit and other northern cities. Franklin and King had been friends for years, and when King visited the city, he dined with Franklin and his family. When plans were being made for the walk, Franklin asked King to be the keynote speaker.

Close to 125,000 people marched in solidarity down Woodward Avenue, Detroit's Main Street, and throughout the Motor City's downtown area. The walk ended at Cobo Hall, the city's premier convention center on the banks of the Detroit River, where a rally was held. Attendees were welcomed by the DCHR leaders, and Detroit's mayor Jerome Cavanaugh then listened to several speeches. One was from United Auto Workers president Walther Reuther. In the early 1960s, Detroit was a major manufacturer of automobiles and an economic engine for the city and the nation. The union was at the forefront of labor issues at Detroit auto manufacturing plants, and black autoworkers led the way for economic and social equality at the UAW. With so many black autoworkers in the Motor City, Reuther's attendance was critical. In his address, Reuther maintained that political and economic opportunities were a right for all workers and all Americans. However, King was the star. Standing at the podium, King declared that "now is the time to make real the promises of democracy. Now is the time to transform this pending national elegy into a creative psalm of brotherhood. . . . Now is the time to lift our nation from the quicksands of racial injustice to the solid rock of racial justice. Now is the time to get rid of segregation and discrimination" (Stateside Staff 2020).

In 1957, King and Melvin Arnold, a publisher, spoke about a book of sermons. Several years later—1962 and 1963—and despite some reluctance, King buckled down and wrote when he could in. *Strength to Love* was published in June 1963 and featured fourteen sermons he delivered at Dexter Avenue Baptist Church, Ebenezer Baptist Church, and other churches and venues nationwide. The *New York Times* announced its publication several weeks before it was released and referred to it as "addresses on Dr. King's thesis that racial integration can be achieved through nonviolent action" ("Books and Authors" 1963). As a compilation of sermons, they show how King understood his Christian faith and used it as a lens through which to see and a framework by which to understand twentieth-century society. The book was written and published to appeal to

> ### Cultural Connection: Cold War and Civil Rights
>
> The Cold War greatly influenced American race politics and the African American quest for civil rights. On one hand, the struggle with the Soviet Union brought questions of racial equality to the forefront and improved the government's civil rights record. It provided the civil rights movement with leverage with the government. On the other hand, it restrained the civil rights movement in its activities. The Cold War made civil rights an international issue.
>
> In the escalating struggle for world leadership and allegiance in the destabilized or newly evolving nations, propaganda and image played an ever-growing role. To influence emerging nations in Asia and Africa, the Soviet Union attempted to spread distrust of the United States and its claim of world leadership of freedom and democracy. The Soviet Union disseminated America's persistent human rights violations. American propaganda constructed a story of constant racial progress. The continued existence of segregation and the recurring protest and violence against African American rights, particularly in the South, created problems with the constructed image of racial change and progress. It was argued that these were individual cases in restricted areas that proved racial progress was only possible in a democracy.
>
> Many African Americans believed that supporting the American anticommunist foreign policy would result in the government fighting domestic discrimination. In their civil rights activism, the African American community felt connected to the emerging nations' struggle against colonialism that was simultaneously taking place. The African American civil rights movement was well aware of the international interest in and importance of American race relations. Petitions on American segregation and racial discrimination to the United Nations furthered the internationalization of racial issues in the United States.
>
> In its activism, the civil rights movement attempted to make use of the Cold War discourse to pressure for civil rights actions of the government. From Walter White and the NAACP to Martin Luther King, major civil rights leaders made use of Cold War discourse to influence the domestic audience on issues of civil rights. They argued for the necessity of racial reform if the United States wanted to win the support of the international community, the newly emerging nations of Asia and Africa in particular, and effectively contain the international and national spread of communism.
>
> Source: Christine Knauer, "Cold War and Civil Rights," in Leslie Alexander and Walter Rucker, ed., *Encyclopedia of African American History*, vol. 3 (Santa Barbara, CA: ABC-CLIO, 2010), 711–713.

progressive Christian congregations and communities of the period; however, its messages have challenged and changed people's lives and perspectives regardless of religious beliefs.

"The Death of Evil upon the Seashore" was discussed in chapter 2, while chapters 3 and 4 discussed "A Knock at Midnight" and "A Tough Mind and Tender Heart," respectively. Chapter 5 included summaries of "Paul's

Letters to American Christians" and "The Man Who Was a Fool." "How Should a Christian View Communism?" is a revision of the sermon "Can a Christian Be a Communist?," considered in chapter 6. What follows is a brief discussion of the other sermons in *Strength to Love*.

In "Transformed Nonconformist," King considers the work of poet and educator Henry Wadsworth Longfellow; founding father and third president, Thomas Jefferson; transcendentalist Ralph Waldo Emerson; poet James Russell Lowell, seventeenth-century English Puritan cleric Paul Bunyan; and the philosopher and theologian, Julius Seelye Bixler. King uses Roman 12:2 as his primary text: "And be not conformed to this world: but be ye transformed by the renewing of your mind, that ye may prove what is that good, and acceptable, and perfect, will of God" (King James Version). Here, Paul, Jesus's disciple and one of the earliest Christians, is speaking to the growing Christian minority residing in the Roman Empire and warns them not to succumb to the allure of pagan Roman culture and society but to follow the teachings of Jesus. Centuries later, like Paul, King challenges modern Christians to follow the teachings of Jesus, a man he calls the "world's most dedicated nonconformist," and become constructive, creative, and disciplined dissenters from the status quo to create and sustain a society of generosity, love, and respect (King, *Strength*, 2010, 13). Too often, he says, individuals are persuaded to follow the crowd, take the easy way out, or silently accept what their peers say and do. Such conformity led southern white moderates to be silent and refuse to openly reject racial segregation for fear of retribution. Domestically, the fear of challenging the inequitable distribution of wealth and outmoded capitalist tenets created unimaginable poverty for millions throughout the nation. In international politics, an unrealistic balance between the East and the West kept the world on the precipice of war and self-destruction.

King critiques American Christians and their religious institutions. For so long, he declares, they have been willing to abandon Jesus's nonconforming ideas for the sake of economic gain. He compares some of his religious colleagues to Pontius Pilate, the Roman governor of Judea who presided over Jesus's crucifixion. After Jesus's arrest and detention, Pilate initially pardoned him but was later swayed by the crowd to execute Jesus. Religious leaders, such as Pontius Pilate, fail to follow their principles and faith and instead choose to follow the ephemeral tastes of their parishioners and society and sacrifice their principles on the altar of convenience and affluence. To become creative nonconformists and "transformed by the renewing of your mind," King maintained, Christians must be open to the transforming power of God and be ready and willing to "courageously do battle for truth" for the survival of human civilization (King, *Strength*, 2010, 19).

"On Being a Good Neighbor," he uses Jesus's Parable of the Good Samaritan that is found in the tenth chapter of the Gospel according to Luke:

> And Jesus answering said, A certain man went down from Jerusalem to Jericho, and fell among thieves, which stripped him of his raiment, and wounded him, and departed, leaving him half dead. And by chance there came down a certain priest that way: and when he saw him, he passed by on the other side. And likewise a Levite, when he was at the place, came and looked on him, and passed by on the other side. But a certain Samaritan, as he journeyed, came where he was: and when he saw him, he had compassion on him, And went to him, and bound up his wounds, pouring in oil and wine, and set him on his own beast, and brought him to an inn, and took care of him. And on the morrow when he departed, he took out two pence, and gave them to the host, and said unto him, Take care of him; and whatsoever thou spendest more, when I come again, I will repay thee. (Luke 10: 30–35, KJV)

King had used the parable before in other sermons, including "It's Hard to Be a Christian" in early 1956, at the beginning of his ministry, where he argued that the Samaritan provided a clear example of how one should conduct oneself to ultimately serve Christ.

In "On Being a Good Neighbor," King says that the Samaritan is a clear example of what a good neighbor can be and how to serve one's neighbors and ultimately serve humanity. The Samaritan was a good neighbor because he possessed universal altruism. His selfless concern, kindness, and assistance were provided without regard to his immediate family, kin, clan, religion, or tribe. It was wide ranging and comprehensive in scope and transcended arbitrary social groupings. He also had a dangerous altruism in that he put his life in potential jeopardy to save another person. The road between Jerusalem and Jericho was a treacherous one, traveled by those seeking to cause harm to and rob others. The Samaritan, like the priest and the Levite, could have turned a blind eye and left the man for dead; instead, his selfless concern for the welfare of others moved him to help, knowing quite well that he could have suffered the same fate as the man he was assisting. King goes on to say that the Samaritan had an excessive altruism in that he went "far beyond the call of duty" (King, *Strength*, 2010, 28) and did more than he was obligated to do. Not only did the Samaritan stop, tend to the man's wound, put him on his pack animal while probably walking beside him, and deliver him to a safe place to recuperate but he also paid for the stranger's care.

Like the Samaritan, Americans need to adopt a universal altruism, King said. When they do, they will move beyond their parochialism to question some of the basic tenets of society, including racism, poverty and economic inequity, and jingoism. Using the Samaritan as the epitome of neighborliness who risked his life for a stranger, white and black Americans must be willing to risk their power, privilege, and social status in the struggle for African American equality. Further, the Samaritan's excessive altruism provides a useful model for desegregation efforts. When followed, civil rights laws would bring about a desegregated society. However, a desegregated society is far from a brotherhood. By having excessive altruism, by going beyond the letter of the law and tackling "fears, prejudice, pride, and irrationality," the good neighbor participates in true integration and helps transform society. Being a good neighbor is possible, he submits, when we challenge ourselves and put others first with true compassion.

Jesus's crucifixion is recounted in "Love in Action": "And when they were come to the place, which is called Calvary, there they crucified him, and the malefactors, one on the right hand, and the other on the left. Then said Jesus, Father, forgive them; for they know not what they do" (Luke 23: 33–34, KJV). King posits that Jesus's words right before his earthly death have meaning for Christians and humanity in general. Rather than seek revenge when someone has wronged or mistreated us, run afoul of the law, or broken the rules, customs, and mores of our society, one should practice forgiveness so that forgiveness becomes part of one's "permanent attitude" (King, *Strength*, 2010, 33). King calls on the reader to forgive the cheating politician, accept the unwed teen mother, and show mercy to the murderer, because forgiveness is part of a Christian love that will transform society.

Dying on the cross, Jesus also said that those crucifying him were spiritually blind. Like many members of Roman civilization, segments of Western civilization suffered from intellectual, political, and spiritual blindness. Such blindness led to the creation and expansion of slavery in the Western hemisphere from the fifteenth to the nineteenth centuries and Jim Crow and racial segregation in the South in the twentieth century. It also led to men who "still feel that war is the answer to the problems of the world," the Cold War, and nuclear stockpiling (King, *Strength*, 2010, 36). War had no place in human society, according to King, for it only led to destruction, physical death, broken hearts, and the illusion of safety and peace. As Jesus has been said to give sight to the physically blind, the church, King says, can provide the cure for the spiritual blindness plaguing the nation by being a beacon of kindheartedness and conscientiousness. When the church embraces its moral obligation to guide humanity, its congregants and followers will aspire to search for intelligence and spiritual and scientific truth regardless of their academic training and pedigree, otherwise, the nation and the world suffered the risk of devolving into chaos and social self-destruction.

"Shattered Dreams," "Our God Is Able," "Antidotes to Fear," and "The Answer to a Perplexing Question" are testimonies of faith. King declares that God is the "great benign power in the universe" ever present in human affairs (King, *Strength*, 2010, 117). Like the apostle Paul, who dreamed of spreading the gospel in Spain but ended up in a prison cell in Rome with an unyielding hope, a mature faith in God can help a person weather life's storm, conquer fear, and transform shattered and broken dreams into occasions to aid in God's unfolding eternal and unknowable plan. He admits that evil exists in the world and evil men commit evil deeds, but God's power eventually conquers evil and works through the lives of men and women to bring about justice, love, and equality. Toward the end of "Our God Is Able," King ends the homily with a story from his early ministry in Montgomery during the Montgomery bus boycott. White supremacists routinely harassed him and issued death threats. One night after he and Coretta went to bed, he received a threatening phone call ordering him to leave town. At his wits' end and not knowing what to do, he prayed aloud, asking God for strength and inner peace. He remembers feeling a divine and comforting presence that he had never felt before and, from that experience, says he gained the confidence to continue leading the boycott. For King, God is not an abstract, philosophical idea to be debated; instead, like African American ministers before and after him, God was a liberator of the oppressed.

Writing for *Commentary*, a magazine of political opinion shortly after the publication of *Strength to Love*, Staughton Lynd, the peace and civil rights activist said that the book "is best approached, not as an intellectual discourse, but as a spiritual handbook for Christians seeking to overcome hate and . . . fear and despair" (Lynd 1963). For half a century, the book has been required reading for seminarians and students of African American history.

On July 5, King was interviewed by several journalists for an internationally circulated U.S. Information Program press conference. The journalists included George Enninful, a reporter for the Ghana News Agency; William Workman, associate editor of South Carolina's *State* newspaper, T. V. Parasuram, correspondent for the *Indian Express*; as well as program moderator Robert Lodge. During the interview, he explained the history and gains of the civil rights movement and his hope for President Kennedy's upcoming civil rights legislation. King was thoughtful and measured in his statements and responses to questions and posited that African Americans should not be discriminated against in public and private institutions maintained and supported by black and white taxpayers' dollars. When Enninful asked him about Kennedy's proposed civil rights legislation, King responded in a similar fashion to his *New York Amsterdam News* columns, stating that Kennedy's bill and work on civil rights went further than his predecessor's but did not go far enough in dealing with blatant and rampant discrimination against black people throughout the nation.

In response to Robert Lodge's questions about the best strategies to achieve integration, King noted that whites needed to be persuaded to change their attitudes toward blacks, but the power of persuasion was just one tool. For blacks to obtain and practice their constitutional rights, they required judicial decisions, executive orders, and congressional legislation, because changing attitudes could take generations, while changing behaviors by laws was immediate. Later in the press conference, King discussed and defended his "Letter from Birmingham Jail" and placed the civil rights movement within larger worldwide movements against oppression and colonialism. At the end of the press conference, King highlighted the importance of nonviolent mass protests and demonstrations to challenge the forces of segregation and told the panel that this was the purpose of the March on Washington.

Several days later, on June 9, King's interview on *Open End* with David Susskind aired on WPIX-TV in New York City. The interview was unlike any other to date because of its length. The two spoke for close to two hours, allowing King to cover a variety of topics and delve deeper into issues more than he had the opportunity to do in other interviews, press conferences, and media appearances. He spoke about the Birmingham campaign and its influence on the larger civil rights movement throughout the nation, the effectiveness of Kennedy's justice department, Kennedy's past reluctance in advocating for black civil rights and his proposed civil rights legislation, the March on Washington, the integration of colleges and universities in Alabama and throughout the South, his continued commitment to the philosophy of nonviolence, the United States' image throughout the world, his disappointment with southern white moderates and their lukewarm support of the black struggle, tokenism, the Nation of Islam and black nationalism, the inadequate response of the Eisenhower administration in the field of civil rights, the power of economic boycotts of stores and establishments that discriminate against black people, black partisan politics, and African American discontent and impatience with the slow pace of social and economic change in every section of the nation, including northern and western cities. In analyzing the racial dilemma in the nation, he noted that the slow pace of change created openings for more radical black organizations that did not embrace nonviolent mass resistance. The only way to avoid violent uprisings in black communities and cities throughout the nation was with robust federal investment and programs in those communities.

The August 28, 1963, March on Washington for Jobs and Freedom is perhaps the best-known event of the modern civil rights movement. One of its organizers, A. Philip Randolph, called it "a new beginning not only for the Negro but for all Americans who thirst for freedom and a better life" (Bagwell and Walker 2004). The March on Washington, organizers insisted, would encourage President Kennedy and force an intransigent Congress to pass civil rights legislation that would offer further protections for African Americans' constitutional rights and improve their quality of life. In 1962, all the major civil rights organizations, including the Student Nonviolent Coordinating Committee, the SCLC, the Congress of Racial Equality, the National Urban League, the National Association for the Advancement of Colored People, and the Negro American Labor Council agreed to lend their support to the March. Randolph asked Bayard Rustin to be the deputy director of the March and help him plan and carry it out.

During the morning's entertainment portion, Ossie Davis, the actor, playwright, and civil rights activist, worked as a master of ceremony. On the day of the march, he presented the audience with leading actors, musicians, and entertainers who supported the cause of civil rights. Shortly after 2:00 p.m., the formal and overtly political session of the March on Washington began with a lineup of speakers that showed the complex link between the religious and secular aspects of the black freedom struggle. King provided the last speech at the March on Washington, which was for many the highlight of the day.

Since the March on Washington, King's remarks have come to be known as the "I Have a Dream" speech and a masterful work of rhetoric. Snippets of his speech have been read and viewed by millions all over the world. However, it was not the first time King had shared his dream. In November 1962 in Rocky Mount, North Carolina, he gave an early version of "I Have a Dream." The crowd at the Great March in Detroit heard a version in June 1963. According to Wyatt T. Walker, one of King's advisers, "[t]he night before [the march] Andy Young and I were working on a new climax because we thought the 'I Have a Dream' part was tired. We heard it 25, 30 times" (Bagwell and Walker 2004). On that late afternoon in August, King could feel the mood of the crowd and had an attentive congregation. Like the trains that took millions of black people from the South to the North and brought so many from their hometowns and cities to the nation's capital, King started slow and then picked up momentum. His remarks encouraged the multiracial crowd to dream of a more just America.

The March was seen as a resounding success for most of the 250,000 attendees as well as civil rights leaders and the Kennedy administration. King and other civil rights leaders met with President Kennedy and held a press conference after the March. All agreed that it was peaceful, orderly, well organized, and inspiring. They all celebrated the fact that there were no incidents of violence throughout the day. The March on Washington for Jobs and Freedom was a momentous day in the lives of African Americans and the nation. It was many things for many people, a coming of age for a generation, the capstone of the modern civil rights movement, and an end to the age of mass protest.

> ## CULTURAL CONNECTION: CIVIL RIGHTS MUSIC
>
> The freedom song or civil rights song generally was simple in its construction, initially adopted from spirituals, hymns, and gospel songs, and consisted of texts that progressed from freedom in a more abstract form to specific activities used to achieve it. Familiar songs taken from the black church, such as "I Ain't Gonna Let Nobody Turn Me Around," "Wade in the Water," or "We Shall Not Be Moved," had their texts modified to fit movement activities. One of the best-known examples of this is the song "We Shall Overcome," which was based on a hymn written by Rev. Charles Albert Tindley in 1905. Whereas Tindley wrote, "I will overcome someday," in the name of solidarity, it evolved into "We *shall* overcome." "Shall" probably replaced "will" to avoid alliteration for ease of diction. This song became the anthem of the movement and, in time, it became associated with Martin Luther King Jr. These songs also convey tactics and key values of the movement, and, as song leader and activist Bernice Johnson Reagon recounted later, music became "one of the best records . . . of transformation of consciousness in the ordinary people, the masses, who took part in the movement."
>
> By 1963, two broadly conceived categories defined the idiom of the freedom song. They were the songs adapted from spirituals or gospel songs that were used as part of movement activities and professionally composed topical songs that commented on protest events from a sideline perspective. This latter category developed first in the folk community through such artists as Pete Seeger, Bob Dylan, and Joan Baez. In the mid-1960s, however, singer and pianist Nina Simone began writing and performing songs that could be viewed as extensions of the work of the aforementioned folk artists. Simone, whose musical style defies category, was significant in voicing the changing rhetoric of the movement especially as resistance became more violent and bloody. In 1964, Simone, spurred by television reports of the bombing of the Sixteenth Street Baptist Church in Birmingham and the deaths of four little girls, wrote "Mississippi Goddamn." Simone would continue writing and performing songs that spoke to the movement, including "Ol' Jim Crow," "Mr. Backlash Blues," and "I Wish I Knew How It Would Feel To Be Free." Simone's songs and performance marked a considerable shift in black popular music's relation with the movement and also in the rhetoric of the movement, which by 1966 was moving more to the militancy of black nationalism.
>
> Source: Tammy L. Kernodle, "Civil Rights Music," in Emmett G. Price III, Tammy L. Kernodle, and Horace J. Maxile Jr., ed., *Encyclopedia of African American Music*, vol. 1 (Santa Barbara, CA: ABC-CLIO, 2011), 204–205.

Less than three weeks after the March on Washington, King returned to Birmingham. He left the Magic City in May, optimistic about the success of the campaign there and the desegregation plan that it brought about, but he returned in mid-September in a somber mood. At 10:24 a.m. on Sunday, September 15, as children and adults were readying themselves and the church for worship, a bomb ripped through the Sixteenth Street

Baptist Church. Among the dead were three fourteen-year-old girls and an eleven-year-old girl: Addie Mae Collins, Denise McNair, Carole Robertson, and Cynthia Wesley. Scores were injured. Shuttlesworth gave the eulogy for Carole Robertson. On September 18, King gave the eulogy to Collins, McNair, and Wesley. He called the bombing "one of the most vicious and tragic crimes ever perpetrated against humanity." He later said that Collins, McNair, and Wesley "say to each of us, black and white alike, that we must substitute courage for caution. They say to us that we must be concerned not merely about who murdered them, but about the system, the way of life, the philosophy which produced the murderers" (Tisby 2017). Three men, Robert E. Chambliss, Bobby Frank Cherry, and Thomas E. Blanton Jr., all members of the local chapter of the Ku Klux Klan, were eventually tried and convicted of the bombing.

The next day, King was in Washington, DC. He and other civil rights leaders, including Shuttlesworth, Abernathy, Dr. Lucius Pitts, president of Miles College; J. L. Ware, president of the Interdenominational Ministerial Alliance; and Bishop H. I. Murchison of the Christian Methodist Church met with President Kennedy to discuss the situation in Birmingham. In one interaction with President Kennedy, King declared that the city had reached a "state of civil disorder." The group made several suggestions to Kennedy during the meeting, including deploying federal troops into Birmingham to protect black citizens there. Kennedy listened to their ideas but did not follow through. In his *Autobiography*, King says that he left feeling hopeful that the Kennedy administration would act decisively. Shortly after the meeting with Kennedy, however, hopes were thrashed as the federal government continued to allow indiscriminate violence to reign in the city. "I fear," King wrote, "that from the White House down to ... the city administration of Birmingham, the intent and the intensity of the Negro has been misunderstood" (Carson 1998, 234).

In October, King returned to the lecture circuit to raise funds for the SCLC. On October 27, he spoke at the Bright Hope Baptist Church's groundbreaking ceremonies for their new church and youth center in North Philadelphia. Having spoken at the church before, King was no stranger to Bright Hope and was welcomed with open arms. On November 14, he was at Oberlin College in Oberlin, Ohio, though his speech was brief because he was fighting a terrible case of influenza.

The flu and the assassination of President John F. Kennedy on November 22 interrupted King's speaking engagement schedule. Kennedy's assassination shocked the nation, and following his death, King was asked for comments by a host of reporters and news outlets. On November 23, one day after Kennedy's death, Ray Moore of CBS News interviewed King in his Atlanta home, during which time King praised Kennedy stating that he "came forth with the most comprehensive civil rights bill that we have ever had from any president, and he had a great understanding of the depths and dimensions of the [racial] problem" (Moore 2013). Later King wrote that Kennedy "was assassinated by a morally inclement climate . . . filled with heavy torrents of false accusation, jostling winds of hatred, and raging storms of violence" (Carson 1998, 237). On November 26, he spoke with President Lyndon B. Johnson, offered his support, and told him that one of the best ways to honor Kennedy's legacy would be to pass the civil rights bill and other progressive legislation. The conversation was an amicable one, one that Johnson and King would resume when King visited Johnson at the White House on December 3. The meeting lasted for forty-five minutes, during which time they discussed the civil rights bill being debated in Congress and black voter registration.

King closed the year back on the lecture circuit. On December 12, he was on the campus of Franklin & Marshall College in Lancaster, Pennsylvania. With an audience close to five thousand, it was a record-breaking indoor crowd in Lancaster at the time. He reminded the crowd that "the time is always ripe to do right" (Buckwalter 2019). Days later, on December 18, he spoke on the campus of Western Michigan University as part of the institution's "Conscience of America" lecture series. In his discussion of contemporary movements in social justice, he professed that "[w]e're challenged after working in the realm of ideas, to move out into the arena of social action and to work passionately and unrelentingly to make racial justice a reality" ("Dr. Martin Luther King Jr. 1963" n.d.).

The year 1963 brought King a new child, a stint in jail, a successful publication, high-profile television appearances that brought more attention to the civil rights movement, the March on Washington, and despite Kennedy's death, the hope of broad and expansive civil rights legislation. Fatigued, King returned home to Atlanta in late December to spend the days between Christmas and New Year's with Coretta and his four children. Except for a speech at a protest in downtown Atlanta, he stayed home resting as best he could and playing with Dexter, Bernice, Martin, and Yolanda, especially at one of the children's favorite games: jumping off the refrigerator into their father's outstretched arms.

# 8

# The Man of the Year and the Nobel Prize Laureate

In the January 4, 1964, issue of *Time* magazine King was named its 1963 "Man of the Year," the first black American to receive the honor. Calling him the "American Gandhi," the article declares that King "has made himself the unchallenged voice of the Negro people—and the disquieting conscience of the whites." A portrait of King painted by the artist Robert Vickery is on the magazine's cover, and the accompanying article provides a brief history of his upbringing, the Montgomery bus boycott, the campaigns in Albany and Birmingham, and a glimpse into his daily work routine and nationwide speaking tour:

> King rises at 6:30 a.m. and goes to his study for 45 minutes of reading. Then he has fruit juice and coffee for breakfast, and at 9 o'clock drives to his office. . . . There he goes to work in a 16-ft. square room filled with perhaps 200 volumes on Negro and religious subjects; he checks his mail (about 70 letters a day), writes his speeches and sermons, confers with aides and, by telephone, with civil rights leaders around the country. He usually eats his lunch at his desk, then continues working, often until 2 or 3 o'clock the next morning. . . . King spends his time in airplanes, journeying to the far corners of the U.S. to speak and preach to huge audiences. He traveled about 275,000 miles in 1963 and made more than 350 speeches. ("America's Gandhi" 1964)

King and his inner circle at the SCLC were excited about the honor, because it showed that their work was not going unnoticed and was even supported by certain segments of the white population throughout the nation.

He, James Farmer, Roy Wilkins, and Whitney Young met with President Johnson on January 18 to discuss the civil rights bill, which was stalled in the House Rules Committee, and Johnson's Great Society programs to fight poverty. Two weeks earlier, during his first State of the Union address, Johnson laid out his plan to use federal resources to assist Americans who had not benefited from the American dream. Called the Great Society, Johnson declared an "unconditional war on poverty" through programs that focused on youth and the elderly. During the meeting, King offered Johnson his support, as he had done in November, and was hopeful that federal intervention could improve the economic outlook for African Americans.

A couple of days later, King went to In the Oaks, a retreat center owned by the Episcopal Diocese in Black Mountain, North Carolina. There, SCLC leadership met to unwind and plan their next mass action campaign. Between ping-pong games, softball matches, and card games, there was considerable debate within the organization about next steps. White elected officials and business leaders were dragging their feet on integration efforts in Alabama, and some thought the organization should return to Alabama's largest city to demonstrate. Others felt that the situations in Dansville, Virginia, or Atlanta, Georgia, required their attention. They also discussed FBI surveillance, the potential of FBI infiltration, and FBI director J. Edgar Hoover's attempts to link the SCLC with a communist conspiracy. They left the retreat after several days a bit rested but not renewed and with no clear idea of what their next campaign would be.

King returned to what appeared to be a nonstop fundraising tour and speaking engagements in the winter of 1964. His speeches contained the same content as those he gave before, but the audiences were different. It was a cold day in Milwaukee, Wisconsin, in late January when King addressed a standing-room-only crowd of 6,300 people at the Milwaukee Auditorium and spoke about the importance of the civil rights legislation being debated in Congress and the continued need for nonviolent direct action. On February 5, he delivered "The American Dream" at Drew University's convocation in Madison, New Jersey, at the invitation of George D. Kelsey, a professor of Christian ethics and one of King's mentors when he was a student at Morehouse. Several days later, on February 9, he was back in the Big Apple as the first speaker of the New School's American Race Crisis lecture series, where he delivered the address "The Summer of Our Discontent" and spoke about the trials, tribulations, and successes of the Birmingham campaign. King was at home at the New School. Founded by progressive intellectuals in 1919, the university was known for challenging the timidity of other institutions of higher learning and teaching their students to work for social change throughout society.

After his talk at the New School, he readied himself for his trip to Hawaii to speak to students and faculty at the University of Hawaii at Manoa. The institution was established in 1907 and became a university in 1920. Thirty-nine years later, on August 21, 1959, Hawaii became the fiftieth state. His presence was welcomed by the university and the community. On February 19, with a traditional Hawaiian lei over his dark-colored suit, he spoke to close to ten thousand people about "Progress toward Desegregation" at an outdoor theater as part of the university's Civil Rights Week. Those who did not have seats to hear him sat on the adjacent lawn outside of the Andrews Outdoor Theatre. A local newspaper, *Ka Leo O Hawai'i*, reported that "a good number of the University students cut their classes to hear Dr. King, the president of the Southern Christian Leadership Conference, and found themselves wedged in next to faculty members, high school students and local citizens." One of the attendees at King's talk was Simeon R. Acoba Jr., a twenty-year-old political science student who would later become a state Supreme Court justice in Hawaii. Recalling King's visit years later, Acoba remarked that his presence "expanded beyond campus, as many public officials, the editors of the two major newspapers, labor unions, the Honolulu Chamber of Commerce, churches and many others were engaged" *(Ka Leo* Staff 1964).

King also visited Hawaii to relax in its tropical climate. Throughout 1963, he had traveled tens of thousands of miles by plane, train, and automobile throughout the continental United States planning demonstrations, attending presidential meetings with two different administrations, and running one of the most important civil rights organizations in the nation. He had experienced exhaustion while working in Alabama and wanted to avoid the condition again. A break in the fiftieth state, with its average daily temperature in the eighties and ocean waves crashing on the beach, was what Mother Nature and maybe God wanted for him. However, his vacation was short-lived, and he returned to his busy speaking tour.

On March 9, King arrived at the First African Baptist Church in Tuscaloosa, Alabama, where Rev. Theophilus Y. Rogers Jr. was the pastor. It was his second visit to First African in less than a year, having preached at Rogers's installation as pastor the previous August. Later that month, King spoke at the Klein Memorial Auditorium in Bridgeport, Connecticut, in support of the pending civil rights legislation in the Senate and attended the groundbreaking ceremony for a fifty-unit, federally funded apartment building at Martin and Nelson Streets in Hartford, Connecticut, sponsored by the Mount Olivet Baptist Church. During the last week of March, he visited Washington, DC, to listen to the Senate debate the civil rights bill and speak with senators supporting the bill about strategies moving forward. It was during this brief stint in Washington that he had a chance meeting with Malcolm X.

Malcolm X had risen through the ranks of the Nation of Islam (NOI) to become its national spokesperson and leading black nationalist thinker. Infighting within the NOI and Malcolm's desire to create his own political organization led him to leave the NOI and create the Organization of Afro-American Unity (OAAU) in New York City. It was the first and only meeting between the two leaders, though they had read and spoken about each other for years. King was holding a press conference in the hallway when Malcolm walked up to him with his hand extended and King took it. Photographers captured the moment: King and Malcolm are shaking hands, smiling at one another. For those in the movement, the image was a symbol of hope: two branches of the black freedom struggle coming together. The hopes of a working relationship between King and Malcolm X or the SCLC and the OAAU were dashed when Malcolm was assassinated on February 21, 1965, less than one year after the fortuitous meeting.

King continued his speaking tour in April. On April 13, King was in Winston-Salem, North Carolina, and spoke at the Goler Metropolitan African Methodist Episcopal Zion Church to support voter registration drives in the city. He also visited Wake Forest University, which had recently integrated in September 1962. When it admitted three black students in the fall of 1962, it was the first major private, southern university to integrate. He was in the sunny climate of central California and the Las Vegas desert in late April. The Stanford Civil Rights Secretariat, a student group at Stanford University, organized the Western States Civil Rights Conference at the University from April 23 to 24, where King was one of the keynote speakers along with Robert Moses of the Student Nonviolent Coordinating Committee (SNCC). The predominantly white student audience was interested in events in the South and looking for opportunities to hear about and become part of the larger movement there.

On April 26, King was in Las Vegas, Nevada, where he spoke at the local chapter of the NAACP's Freedom Banquet and a public rally. He discussed the pending civil rights bill on Capitol Hill and encouraged his listeners to urge their state senators to support the bill and maintain a commitment to nonviolent, direct action. Esther Langston, the secretary of the Las Vegas NAACP branch, said that King's words were uplifting. Ida Gaines, a local activist who attended his talk, recalled that "he hit some of the high points of what people really wanted to hear from him. He was very encouraging and uplifting" (Przybys 2018). During the 1950s and early 1960s, black Nevadans mounted desegregation campaigns throughout the Silver State, which was often referred to as the "Mississippi of the West," and King's

### Cultural Connection: COINTELPRO

Between 1956 and 1971, the Federal Bureau of Investigation conducted a series of domestic covert action programs, COINTELPRO, which discredited, disrupted, and neutralized leaders, members, and supporters of social movements that threatened the social, political, and economic status quo. Launched in 1961, the COINTELPRO-Socialist Workers Party (SWP) singled out black SWP political campaigns for disruption and attempted to block a developing political alliance with Malcolm X's OAAU. Launched on August 25, 1967, the COINTELPRO-Black Nationalist Hate Group Operation (BNHG) formally institutionalized previously ad hoc covert operations that had targeted groups such as the Nation of Islam and the SCLC. These operations had aggravated factionalism in the NOI, exposed "links" between SCLC activists and the Communist Party, and attempted to expose Martin Luther King Jr.'s sexual affairs to induce him to suicide. Consisting of 360 documented operations, COINTELPRO-BNHG targeted groups that engaged in civil disobedience, picketing, or antiwar activity; advocated separatism, self-defense, or revolution; or associated with other COINTELPRO targets.

FBI agents used surreptitious entry, electronic surveillance, and informants to acquire and covertly distribute material to police, Congress, the media, elected officials, landlords, college presidents, and the Internal Revenue Service. By covertly distributing intelligence information and mailing derogatory and scurrilous communications, agents prevented activists from gaining respectability among white liberals, moderate blacks, and other movement people. To discredit activists and organizations, agents alerted local police officials to targets' plans and activities so that they could arrest activists on pretexts. To disrupt personal lives, agents sent anonymous communications to spouses, alleging activists' infidelity with traveling companions and coworkers. These operations thwarted fundraising, recruiting, organizing, and favorable publicity; prevented coalition building; and harassed movement leaders.

To capitalize on ideological, organizational, and personal conflicts; create factionalism; and provoke conflict between organizations, FBI agents made anonymous telephone calls and created counterfeit movement literature, cartoons, and other national communications. Alleging misconduct, provoking ridicule, snitch-jacketing activists as informants, and alleging the existence of assassination plots, such communications framed effective movement leaders as embezzlers, charlatans, informants, and provocateurs. Such tactics exacerbated divisions among white leftists and black revolutionaries, between moderates and radicals, and between advocates of public positions on nonviolence versus self-defense.

Source: John Drabble, "COINTELPRO," in Leslie Alexander and Walter Rucker, ed., *Encyclopedia of African American History*, vol. 3 (Santa Barbara, CA: ABC-CLIO, 2010), 709–711.

visit acknowledged their work and gave inspiration to those who had struggled for racial justice there.

Back in Atlanta on May 4, King convened the SCLC staff to resume conversations about the organization's next major campaign. James Bevel recently returned from Montgomery and wanted the organization to implement another full-scale assault against racism and segregation in Alabama, because businesspeople and white moderate city officials had not fulfilled their promises to desegregate the city, and black Birmingham residents were ready to protest and use nonviolent direct action again. John Gibson, Hosea Williams, and Wyatt Walker wanted the SCLC to commit its time and energy to St. Augustine, Florida, a city on the northeast coast of the Sunshine State. Founded by Spanish colonists in 1565 and known for its Spanish architecture, it is the nation's oldest settlement. Four hundred years later, St. Augustine was a stronghold of segregation and racial violence against black residents. Walker argued that a nonviolent campaign there could be a "beautiful prelude for the long, hot summer" of protests and discontent throughout black America (Garrow 1986, 326). King and the staff eventually agreed with Walker and Williams's rationale, and after his return from a speaking engagement at Bowdoin College in Maine on May 6 and from making time for his wife and children, he and Walker visited St. Augustine on May 18 and May 25 to lay the foundation for a movement there. At a mass meeting on the evening of May 18, he told the audience that the SCLC was committed to assisting them in their endeavor to be free. Leaving Walker in charge, King left the Ancient City to embark on a western-speaking tour that would take him to major cities in California and Arizona.

During his appearances in California, he advised his listeners to support the pending civil rights legislation in the U.S. Senate and spoke in favor of the Rumford Fair Housing Act, which banned racial discrimination in selling real estate or rental properties throughout the state. White reactionaries opposed the Rumford Act and were poised to have California Proposition 14, an initiative that sought to overturn the Rumford Act, on the November ballot. In San Diego on May 29, King spoke to students, faculty, and staff at California Western University, now Point Loma Nazarene University, and San Diego State University. According to a local news report the day after his talks, "he told the students they should be as indignant about racial discrimination in housing and employment in California as they are about the bombing of Negro homes and churches in the South." He also asserted that "it would be a setback for American freedom and the entire structure of justice if the Rumford Act in California were repealed" ("From the Archives" 2019).

On May 31, King was the keynote speaker at Religious Witness for Human Dignity, an interfaith gathering of Protestants, Catholics, and

Jews held at the Los Angeles Coliseum. Again, he publicly supported the civil rights bill in the Senate and told the crowd that "now is the time to open the floodgates of opportunity and allow an avalanche of justice to pour upon us" (King n.d.). The next day, June 1, he was in Fresno, California, two hundred miles north of Los Angeles, where he spoke at Ratcliffe Stadium on the campus of Fresno City College and participated in a march supporting the Rumford Act. Walking under a banner reading "Clergymen for Fair Housing," he led a contingent of his followers through the streets of Fresno to bring attention to the need for affordable housing in the San Joaquin Valley. He was in Tempe and Phoenix, Arizona, on June 3, at the Goodwin Stadium at Arizona State University and the Tanner African Methodist Episcopal Church, respectively, and reminded the audience that all life regardless of race, class, and creed are interconnected and that black people "were not the only ones who confront oppression in this country; the American Indian, the Mexican, the Puerto Rican and others confront the problems [of racial injustice]" (King n.d.). When he spoke at the 1964 Republican National Convention on June 7 at the Cow Palace in San Francisco, California, to convince the party to adopt a more robust civil right and an economic plan for the poor, it was clear that King's concerns extended beyond issues of racial justice into the realm of economic justice. He spoke not just for black America but was becoming a champion for all Americans who had been ignored by politicians, lobbyists, corporations, and the military-industrial complex. Writing about the 1964 Republican Party in his *Autobiography*, King lamented that the "Party had taken a giant stride away from its Lincoln tradition" (Carson 1998, 253).

He returned to the South after his West Coast and southwestern speaking tour, physically worn out and tired. For the most part, during the first five months of 1964, King was absent from the family, and his time away from home caused a strain on Coretta because she was the sole caretaker of four children under the age of ten. She had the help of King's parents and the Ebenezer Church community, but that was no substitute for an active and present husband and father of her children. Perturbed by tensions with his wife over his absentee parenting, he went to St. Augustine to assist in the movement there.

Much had happened in his absence. Wyatt Walker, SCLC staff, and the local black community had organized demonstrations in St. Augustine, including wade-ins at a local segregated beach; members of the Ku Klux Klan and the notorious white supremacist J. B. Stoner had descended upon the city to instill fear in the protesters, and the beachside cottage the organization rented for King had been riddled with bullets. He arrived on June 10, and on July 11, King, Ralph Abernathy, Bernard Lee, and others went to the restaurant at the Monson Motor Lodge, a popular tourist destination that served African Americans, but only the black servants of affluent whites in a segregated area. James Brock, the owner, met King and his entourage at the entrance, refused them service, and asked them to leave. King refused and was eventually arrested by the chief of police and sheriff for trespassing and a variety of other offenses. It was his third arrest for his civil rights work and landed him in jail for two days until he was released on June 13. For days, the movement was at an impasse where peaceful, nonviolent integrated protesters marched and were met by violent white racists. In one incident black and white protesters organized a swim-in at the Monson Motor Lodge, and Brock poured chemicals in the pools to expel them.

King worked in the background trying to secure an agreement. A grand jury proposed that a biracial committee be formed to plan and eventually institute a desegregation plan after King and the SCLC left St. Augustine and protests stopped for thirty days. He rejected the offer and counterproposed that a biracial committee be formed and KKK violence be contained immediately. When negotiations stalled, Florida governor C. Farris Bryant stepped in and created a temporary four-person biracial committee on June 30. King had won a battle with the creation of the committee, but it was only a partial victory, as the committee lacked the power to enforce desegregation. Partial victory or not, the SCLC had once again proved the power of nonviolent, direct action in challenging segregation.

A major victory and culmination of King's travels and lobbying arrived on July 2 when President Johnson signed the Civil Rights Act of 1964 that banned racial discrimination in public accommodations throughout the nation. King was in Washington when the bill became law. In one iconic photo from the day, he is standing directly behind Johnson as Johnson affixed his signature to the law. In another, he graciously receives one of the seventy-two pens Johnson used.

While the drama in St. Augustine unfolded, *Why We Can't Wait*, King's third book, was published by Harper & Row on June 9. Announcing the book's publication, the *New York Times* described it as "a statement of Dr. King's philosophy of nonviolence as the course to be followed by Negroes in struggling for their rights" ("Books—Authors" 1964). Stanley Levison, King's longtime adviser and confidante, negotiated the contract for the book, and King wrote it with professional ghostwriter and businessman Al Duckett throughout the latter half of 1963. Duckett had a hand in writing many of King's speeches and worked with black political and sports figures, including Jackie Robinson. However, King was unhappy with the pace and tone of the work and, with Levison's help, replaced Duckett with Nat Lamar, a young Harvard graduate, fellow Atlantan, and freelance writer in the autumn of 1963. Lamar eventually left the project and Hermine Popper, the editor, short story writer, and critic who had worked with

King on *Strive toward Freedom* was hired to assist King with putting the final touches on the book in the spring of 1964.

*Why We Can't Wait* can be understood in three parts. Part one, the first two chapters, discusses the history of race relations and African American political and economic life in the late nineteenth and early twentieth centuries. Together they provide readers the why: why black people in Birmingham were willing to risk life and limb to obtain their constitutional and, according to King, God-given rights. Chapters 3 through 7, the second part, recounts the how: how black Birmingham residents, with the help of the SCLC, challenge segregation and white racists in the Magic City and how the campaign influenced the larger black freedom struggle during the summer of 1963, the "summer of our discontent." Chapter 5 contains King's famous "Letter from Birmingham Jail" in its entirety. Chapter 8, the book's third part, offers creative approaches that the nation can take to "radically readjust" its contemporary attitudes and stances toward blacks and provide "compensatory consideration" for the discrimination African Americans endured since the nation's founding (King, *Why We Can't Wait*, 1964, 124). Rather than reparations for centuries of unpaid labor and exploitation, King called for a massive federal spending program called the Bill of Rights for the Disadvantaged. Modeled after President Franklin Roosevelt's G.I. Bill, the Bill of Rights for the Disadvantaged would be open to white and black Americans and offer job training, federally backed mortgages and loans, educational opportunities, medical care, and other resources that would be used to "attack the tenacious poverty which so paradoxically exists in the midst of plenty" (King, *Why We Can't Wait*, 1964, 129).

*Why We Can't Wait* was favorably received. Nelson Rockefeller, the governor of New York state and SCLC supporter called the book incisive. Daniel Poling, the white evangelical minister and editor of the *Christian Herald* said King's third book was "one of the most eloquent achievements" of 1964. Saunders Redding, the author and professor of creative writing at Hampton Institute, now Hampton University, in Virginia reviewed the book for the *New York Times* in July. The "most effective message of *Why We Can't Wait* comes in those dramatic chapters in which the author relates the story of 'Bull Connor's Birmingham' and illustrates it with those brutal, obscene photographs that nearly the whole world saw, and seeing, turned away from in speechless shame and horror" (Redding 1964).

While the SCLC was assisting black residents in St. Augustine, Florida, the Council of Federated Organizations' Freedom Summer was well underway. The Council was an umbrella organization in Mississippi comprised of SNCC, the National Association for the Advancement of Colored People, and the Congress of Racial Equality. The Freedom Summer was a project geared to energize and intensify voter registration, create freedom schools and community centers, and organize a predominantly black political party, the Mississippi Freedom Democratic Party (MFDP). The MFDP's attempt to unseat the Mississippi Democratic Party at the 1964 Democratic National Convention was an attempt to influence national politics. Mississippi's statewide exclusion of the majority of African Americans from voting meant that the Mississippi delegation to the convention was not a democratically chosen group or reflective of the state's population and was, therefore, illegitimate. Most of the sixty-eight members of the MFDP delegation were black and represented a cross section of black Mississippians—sharecroppers, farmers, domestics, teachers, and clergy. Four delegates were white. The purpose was to dramatize to the nation the disfranchisement of millions of African Americans throughout the nation during a presidential election.

King was not part of the MFDP and did not participate to any meaningful extent in the Freedom Summer, but he toured Mississippi in late July and supported the idea of the MFDP. When the MFDP delegation went to the Democratic National Convention in Atlantic City from August 24 to August 27, they conscripted King to help negotiate on their behalf with the Johnson administration and Democratic National Committee operatives. In one negotiation session, he told the credentials committee that "seating [the MFDP] would become symbolic of the intention of this country to bring freedom and democracy to all people" (Carson 1998, 252). Initially Johnson dismissed the MFDP and argued that their campaign to unseat the white Mississippi delegates was a dangerous ploy that could lead to the defection of white southern Democrats and the election of his Republican rival, staunch conservative Barry Goldwater. King was in a bind: he supported the MFDP but did not want to wrinkle his relationship with Johnson and thereby limit any future assistance that the Johnson administration could provide to the black freedom struggle if LBJ won the presidency.

In a stunning turn of events, after hours and days of political wrangling, King, Bayard Rustin, Roy Wilkins, Al Lowenstein, Joseph Ruah, Lyndon Johnson, and high-ranking members of the Democratic Party brokered a compromise: two members of the MFDP, Aaron Henry and Ed King, would be seated with the all-white delegation, who would be required to take a loyalty oath, pledge allegiance to the National Democratic Party, and support Johnson as the party's presidential candidate. All other MFDP delegates would be designated convention guests. King understood the compromise and its acceptance as politically expedient. No one would get everything they wanted in the short term, but in the long run, black people would have a friend in the White House. The MFDP rejected the plan, the all-white delegation was seated, Johnson became the party's presidential candidate, and he went on to be elected president.

After the Democratic National Convention, King returned to Atlanta to prepare for a tour of Europe with Coretta and Ralph and Juanita Abernathy. On September 13 and 14, he was an honored guest of West Berlin's mayor Willy Brandt. He visited the Berlin Wall, spoke at an event commemorating the life and legacy of John F. Kennedy, delivered a sermon at the Waldbühne, an amphitheater in West Berlin, and later addressed a large audience in East Berlin at St. Mary's Church. Several days later he was in Rome, where he and Abernathy had an audience with Pope Paul VI. Pope Paul VI was elected pope in June 1963 and served in the position until his death in 1978. The Archbishop of Atlanta, Paul Hallahan, arranged the twenty-five-minute meeting during which time King, Abernathy, and the Pope discussed race relations through an interpreter. Speaking to Paul Hoffman of the *New York Times* after the meeting, King said that "the Pope made it palpably clear that he is a friend of the Negro people and asked me to tell the American Negroes that he is committed to the cause of civil rights in the United States" (Hoffman 1964). After their meeting with Pope Paul VI, the Kings and Abernathys spent a couple of days in Madrid, Spain, and then London, England, to promote *Why We Can't Wait* before returning to Atlanta.

Back home, King resumed his speaking tour. Between October 7 and 11, he was in Philadelphia, Pennsylvania, as the keynote speaker at the Sound of Freedom, a program sponsored by Greater Philadelphia Citizen Committee, and in Newark, New Jersey, and New York City. Following those visits and at the invitation of the St. Louis University Student Government, he was in St. Louis, Missouri, speaking to eager students, staff, and faculty at the oldest university west of the Mississippi. "While the law can't change the hearts of men," he told the audience of close to four thousand, "it does change the habits. And, in time, habits change attitudes" (Edgell 2018). King returned home from St. Louis fatigued and with fever, and on Tuesday, October 13, checked himself into St. Joseph's Infirmary, one of Atlanta's first hospitals, under the care of Dr. Asa Yancey, a preeminent black physician and health educator, who prescribed hospital bed rest, a change of diet, and sleeping aids.

The next day, while King was still in the hospital, Coretta called and told him he had won the Nobel Peace Prize. The prize was inaugurated in 1901 through Dr. Alfred Nobel's last will and testament that his wealth and estate be used for "prizes to those who, during the preceding year, have conferred the greatest benefit to humankind" ("The Establishment of the Nobel" n.d.). King realized that he was being considered for the honor when Nobel officials reached out to him requesting additional copies of his articles and books weeks before, but as he sat fatigued and foggy from sleeping pills, he slowly absorbed the news, and reporters and photographers were on hand to cover the moment. He told the *New York Times*, "I was not fully awake" and "for a while I thought it was a dream, and then I realized it was true" ("Man with a Dream" 1964). *Jet* Magazine featured King on the front page of its October 29 issue with the headline "Rev. M.L. King: Crusade for Love and Peace Leads to the World's Most Rewarding Honor." Telegrams of congratulations and support poured in, and when the SCLC inner circle and King's family joined him in his hospital room to celebrate the news, he told them and reporters that the real winners of the Nobel Prize were those African Americans on the front lines of nonviolent mass resistance to racial injustice and that the $54,000 prize money would be donated to the civil rights movement.

King left St. Joseph's infirmary on October 14 and ended his recuperation to spend late October and early November conducting a nationwide and thinly veiled get-out-and-vote-for-Lyndon-Johnson campaign that often featured him on a flatbed truck crisscrossing black neighborhoods and urging residents to exercise their right to vote. He was due in Oslo, Norway, in early December to receive the Nobel Prize and deliver a lecture at the University of Oslo, so when he was not stumping for Johnson's campaign or worrying about a potential FBI smear campaign to undermine him, he was writing, rewriting, and editing his Nobel acceptance speech.

He left for Europe on December 4 with a large group of supporters and loved ones, including Coretta, his parents and siblings, SCLC staff, Bayard Rustin, and a host of others. Before Oslo, the group stopped in London, where King met with activists, politicians, and luminaries from newly emerged nations, including India, and preached "The Three Dimensions of a Complete Life" at St. Paul's Cathedral to an eager crowd of three thousand on December 6. St. Paul's was founded in 604 CE and is the home of the bishop of London. Throughout its long history, it has been known as an institution that stands against oppression in all its forms. As it has for centuries, in the twenty-first century, it remains the heart of London's Anglican community. King's oratory left the congregation spellbound, with one observer recalling that "he was actor, poet and preacher all at the same time" (Muir 2014).

On December 7, he spoke about South African apartheid, the recent incarceration of Nelson Mandela, and other black anti-apartheid leaders and compared American segregation with South African apartheid. In both nations, he observed, black people were fighting against intransigent white supremacists, and in both nations, nonviolent mass resistance was an important tool for social change. England, Europe, and the United States, in order to force change in South Africa, could "join in the one form of non-violent action that could bring freedom and justice to South Africa . . . a massive movement for economic sanctions." Such sanctions would entail not buying South African diamonds and an oil embargo to force the white minority of that nation to recognize black South Africans' basic rights and create a multiracial society (King, "Speech on South Africa" 1964).

The King group arrived in Norway on December 8, and King spent several busy days in the Nordic nation holding press conferences, attending receptions at the U.S. Embassy, meeting King Olav of Norway, dining with the mayor of Oslo, receiving the Nobel Prize at the official award ceremony, and delivering the Nobel lecture to an overflowing audience at the University of Oslo.

The lecture and his personal and political journey up to that point demonstrated that King was, indeed, an intelligent and formidable black civil rights leader in the United States, but he was also a champion for oppressed, exploited, and downtrodden people of color the world over. During his lecture, King maintained that the wealthier humanity had become, "the poorer we have become morally and spiritually," and this moral poverty resulted in racism, war, and poverty. Racism and racial injustice were being challenged by "the great masses of people ... determined to end the exploitation of their races and land" in the United States, Africa, Asia, and South America. Despite some progress in the United States on the racial front, including the 1964 Civil Rights Act and the election of President Lyndon Johnson, the United States still had to pass through the wilderness of racism and unequivocally embrace the philosophy of nonviolence and nonviolent peaceful protest. The philosophy and method on nonviolence, King contended, was a necessary prescription for humanity's spiritual poverty.

Poverty and war were the second and third results of humanity's moral deficiency. King compared poverty to a "monstrous octopus" with "nagging, prehensile tentacles in lands and villages all over the world." Grave economic disparities exist between the West and other nations throughout the world and within Western nations themselves, where the rich live in penthouse apartments and affluent, gated suburbs and the poor lives in urban ghettos and rural slums. To tackle poverty and ultimately humanity's soul, King maintained that "wealthy nations must go all out to bridge the gulf between the rich minority and the poor majority." He declares that war in the twentieth century is obsolete because small-scale or international wars only result in bloodshed, destruction for the vanquished, hatred for the victors, and worldwide instability. The method of nonviolence is relevant to relations between nation-states, who should embrace it not just to avoid war but to bring about peace and international brotherhood. Only by tackling these interrelated problems of racial injustice, poverty, and war can humanity redeem and "transform our imminent cosmic elegy into a psalm of creative fulfillment" (King, "Nobel Lecture," 1964).

King realized he was the symbol of the movement and that while the Nobel Peace Prize rewarded him for his patience, exhausting speaking tours to forward racial justice, and courage in the face of white

## Cultural Connection: The Free Speech Movement

In 1964, the Free Speech Movement (FSM) erupted at the University of California, Berkeley—the first massive countercultural protest by college students. Few expected it, and even fewer realized that it would ignite similar protests on other campuses.

Students at Berkeley had for some time felt constrained by university regulations that restricted political expression. They had only one place outside the classroom where they could present their ideas: a small piece of land, called a free speech area, at the entrance of the college on Bancroft Strip. There they made speeches and distributed pamphlets. On September 14, 1964, however, the university announced that it would end the free speech zone. The decision came after several students picketed the nearby *Oakland Tribune* for having engaged in racial discrimination. The newspaper's owner complained about students inciting radicalism, and so the administration decided to crack down.

On campus, discontent grew as angry students claimed that the episode proved that the university, and American society, wanted to crush dissent. On October 1, the tense situation boiled over when university police arrested a student, Jack Weinberg, for violating restrictions on political speech. Dozens of students immediately gathered in front of Sproul Hall, the main administration building, where they surrounded the police car holding Weinberg.

Mario Savio, a philosophy student, addressed the crowd and won recognition as the leader of the protest. About two hundred students soon occupied Sproul Hall, began a sit-in, and did not disperse until the administration promised to establish a committee, which would include faculty and students to study college rules. The protest became known as the FSM later that week, after representatives from several student clubs met and established a formal organization.

On November 20, the University of California Board of Regents eased the speech restrictions, and the crisis appeared to be over. Several days later, however, the administration announced that it would prosecute the protest leaders. In response, on December 2, new sit-ins occurred at Sproul Hall, with four hundred students occupying the building until riot police dragged them out. At the same time, graduate teaching assistants went on strike, and in the turmoil, the college canceled many classes. Finally on December 8, the faculty agreed with the students' demands, and the Regents decided to further extend the right to free speech.

In all, the students sought freedom of political expression and some educational reforms. On campuses across the nation, students held Berkeley-style protests in reaction to oppressive conditions. By 1966, the FSM would disband and be replaced by radicalized movements disgusted with liberal moderation and by a hippie culture that rejected political action as futile.

Source: Neil Hamilton, "Free Speech Movement," in Michael Green and Scott Stabler, ed., *Ideas and Movements That Shaped America*, vol. 2 (Santa Barbara, CA: ABC-CLIO, 2015), 431–433.

supremacist violence, he was just a trustee of the award. The Nobel Peace Prize was an international moral victory for the civil rights movement and all nonviolent struggles against racialized oppression.

After leaving Oslo, King went to Stockholm, Sweden, for a two-day visit, and then Paris before returning to the United States with a renewed sense of purpose. He started the year as the "Man of the Year" and ended the year as the youngest person to ever receive the Nobel Peace Prize up to that time. With all the accolades and awards he had earned throughout the years, he could have rested on his laurels and become a distinguished professor of religion or philosophy, an aspiration of his since theology school. He had many offers and could have written his own ticket to whatever university he wanted, but America was still wandering through a spiritual and moral wilderness, and it needed a guide. The 1964 Civil Rights Act addressed issues of racial discrimination, and President Johnson had made the eradication of poverty one of his top priorities, but black people and other people of color continued to experience systemic racism, the poor remained invisible despite the nation's economic prosperity, and America was still at war in Vietnam. The three evils of racism, poverty, and war meant that King needed to continue his work and do what SCLC stated as its goal: to save the soul of America. That work eventually took him and the SCLC to Selma, Alabama, to confront continued racism and noncompliance with the 1964 Civil Rights Act.

SNCC had been in Selma throughout 1964 urging black residents to vote through voter registration drives but with minimal success and limited funds, so black residents of Selma requested assistance from the SCLC. Though based in Montgomery, fifty miles away from Selma, James Bevel of the SCLC had also been working with Selma residents throughout 1964, laying a foundation for the organization's efforts there in 1965. During a planning session after Christmas, King and his SCLC associates agreed to begin a campaign working with SNCC on January 2 at a mass meeting at Brown Chapel AME Church, a Selma congregation with origins dating back to the Reconstruction era. King spoke to hundreds of black activists and supporters from Selma. He told them why the SCLC was there and what their intentions were: to oppose the continued, illegal segregationist policies of the Queen City and to register blacks to vote. He later wrote that Selma was "to 1965 what Birmingham was to 1963" (Carson 1998, 271).

Selma, Alabama, is located near the banks of the Alabama River and is the political and judicial center of Dallas County. In 1965, over half of the residents of Dallas County were African American, but less than 2 percent were registered to vote because of discriminatory policies in the county. SCLC's strategy was to send scores of well-dressed black men and women to the courthouse to register to vote on a daily basis, wait for the county sheriff, Jim Clark, to resort to violence in turning them away, and dramatize for the ever-present news agencies the illegality of Clark's and Selma's racial discrimination. In one instance, on January 25, black applicants were seeking to register to vote when Clark and his deputies began pushing them on the sidewalk. Unbeknownst to Clark, Annie Lee Cooper, a black, middle-aged woman was in no mood to be pushed around. As Clark approached her, she punched him in the head and was tackled by deputies and beaten over the head by Clark's billy club. Clark showed no remorse for his police brutality, and he and his deputies continued to arrest black applicants. By late January, hundreds of marchers had been arrested in Selma and surrounding towns, and King decided it was time to be arrested and bring national attention to voter suppression in Selma.

On February 1, King spoke at Brown Chapel and told the crowd that if "Negroes could vote . . . there would be no Jim Clarks" or "oppressive poverty directed toward Negroes" and then led 260 marchers comprised mainly of young people to the courthouse (Herbers 1965). They marched only a couple of blocks until they were arrested for parading without a license. In custody, King refused to post bail and remained in jail for the rest of the week. On Friday, February 5, he published a letter in the *New York Times* saying that "when the Civil Rights Act of 1964 was passed Americans were lulled into complacency because they thought the day of difficult struggle was over." With so few black people registered to vote in Dallas County, Alabama, he added derisively that "there are more Negroes in jail with me than there are on the voting rolls" (King, "Letter . . . from a Selma, Alabama Jail," 1965). Shortly after his release, King was in Washington, DC, lobbying Vice President Hubert Humphrey, Attorney General Nicholas Katzenbach, and President Johnson about the possibility of passing voting rights legislation. Refusing to wait and play politics, King, the SCLC, and SNCC brainstormed for weeks about ways to bring about a national conversation about voter suppression and discrimination. Although SNCC rejected the idea, the SCLC decided upon a march from Selma to Montgomery.

Governor George Wallace prohibited the fifty-mile march that would span several days, but on March 7, hundreds of marchers assembled at Brown Chapel to make their mark in history. King was tending to church business at Ebenezer, so John Lewis, the chairperson of SNCC, who participated despite his organization's disapproval, and Hosea Williams, SCLC's director of voter registration, began the march. To get out of Selma, head east, and begin their long journey to Montgomery, the marchers had to cross the Edmund Pettus Bridge, a four-lane arched steel bridge on U.S. Route 80 spanning the Alabama River. The bridge was named after a Confederate Civil War officer who became a post-Reconstruction U.S. senator from Alabama and a late nineteenth-century Ku Klux Klan leader.

On the bridge, the marchers were stopped by Alabama state troopers who were wearing gas masks and wielding nightsticks. The troopers ordered the marchers to disperse, go home, or return to Brown Chapel, but the marchers refused. After a final warning, the troopers, many of whom were on horseback, moved in, pushing the crowd with nightsticks, firing canisters of tear gas, and beating the peaceful protesters to force them back across the bridge. No one was spared: men, women, and children suffered the blows of the troopers. The fiasco was filmed by national news outlets for the nation to see that evening and came to be known as Bloody Sunday.

King returned to Selma and prepared to lead the march to Montgomery on March 9. The ranks of the marchers had swelled to two thousand blacks and whites and included clergymen, politicians, and union officials from around the nation, but federal judge Frank Johnson, in Montgomery, prohibited the march. King was at another crossroad. To continue the march meant that he would violate a federal injunction, lose federal support, and ultimately alienate President Johnson. To not march meant that he would lose the support of the people he promised to lead, and he would appear spineless. King compromised. The marchers left Selma, walked across the bridge, and were stopped by Alabama state troopers. This time the lead group knelt in prayer, led by Ralph Abernathy; then King turned the marchers and led them back to Brown Chapel. Over the next twelve days, plans were made to continue the march, and the merits of the march were debated in federal court. Eventually, Judge Frank Johnson decided that the marchers had the right to march from Selma to Montgomery. On Sunday, March 21, over three thousand assembled at the Brown Chapel and began their journey, with King at the head of the group walking arm in arm with clergymen. They were not stopped by Alabama state troopers; instead, they were protected by the Alabama national guard by the order of President Johnson.

On March 25, the weary marchers made their way to a rally in the heart of Montgomery. Rain, blistered feet, aching joints, and death threats made their fifty-mile journey a challenging trek, but they were overjoyed to reach the steps of the State Capitol building, where King delivered an impassioned speech: "How Long? Not Long." How long will it take to create a "society to be at peace with itself" he asked. "Not long, because the arc of the moral universe is long, but it bends toward justice" (Carson 1998, 286). It had been ten years since King was installed as pastor at Dexter Avenue Baptist Church in Montgomery and ten years since the Montgomery bus boycott. He began as an intelligent and unknown black preacher in a small southern city and became the moral conscience of the nation. As he stood on the podium addressing the crowd of nonviolent pilgrims on that mild March afternoon, he remembered the victories and setbacks of the movement and reminded the audience that they "must keep going" (Carson 1998, 285).

King and the Selma movement brought the issue of voting access and voting suppression to the nation's attention and encouraged President Johnson to use his position to push for new voting rights legislation. On March 15, in an address to Congress, Johnson declared that all Americans regardless of race must have the right to vote, and five months later, on August 6, he signed the Voting Rights Act of 1965, which prohibits tactics used to prevent people from voting, including literacy tests.

King's leadership and the devotees of nonviolence had made progress in school integration, forced the integration of interstate transit, desegregated city buses throughout the South, brought the issue of racial injustice to the forefront of American politics, and encouraged politicians to pass civil rights legislation and the Voting Rights Act. However, racism, poverty, and war continued, so despite the success of the civil rights movement, King continued his work and broadened his perspective and approach.

# 9

## Going to Chicago

The Selma campaign and its attendant duties were rewarding but tiring, and King rarely slept for more than four hours per night, so in early April 1965, he took a vacation in Miami, Florida, and the Bahamas. During that early spring, he and the Southern Christian Leadership Conference (SCLC) flirted with the idea of an economic boycott of Alabama that would disrupt the flow of federal funds to the Cotton State, halt the transportation of the state's goods by truckers, and discourage the purchase of any goods and items made in the state. King thought the boycott was a necessity akin to the Montgomery bus boycott, and he explained his reasons and meaning in a *New York Amsterdam News* article on April 10. The purpose of the boycott was to bring an end to the daily reign of terror blacks faced in the state. In response to a question of whether the Alabama boycott would hurt its black residents, he indicated that black people in the state have "accept[ed] suffering, sacrifice, and temporary hurt in order to relieve the larger and psychological hurt." Since they were "hurting and suffering so severely [the boycott] couldn't be much worse" (King, "The Boycott Explained," 1965). Despite his best effort, however, he and the SCLC received no support from other civil rights organizations or white moderates, so they dropped the idea to support SCLC's expansion into northern and western urban areas to bring attention to segregated housing, poverty, and segregated schools there. Initially they were unsure which city to focus their attention on, so King toured several cities.

He visited Boston from April 22 to April 24, where he met with the state legislature, the mayor of Boston, and community groups. At a joint session of the Massachusetts Legislature at the Massachusetts State House, he maintained that "we see subtle forms of discrimination in all of our communities, expressed in housing discrimination, de facto segregation, in the public schools, and expressed in job discrimination and unemployment" and called "upon the Great Legislature of the Commonwealth of Massachusetts to be maladjusted until the good society is realized" (King, "Address of Reverend," 1965). From there he went to Roxbury, the predominantly black neighborhood in Boston, visited an overcrowded school and spoke with concerned parents before touring a dilapidated tenement occupied by black residents. At an evening Passover event at Temple Israel in Boston's Back Bay neighborhood, he told the predominantly white audience that "we are involved in a great and momentous struggle right now to get rid of the tragic yoke around us so long. We must remove the pharaohs who still have hardened hearts" (Levey, "Dr. King Appeals for Brotherhood," 1965).

The next day, King led thousands of marchers from Roxbury to the Boston Common, where he spoke to a crowd estimated at twenty-two thousand, one of the largest demonstrations in the city's history. His designated driver, Roxbury resident Arnold Walker, remembers "walking with solemn deliberation from the William E. Carter playground in lower Roxbury, down Columbus Avenue to the Parkman Bandstand on Boston Common" (Sharif 2012). At the rally, King declared that "now is the time to make real the promise of democracy" and "make brotherhood a reality" (Levey, "Dr. King Appeals for Brotherhood," 1965). Before leaving Beantown, King and Massachusetts SCLC president Virgil Woods met with Boston's mayor, John F. Collins, and presented him with a list of grievances that included housing issues, code enforcement, economic welfare, community upkeep, and needed anti-poverty work in Boston's black community. His visit was a resounding success. One Bostonian remarked that King's presence and approach "served to heighten the drama of the plight of Boston's Negroes" and to "show that Selma exists in Boston" (Dudley 1965).

Several days later, King was in Southern California. On April 27, he was in the City of Angels again speaking to students, faculty, and staff at the University of California, Los Angeles, where he delivered an address entitled "Segregation Must Die" and reminded the audience of five thousand that "things don't change on their own, things don't change by waiting for them to change; they change through actions of good people" (Regents of the University of California 1965). After a brief time with his family in Atlanta, King went to Philadelphia in early May. He and the SCLC decided that Boston was not the proper place to stage their first northern campaign and scouted out the City of Brotherly Love. Local politics on the ground in Philadelphia were not suitable for nonviolent, direct action to confront northern poverty or de facto segregation in schools and employment there. King also visited Washington, DC, but found the nation's capital unsuitable for the organization's first foray outside of the Deep South.

On July 6, on a sweltering Chicago day, King arrived in Chicago to speak with the predominantly white fifth General Synod of the United Church of Christ, after which he met with Al Raby, a devoted local teacher, activist, and chairmen of the Coordinating Council of Community Organizations (CCCO), who asked King to help them in their efforts to desegregate Chicago public schools. The discussion was meaningful, and King promised to return within weeks. Chicago had been a destination for black migrants from the Mississippi Delta for decades during the early twentieth century, and by 1950, the city's South Side neighborhood was often referred to as the "Negro Metropolis" because it was home to the city's black cultural and intellectual elite. Black economic achievement in the city provided opportunities for blacks to move throughout the city, but residential and educational prospects were limited. King returned to the Windy City on July 23 to consult with local activists and conduct a tour of the city's black neighborhoods. After fruitful meetings in Chicago and conversations with the SCLC staff, Chicago became the site for the organization's northern city campaign.

Chicago was not like any southern city, and King could not count on blatant racist attacks by the police to garner publicity the way he could in his previous campaigns. Northern white moderates were not easily condemned for de facto segregation, so careful planning was needed to create an effective movement. The organization took the summer and autumn of 1965 to develop a plan. Its activity in Chicago was delayed briefly by a violent black uprising in the Watts neighborhood of Los Angeles.

King arrived in the City of Angels on August 17 at the request of black Los Angeles clergy who wanted his assistance in quelling the violence and negotiating with Mayor Sam Yorty and Police Chief William Parker. After a press conference, where he explained his reasons for being in Los Angeles and condemned the violence of the riot and the poverty, economic insecurities, and police violence that led up to it, King toured the ravaged neighborhood and met with local black residents and activists. He listened intently as he toured Watts even as some accused him of not knowing the extent of structural racism in Los Angeles or the lived reality of black Angelenos. One gentleman from Birmingham, Alabama, who had lived in Los Angeles for several years told King that the politics of Birmingham were incomparable to Los Angeles. Repeatedly, King declared that blacks in Los Angeles were not free, just as blacks in Alabama were not free, and said that he would use his power and influence to encourage California governor Edmund Brown and Los Angeles mayor Sam Yorty to meet with them to hear their grievances.

> ### Cultural Connection: Long, Hot Summer Riots, 1965–1967
>
> The term "Long, Hot Summer" is often applied to the riots occurring in the United States during the spring and summer months of 1965, 1966, and 1967. These violent disturbances often began in hot weather, often required the assistance of the National Guard, and caused much financial damage, many arrests, and many deaths. They helped point out to the nation the discrimination still prevalent at the time as well as the reforms needed to heal a nation divided by race.
>
> On August 11, 1965, in the Watts neighborhood of Los Angeles in the middle of a summer heat wave, a simple incident ignited a major riot. A highway patrolman stopped a speeding black driver and arrested him for driving under the influence. A mob started to congregate, and events escalated. Passing white motorists were dragged out of their cars and beaten; automobiles were overturned and set on fire. Eventually, the National Guard had to be called in to restore order. In all, thirty-four people were killed, nearly four thousand people were arrested, and there were $35 million in damages.
>
> In the spring of 1966, emotions again flared in Watts, although not to the extent they had the previous year. But in July, Chicago exploded with rock throwing and firebombing. Three people were killed by stray bullets, and there were 533 arrests. In all, forty-three different cities had racially violent events in 1966.
>
> In 1967, nearly 150 cities had racial disturbances. Those in Detroit and Newark (New Jersey) were major. Lasting from July 14 to July 17, the riots in Newark began in the Central Ward and spread into the downtown area. In the end, there was $10 million in damage, 725 people injured, 1,500 arrested, and twenty-three people killed. The Detroit riot began on July 23 and lasted for five days. The flash point for the violence was the arrests of eighty-two people who were at an after-hours bar celebrating the return of two Vietnam War veterans near the home of Danny Thomas, a Vietnam veteran who had been killed by a gang of white youths. In the end, there was $22 million in damage, 1,189 people injured, 43 people killed—the youngest was four years old and the oldest sixty-eight—and 7,000 people arrested.
>
> As a result of all the violence, President Lyndon Johnson appointed a Commission on Civil Disorder on July 28, 1967, to be chaired by Governor Otto Kerner of Illinois. The famous conclusion states, "Our nation is moving toward two societies, one black, one white—separate and unequal."
>
> Source: William P. Toth, "Long Hot Summer Riots, 1965–1967," in Leslie Alexander and Walter Rucker, ed., *Encyclopedia of African American History*, vol. 3 (Santa Barbara, CA: ABC-CLIO, 2010), 863–864.

Before returning to Atlanta to resume planning the Chicago campaign, King and Bayard Rustin met with Yorty and Parker and discussed police brutality against the city's black residents, poverty, and endemic racial prejudice in the city. He suggested the creation of a civilian review board of the police, but as expected, white city leaders denied any existence of racial discrimination in their city, ignored his proposals, and even questioned

King's presence in the city. When he left LA, King concluded that the riot was less about race relations and more about economic concerns. He wrote about the violence in Watts in his August 28 "People to People" column in the *New York Amsterdam News* stating that the "riots grew out of the depths of despair which afflict a people who see no way out of their economic dilemma" (King, "Feeling Alone in the Struggle," 1965). To avoid such national crises as the Watts riot in the future, King declared that black people needed real economic stability, an issue he would continue to pursue throughout 1965 and 1966.

King crisscrossed the country delivering speeches and raising money for the SCLC as he and the organization continued planning their Chicago movement, also called the movement to end slums. In September, he took to the black press again to explain "Why Chicago Is the Target." It was neither personal aggrandizement nor ego that took King and the SCLC to Chicago but rather "existing deplorable conditions and the conscience of good to the cause" that called them to the city. As a man of faith and one who cared about the well-being of African Americans throughout the nation, including the North, he vowed to "commit as much of [his] personal and organizational resources to the [cause] as humanly possible" (King, "Why Chicago Is the Target," 1966).

He was in New York City on November 14, speaking at Harlem's Abyssinian Baptist Church's 157th anniversary at the request of its pastor and U.S. congressman Adam Clayton Powell Jr. Having been raised in Atlanta and having challenged white supremacy, he was quite aware of intransigent, structural racism, but his trip to Watts and his continued unfolding as a leader and moral conscience of the nation made him begin to see structural, intransigent poverty and economic exploitation throughout the nation and the nation's ongoing war in Vietnam as major social problems.

On November 23, he spoke at the University of Milwaukee to a sold-out audience. At a press conference there, he noted that racism in the South in places such as Alabama must be challenged and overcome along with de facto segregation in public schools and black poverty in places such as Milwaukee. Necessary economic reforms in northern urban areas required raising the basic minimum wage to $1.75; within weeks, after closer examination, he called for a minimum wage of $2.00. This minimum wage needed to be extended to millions of workers not categorized as minimum-wage workers, including domestic and childcare workers, many of whom were underpaid black women.

Several days later, he joined his wife in Detroit, Michigan, at New Bethel Baptist Church; she was there speaking out against the war in Vietnam. In her remarks, Scott King encouraged the peace movement and the civil rights movement to work together. King had made comments about the need for U.S. negotiations with the Viet Cong and worldwide disarmament earlier that year but was met with discontented reporters, who were only interested in his racial commentary, and the Johnson administration, who disliked King's comments about Johnson's foreign policy. In response to the negative press and political pressure, King toned down his comments and reversed course on a nationwide letter campaign he proposed in which concerned Americans wrote to their elected officials to encourage them to change course in Vietnam. In time, however, he would become more vocal about the Vietnam War and the need for changes in American foreign policy; in the interim, Scott King spoke vociferously about the need for an end to a war which seemingly had no end.

The Chicago movement kicked off in early January 1966 with a press conference during which King maintained that "the Chicago problem is simply a matter of economic exploitation. Every condition exists simply because someone profits by its existence. This economic exploitation is crystallized in the slums." Using James Bevel's approach, King went on to compare black ghettos to internal colonies and European colonialism in parts of Africa. Without giving finer details of the nonviolent, direct actions to take place throughout the city by the SCLC and CCCO, King revealed that the movement would be a multifaceted one that pressured city, state, and federal agencies and assisted the social and political development of black residents who resided in the slums (Southern Christian Leadership Conference 1966). Several weeks later King, Coretta, and members of the SCLC staff moved into a run-down, third-floor, four-room apartment in the Lawndale neighborhood on Chicago's black West Side.

The apartment was without light or heat and had not been maintained by the landlord, but they settled in and acquired a few sparse accommodations from donations and a secondhand store. Living in the community, King welcomed poor black neighbors into his home to talk about the challenges they faced, and black neighbors welcomed him into the neighborhood. On one evening shortly after he took up residence in the community, the leaders of the Vice Lords, a local black gang, visited King and walked around the community with him. When he had spare time, he visited pool halls where local blacks would hang out, to hear about their experiences. One black Chicago resident writing in the *Chicago Defender* commented that King's "living, even for just a little while, among the poor, he will be in a better position to tell Mr. Charlie what he ought to do about the Negro problem" ("King Wins Approval" 1966). At times the black residents asked him for help. On one cold night when the temperature dipped well below zero and the heat had not been turned on, residents asked King for help, and he and the SCLC purchased coal to burn in the building's furnaces. Entrenched black leadership, including black preachers who had been cogs in Mayor Richard Daley's complicated political machine and often received his patronage, wanted King to leave the city.

With his third-floor, four-bedroom flat as his primary residence, King continued his civil rights work by traveling and speaking on behalf of the SCLC. On February 10, 1966, he visited the campus of Illinois Wesleyan University in Bloomington, Illinois, and lectured on the contemporary state of race relations. The lecture discussed the history of race relations, King's commitment to nonviolence, and the economic earning disparities between black and white families. King reminded the audience about the Greek ideas of love and the need to be politically and socially maladjusted. He also updated the audience about recent and current developments in the African American civil rights movement. The takeaway from his comments was that the United States must do better to support, include, and guarantee the safety, health, and well-being of its poor black citizens, whose ancestors helped create and ensure the nation's wealth.

He was concerned about criticisms from Chicago's black political and religious leaders so King appealed to the larger black community through the *Chicago Defender*, Chicago's most important black newspaper of the era. In early 1966, he began writing "My Dream," a weekly column for the paper similar to his weeklies in *The New York Amsterdam News* and *Ebony*. In his "My Dream" column, published on February 12, he laid out the reasons for his presence and the SCLC approach. Slums, he wrote, allowed for the "involuntary enslavement" of millions of African Americans in Chicago, a situation they had endured for decades, despite the city's moniker as the "Promised Land" for southern-born migrants. Opposing slavery in all its deleterious forms, King said he was called to act as a man of faith. Further, Chicago offered a unique political opportunity to expand the civil rights movement into the economic realm and experiment with nonviolent direct action in a northern city to see if it could be useful in other locations. In working in the city, he said, rather than just help the African American residents of Chicago, he sought to "arouse them to the realization that they have the spiritual, moral, political and economic force with them to enable them to help themselves" (King, "My Dream," 1966).

In mid-February, the SCLC and CCCO implemented a new tactic. Residents of a nearby dilapidated building close to King's Chicago apartment approached him and reported that their rodent-infested apartments had no heat and that necessary repairs had not been made. After doing their research, King and the SCLC assumed "trusteeship" of 1321 South Homan Avenue. Trusteeship called for tenants to submit their monthly rent payments not to the eighty-one-year-old landlord but to the SCLC, who would hire residents to make necessary repairs and pay them a fair minimum wage for their labor. King spent several days with Raby, Coretta, and the SCLC staff all dressed in work clothes, shoveling coal and repairing what they could. They knew that assuming trusteeship of the property was an experiment and intended to use it to help determine the "kind of creative social planning that might reverse this trend of degradation of our nation's cities and contribute to the kind of community awareness that will bring new life and new hope to the slums of this city" (Washington 1966).

Such creative social planning also encouraged King to meet with Elijah Muhammad, the spiritual leader of the Nation of Islam who made the city his home. The organization's national headquarters was also in Chicago. To come to Chicago and not meet with the elderly Muhammad would have caused many black Chicagoans to doubt the sincerity of the Chicago freedom movement. Despite negative depictions of the NOI in the mainstream media, black people in the city knew that the black Muslims had created businesses in their neighborhoods and helped rehabilitate many who had been incarcerated. The NOI did not believe in integration and proposed that the solution to the race problem in the United States was the creation of an independent black nation in portions of the South. They also openly advocated self-defense and had a well-trained security force, the Fruit of Islam. Despite King and Muhammad's political and religious differences, they had a cordial meeting, agreed that blacks had been systematically isolated in ghettos, and vowed to work together to create more residential opportunities for blacks and improve the slum areas.

During the early part of March, King and the Chicago movement worked feverishly to organize a gala to raise funds to continue their work. On March 12, close to thirteen thousand people attended the Freedom Festival at the city's International Amphitheater and were entertained by some of the most important black entertainers and activists of the 1960s. Sidney Poitier and Al Raby were the masters of ceremony. By 1966, Poitier had become an international film icon, having starred in over twenty films, and was the first black actor to receive an Academy Award, for his portrayal of Homer Smith in *Lilies of the Field.* Poitier's activism dates to the early 1950s when he and other activists, including the singer and Shakespearean actor Paul Robeson, charged the U.S. government of genocide against African Americans.

Entertainment was provided by Mahalia Jackson, Elizabeth Lands, Harry Belafonte, and Dick Gregory. Jackson began singing gospel music when she was four and made her first gospel recording in 1934. She appeared on the *Ed Sullivan Show* in 1952, where she received national attention as one of the greatest gospel singers of her generation; she first met King at a National Baptist Convention in 1956 and became his favorite gospel singer. Jackson performed several gospel tunes at the festival, reminding her listeners that their work to end slums in Chicago was part of God's larger plan for freedom and equality. Elizabeth Lands was a noted rhythm and blues singer who began her recording career at Motown in the early 1960s. As the civil rights movement gained traction, Lands joined with Harry Belafonte at SCLC benefit shows and performed with Mahalia

Jackson at the legendary Carnegie Hall in New York City. Belafonte began his acting career in Harlem, New York, before becoming a star on Broadway, where he won a Tony Award for his acting in *John Murray Anderson's Almanac* in 1954. Throughout the 1950s and 1960s, he performed and recorded several calypso albums, having become a popular black folk singer. During the festival, he performed his smash hit "Matilda." It tells the story of a heartbroken man whose girlfriend stole $500 from him and went to Venezuela. During the refrain, "Matilda, Matilda," Belafonte had the excited audience up on their feet singing along. Gregory was a Chicago resident and comedian who had participated in other SCLC campaigns throughout the South. During his routine, he encouraged the audience to laugh at themselves while staying committed to the civil rights struggle.

King was the keynote speaker at the event. Throughout January and February, he had been reconsidering and refining his comments about housing discrimination and slums in Chicago, and his remarks at the Freedom Festival were his most direct and insightful. It was easy to look at southern cities in Mississippi and Alabama and point directly to racial discrimination and the violation of African Americans' constitutional rights, he told the audience, but it was necessary to turn attention to racial discrimination in northern cities such as Chicago, where blacks were forced to live in a "domestic colony" where they were "dominated politically, exploited economically, segregated and humiliated at every turn" because of systemic racism in mortgage lending firms, real estate agencies, and racial covenants. Exploitation in housing was directly connected to de facto segregation in schools. Ninety percent of black children in the city's public school system attended underfunded schools that employed uncredentialed teachers and whose populations were almost exclusively black. Living in ghettos meant that black children attended inferior schools and received inferior educations, which eventually led to poor-paying jobs or welfare dependence. To bring about an end to slums and exploitation of blacks in Chicago, King said that it was necessary to organize and participate in "sit-ins, stand-ins, rent strikes, boycotts, picket lines, marches, civil disobedience, and any form of protest and demonstrations that are nonviolently conceived and executed" (King, "Address to the Chicago Freedom Festival," 1966). The Freedom Festival was a resounding feat and brought in close to $100,000 for the movement.

On the day of the festival, the *New York Amsterdam News* ran King's article "Why We Are in Chicago." In it, he responds to black and white Chicago leaders' concerns about his presence in the city. The Chicago freedom movement, he said, was poised to challenge the educational system, building-trade unions, real estate firms, mortgage lending agencies, landlords, Chicago's welfare system, federal housing policies, the judicial system, the Chicago police department, and Mayor Daley's administration and the interlocking and overlapping systems of discrimination these structures created to exploit generations of black residents living in the city. His column condemned several city agencies operating in black ghettos. He likened the school system in black neighborhoods to those in black townships in South Africa, which only educated children to prepare them for menial, low-paying jobs and characterized the police as maintainers of an unequal social order and "enforcers of the present system of exploitation" rather than keepers of the peace. In addition, street cleaning and garbage removal were inadequate. For those reasons, the SCLC and CCCO were "prepared to concentrate all of [their] forces around any and all issues" (King, "Why We Are in Chicago," 1966).

Weeks later, not knowing the racist protests he would endure and witness during the summer when he and his nonviolent supporters marched through white Chicago neighborhoods, he offered "A Prayer for Chicago" in *The Chicago Defender*. The prayer was published on April 16, and in it, he thanked God for a "redemptive nonviolent movement" and asked that Chicago's political leadership "respond to the legitimate discontent and rising expectations" of the city's black and brown populations with "creative and imaginative programs which will rectify the injustices of the past" (King, "A Prayer for Chicago," 1966).

After the productive and lucrative Freedom Festival, King continued traveling the nation speaking and raising money for SCLC. He made stops in New England, the Midwest, and Texas. In each talk, he sought to raise awareness about the structural economic inequality facing millions of blacks in urban northern cities and offered a variety of solutions to intergenerational poverty, including but not limited to an annual income guaranteed by the federal government. SCLC's Operation Breadbasket work in Chicago was led by Jesse Jackson, a theology student, who boycotted and picketed a local dairy company demanding a more inclusive workforce, which led to the hiring of over forty black workers. The campaign provided a necessary victory for a movement looking to gain traction and maintain its appeal to black Chicago residents and white moderates who continued to support the movement. On the heels of the boycott, King announced in late May that the Chicago movement would rally on Soldier Field, a popular sports and entertainment venue, on June 26 to bring together one hundred thousand people dedicated to economic justice and the fundamental transformation of black ghettos nationwide.

Planning for the June 26 event was disrupted, however, when James Meredith was shot on June 6, the second day of his March against Fear, a 220-mile walk from Memphis, Tennessee, to Jackson, Mississippi. Meredith was the first black student enrolled at the University of Mississippi. He was dismayed at continued voter repression in the Magnolia State and wanted to encourage black residents throughout the state and the nation to rid themselves of their fears of whites and white supremacy. King, Stokely Carmichael, from the Student Nonviolent Coordinating Committee, and Floyd McKissick, of the Congress of Racial Equality, held a press conference after Meredith was hospitalized and declared that Meredith's march must continue. Within days, they resumed Meredith's march, accompanied by hundreds of supporters. Law enforcement provided a modicum of security but prevented them from walking on state highways, so the marchers walked alongside U.S. Highway 51 in Mississippi's summer heat and humidity singing, carrying signs, and chanting for freedom. During the march, they often walked by whites who lined the sides of the road spewing racial epithets and waving confederate flags. Along the way to Jackson, organizers registered close to four thousand black voters, including a 106-year-old former slave.

When they arrived in Canton, Mississippi, they set out to pitch their tents near a local black school but were told to leave by local law enforcement and Mississippi state troopers, who had been summoned by white local officials to evict them. During several tense moments, a visibly nervous King, along with Carmichael, stood on the roof of a truck and urged the crowd to maintain unity, remain nonviolent, and fill the jails of the state if they had to. Shortly after his talk, state troopers unleashed a barrage of tear gas, and according to one eyewitness, the situation turned into a "scene of hell with the smoke rising, people vomiting, and crawling around, and choking, and crying" and being kicked and hit by troopers (Blackside, "The Time Has Come," 1990). Carmichael was hit by a tear gas canister, and King, who was choking from the tear gas, helped carry him to safety. The only haven for the marchers that evening was the gym of a nearby Catholic mission.

Sunday, June 26, was the last day of the March against Fear, and King and Carmichael led the marchers from Tougaloo to Jackson, Mississippi, the state capital, where they were met by Coretta and two of the Kings' children. There they held the largest civil rights rally in the state up to that point, twenty-two days after James Meredith started the march. State police stood by to keep the peace, as angry whites shouted epithets and some of the black marchers responded with "Freedom Now" and "Black Power." McKissick, Carmichael, King, and others addressed the crowd. King stated that the dream he had spoken so much about during the last several years had turned into a nightmare, but he continued to have hope that the nation would live up to the ideals laid out in the Constitution. He had participated in the march reluctantly because it took him away from his work in Chicago, but during the demonstration, he and others began to see that the nature of the struggle for black equality was changing. They knew racial discrimination would continue, but congressional legislation and presidential decrees offered some layers of protection and redress.

> ### Cultural Connection: Hippies
>
> The hippie movement took shape in the mid-1960s and had intricate ties to the Beat Generation of the 1950s. The Beats existed as a counterculture that sought to challenge the prevailing norms of American society, and hippies followed this ideology. Hippies rose to prominence in San Francisco, and their ethos spread not only throughout the country but also throughout the world. Much like the Beats, hippies never established a singular message in their movement, though they pushed for allowing everyone to, in essence, do their own thing.
>
> Welcoming so many ideas brought several different facets to the movement. Hippies encouraged drug use, freedom in sexuality, broader musical tastes, a combination of Eastern and Western religious thought, spirituality, and new fashions, among other things. The movement both espoused a counterculture mindset and established the norm of "cool" in culture generally. Although hippies, overall, tended to be white, middle-class males, their openness toward and inclusion of other groups was among their promising facets.
>
> In late 1966, California pushed against hippies by declaring LSD a controlled substance, an obvious attempt to corral the wayward youngsters. The response by hippies was to start hosting be-ins, which was a different way of calling something a concert and a party. The name also implied that to be at a be-in was to be hip, or with the in crowd. This concept existed in a bicoastal manner, as both California and New York held be-in events in the late 1960s.
>
> One of the grand spectacles of the movement was the Woodstock Music and Art Fair, which was held in Bethel, New York, from August 15 to 17, 1969. The festival drew nearly five hundred thousand people to the farmland and featured the following bands: Canned Heat, Richie Havens, Joan Baez, Janis Joplin, the Grateful Dead, Credence Clearwater Revival, Crosby, Stills, Nash & Young, Santana, the Who, Jefferson Airplane, and Jimi Hendrix, among others. Though marred by rain, the event was considered a success, as it contained the mantra of peace, love, and understanding.
>
> Source: P. Huston Lander, "Hippies," in Michael Green and Scott Stabler, ed., *Ideas and Movements That Shaped America*, vol. 2 (Santa Barbara, CA: ABC-CLIO, 2015), 497–500.

Still, with the march's new call for black power, it became clearer to King that African Americans needed "to amass the political and economic strength to achieve their legitimate goals" (Carson 1998, 324). For many, the march from Memphis to Jackson was the symbolic end of the southern civil rights movement.

After the March against Fear, King returned to Chicago. On July 10, with the temperature close to one hundred degrees, tens of thousands of individuals, black and white, gathered at Soldier Field for a Chicago movement rally. The rally was set to begin around 3:00 p.m., but those in attendance arrived several hours early to be entertained by popular local disc jockey Herb Kent, comedian Dick Gregory, musician and Chicago native Oscar Brown, the Andrew McPherson jazz band, and folk singer Peter Yarrow. Coretta Scott King started the rally by singing the national anthem. The Black Power slogan had gained popularity during the March against Fear and convinced many whites that they were no longer needed in the black struggle for equality, but King had been steadfast in his belief and through his work that a multiracial movement of people of goodwill was necessary to ensure black equality, and the audience and speakers on the dais at the Soldier Field rally reflected his approach. Most notable among those joining King on the podium was Ralph Abernathy, his friend and vice president of the SCLC; Edgar Hugh Storer Chandler, the white, Protestant (Congregational) minister and director of the Church Federation of Greater Chicago who supported King and the SCLC in Selma; Ralph Helstein, the Jewish president of the United Packinghouse Workers of America; and Al Raby, of the CCCO. Some in the crowd had heard of the other speakers, but most came to hear the Nobel Peace Prize winner who, though born and raised in Georgia, came to Chicago to put his life and nonviolent ideals on the line to expose contradictions in the Windy City.

His speech was eloquent and challenging. As he had done many times before, he reminded his audience of the importance of nonviolent mass resistance. Speaking to the thousands of black people present and the millions of African Americans not there whose lives and opportunities had not improved despite federal legislation, he said that "we will be sadly mistaken if we think freedom is some lavish dish that the federal government and the white man will pass out on a silver platter while the Negro merely furnishes the appetite." Nonviolent direct action was important, but not enough, he told the crowd. Voting was critical to force Chicago's Mayor Daley to enact measures to address housing discrimination in the city and to force politicians, especially Democrats, to earn black people's votes rather than taking them for granted. It was also necessary to build coalitions with other ethnic groups suffering racial injustice and to work together with progressive whites. "The Negro needs the white man to free him from his fears," and "the white man needs the Negro to free him from his guilt." At the end of the rally, King and thousands of supporters marched to City Hall, and he fastened a list of demands on the doors ("Here's What Dr. King Told Vast Thousands" 1966).

The list of demands was robust and addressed the many overlapping and intersecting social, political, and economic issues and structures that kept Chicago segregated and urged action by real estate brokers and boards, lending institutions, the mayor and city council, the Chicago Housing Authority, local businesses, unions, the governor, the Illinois Public Aid Commission, the Cook County Department of Public Aid, the federal government, and residents of Chicago. The Chicago freedom movement wanted better housing, better education, and better jobs for the city's black and brown population and demanded an open city where people with economic means could move wherever they wanted. To change the city, the movement called for marches, demonstrations, and arrests if necessary.

In the days and weeks after the rally, King, Raby, and members of CCCO and the SCLC met with Mayor Daley and his officials, but negotiations and even side deals were stalled, with neither side wanting to compromise. Recognizing the stalemate, the Chicago freedom movement did as King said at the rally: "Dramatize and expose a social evil" with "the tramp of marching feet" ("Here's What Dr. King Told Vast Thousands" 1966). The movement used a variety of tactics. Sometimes it would send black couples into white real estate firms seeking to rent an apartment or buy a home. After the black couple was denied and told that there were no listings available, the movement would send a white couple into the same establishment, and they would be offered several listings, thereby exposing racial discrimination in housing. In late July and early August, King and the Chicago freedom movement began marching to white real estate agencies demanding a change to such exclusionary practices. The movement also took the struggle outside of the confines of the black slums and into Chicago's all-white neighborhoods to contradict the prevailing myth that blacks chose to live in all-black neighborhoods.

One march took place in the all-white Bridgeport neighborhood where demonstrators marched to Mayor Daley's home. On August 5, King led a nonviolent contingent into the Chicago Lawn section of the city, intending to walk to a real estate office and demand that residential listings be made available on a nondiscriminatory basis. In Marquette Park, a neighborhood in Chicago Lawn, King and marchers were met by a hostile, violent white mob of thousands carrying Confederate flags, white power signs, and swastikas. They were shouting, "We want King," yelling racial epithets, and throwing cherry bombs, rocks, and bricks at the marchers. King was hit in the head by a rock. The Chicago movement wanted to expose white opposition to integration in Chicago, but participants were stunned by the open white hostility, hate, and violence. Andrew Young was present during the march and remembered that "in the South, we faced mobs . . . it would be a couple of hundred—or even 50 or 75. The violence in the South always came from a rabble element, but these were women and children and husbands and wives coming out of their homes becoming a mob. And in some ways, it was far more frightening" (Blackside, "Two Societies 1965–1968," 1990).

Undeterred, the Chicago movement continued its demonstrations. In the weeks after the violence at Marquette Park, movement activists tramped to real estate offices in Bogan Manor, Gage Park, Jefferson Park,

West Elsdon, Evergreen Park, and the Chicago Heights suburb. On August 21, King led a group of marchers into South Deering, a white community in Chicago's far South Side after participating in a discussion about the civil rights movement on *Meet the Press*. Roy Wilkins, Whitney Young, Floyd McKissick, Stokely Carmichael, and James Meredith joined him. During the ninety-minute special broadcast, King spoke on a variety of issues and said to the nation that the Chicago movement had "revealed . . . a blatant, social, hate-filled cancer" that the SCLC was "trying to get rid of" and made clear that racism existed in northern metropolises and was as blatant as discrimination in southern cities (National Broadcasting Company 1966).

By late August, the CCCO and SCLC had exhausted their resources without achieving the outcomes they sought. They also had not obtained support from other civil rights organizations or the Johnson administration. Raby said that the movement "had achieved, not everything we wanted, but everything we could achieve . . . and made the best [decision] we could as honestly as we could" (Blackside, "Two Societies 1965–1968," 1990). King had visited President Johnson numerous times since Johnson took office, and the president sought King's counsel on civil rights issues. King thought, perhaps naively, that Johnson would use his presidential influence to encourage Daley to commit to concrete antidiscrimination policies in housing and education. In fact, Johnson had been in communication with Daley, one of his most ardent supporters, and in one conversation asked Daley, "What shape have you got King in? Is he about ready to get out?" ("Lyndon B. Johnson" 2014).

On August 26, seventy-nine people, including Mayor Daley and members of his administration, realty executives, representatives of mortgage lending institutions, and the Chicago freedom movement met at the historic Palmer House Hotel in downtown Chicago. They signed a ten-point agreement that addressed discriminatory housing policies and practices, reinforcement of the authority of the Chicago Human Relations Commission, whose job it was to ensure real estate agents' compliance with existing regulations, the creation of the Conference of Religion, to assist and further encourage open housing policies, and pledges from city and state agencies to better ensure that welfare allocations and housing offerings did not discriminate. By signing the agreement, Raby and King halted further demonstrations which had disrupted the status quo.

It was not what everyone wanted. Always the optimist, King saw it as a first step in the right direction of a longer process of housing desegregation. Edwin Berry of the Urban League said that they achieved "eight and a half out of nine objectives" ("King, Realty Forces" 1966). Andrew Young saw it as a successful use of nonviolent mass action in a northern urban area and a model for other cities with populations struggling to be heard and recognized. Others, such as community activist Clory Bryant, felt betrayed and excluded. After the summit, she spoke on behalf of many black Chicago residents stating that "we don't care about summits taking place without us.... We want contracts in black and white with some hard answers for us with some signatures and some people we can hold you responsible to and some time frames, but none of this was there" (Blackside, "Two Societies 1965–1968," 1990).

King went back to Atlanta and left Jesse Jackson in charge of Operation Breadbasket, which had been successful in opening employment opportunities for black Chicagoans in factories and retail establishments. He returned in late October only to find that little had been done to enforce the ten-point agreement and threatened to resume protests. What started as a noble endeavor to improve housing options for black and brown Chicagoans ended with empty promises and no means of enforcement. Over the decades to come, the same Chicago neighborhoods that King sought to integrate eventually let blacks and Latinos purchase homes and rent apartments, and then whites fled. As of this writing, Gage Park's population is over 90 percent Latino. Less than 5 percent of Marquette Park's population is white, while blacks make up over 50 percent and Latinos close to 40 percent. South Deering's white population hovers around 2 percent, with blacks making up 65 percent of the community's population. Those of Hispanic origin constitute close to 30 percent of the population. King's optimism and moral compass led him to challenge residential patterns. Little did he know that racism and de facto segregation would change with the times.

Throughout fall 1966, King became less active in Chicago and spent time discerning his positions on national economic issues as they related to impoverished conditions facing millions of Americans and to the Vietnam War. On December 15, he appeared before the Subcommittee on Executive Reorganization, of the Committee on Government Operations, a committee chaired by Democratic senator Abraham Ribicoff from Connecticut, where he urged senators to refocus and rearrange national priorities. Accompanied by Andrew Young, he questioned investments in space exploration while citizens of earth live in slums. "Without denying the value of scientific endeavor," he noted, "there is a striking absurdity in committing billions to reach the moon where no people live ... while the densely populated slums are allocated miniscule appropriations." In speaking about the connection between underfunded anti-poverty programs and the war in Vietnam, he urged the senators to reappropriate the billions of dollars used for "ill-considered warfare" in Southeast Asia and use them for a war on poverty that had become "scarcely a skirmish." As he had done earlier in the year, he also proposed that poverty could be eliminated most effectively through a guaranteed annual income. However, a guaranteed income was part of a larger restructuring of the national economic system that required critical investments in affordable housing and quality education for all Americans. He also noted in an exchange with Senator Ribicoff that the civil rights movement had entered a new stage. In response to the senator's query about a shift in the civil rights movement's focus, King said the movement had entered a new phase that was more focused on "basic economic issues" and "the whole problem of housing and education" ("Martin Luther King and Economic Justice" n.d.).

King returned to Atlanta after the Senate hearing and spent time with Coretta and his growing children: Yolanda, eleven; Martin, nine; Dexter, five; and Berniece, three. He was away from home most of the year, and the children missed their father. It was a marvelous family reunion. However, King was worn out physically, mentally, and perhaps spiritually, and fatherhood, unfortunately, was not the rest he needed, or had in mind. So after attending several meetings in California and New York, he cleared his schedule and departed for Jamaica on January 16, 1967, with Bernard Lee. Coretta would join him several days later. King stayed in Jamaica for several weeks praying, resting, reflecting, and working on his next book *Where Do We Go from Here: Chaos or Community?*

In Jamaica he began to reconsider his stance on America's war in Vietnam. For over a year, he had been reluctant to candidly present his opposition to the war, allowing Coretta's peace work to speak for him by proxy for fear that a bold stance would weaken the civil rights struggle and jeopardize his relationship with President Johnson. Now he decided it was impossible to work for nonviolent change and the poor at home when the nation was violent against poor people at home and abroad. Furthermore, if nonviolence was useful domestically, then it had to be used internationally. Prayer and meditation led him to a new position. He decided to "never again . . . be silent on an issue that is destroying the soul of our nation and . . . little children in Vietnam" (Carson 1998, 335).

# 10

## Beyond Vietnam to Memphis

It had been years since King was able to have such a long, rejuvenating vacation that black middle-class preachers had come to expect, so when he returned to the United States in February 1967, he was invigorated. Despite concerns about how his anti-war stance would go over with black civil rights groups, white moderates and liberals, and the Johnson administration, King followed his conscience and began speaking against the Vietnam War.

On February 25, he joined Alaska senator Ernest Gruening, Oregon senator Mark Hatfield, Minnesota senator Eugene McCarthy, and South Dakota senator George McGovern at an anti-war rally hosted by the *Nation* magazine at the Beverly Hilton Hotel in Los Angeles. King's address, "The Casualties of the War in Vietnam," declared that the needless death of U.S. servicemen, Viet Cong soldiers, and Vietnamese civilians were not the only casualties of the war. America's invasion of and sustained military assault in Vietnam were violations of the United Nations charter, which prohibited member nations from engaging in military campaigns against sovereign, independent nation-states. America's contravention of international law made the United Nations charter a casualty of war. The second casualty of the Vietnam War was the principle that each nation had the right to determine its destiny. By participating in "neo-colonial adventures," King argued, the U.S. government robbed the Vietnamese of self-determination to "perpetuate white colonialism." On the domestic front,

President Johnson's Great Society was the third fatality of the Vietnam War, because the war effort meant that the nation's wealth that could have been used to eradicate poverty was reallocated for destructive purposes. The government allocated $322,000 to kill one enemy abroad while only spending $53 for a poor citizen at home (King, "The Casualties of the War in Vietnam," 1967).

The nation's humility was the fourth casualty of the Vietnam War. Because of a misguided sensibility that "we have everything to teach other nations," King said, "we have some divine, messianic mission to police the whole world." This arrogance and lack of modesty exposed the hypocrisy of the nation's foreign policy, which interferes in Vietnam but remains silent on human rights abuses of the white minority government in apartheid South Africa and modern-day Zimbabwe. The fifth death associated with the war was the domestic assault on free speech. Increasingly, he emphasized, those who questioned U.S. strategies and policies were dubbed unpatriotic, un-American, "quasi-traitors, fools, and venal enemies of our soldiers and institutions" (King, "The Casualties of the War in Vietnam," 1967). King reminded those who suffered persecution because of their anti-war activism that they were not alone. Abraham Lincoln, Ralph Waldo Emerson, and Henry David Thoreau all questioned the legitimacy of war during their times.

Humankind's guaranteed survival was the last casualty of the war. With the proliferation of weapons designed to kill as many people as possible, King pondered humanity's continued dependence on war to solve national and international conflicts and concluded that while humanity's desire for war would continue, war was not necessary to solve humanity's problems. However, if the desire for war, with its saber-rattling, persisted and another world war erupted, which given contemporary international crises seemed inevitable, the only thing left would be "smoldering ashes as a mute testimony of a human race whose folly led inexorably to ultimate death." For the nation to fulfill its higher destiny, King urged the audience to "combine the fervor of the civil rights movement with the peace movement" and "demonstrate, teach and preach, until the very foundations of our nation are shaken" (King, "The Casualties of the War in Vietnam," 1967).

A month later, on March 25, King was teaching, marching, and demonstrating in Chicago against the Vietnam War. After holding a press conference at the Liberty Street Baptist Church, where Rev. Abraham P. Jackson was pastor, King marched with Dr. Benjamin Spock, the noted author, pediatrician, and anti-war activist; Ahmed "Sammy" Rayner Jr., the black alderman from the city's sixth ward; and thousands of other anti-war activists. Carrying signs reading "No More War," "Would Napalm Convert You to Democracy?" "Education, Not Escalation," "Build Schools, Not Bombs," and "War on Poverty Not People," they marched through the

Loop, Chicago's central business district, to the Coliseum, where they held a peace rally. His remarks were like the ones he gave in Los Angeles the month before, and he stressed that the U.S. military campaign in Vietnam was leading the country to a national disaster, because in the name of containing and fighting communism, the nation was "committing atrocities equal to any perpetrated by the Vietcong" ("Dr. King Leads Chicago Peace Rally" 1967).

Throughout March and early April, King and his advisers debated the value and potential negative publicity associated with his participation in a rally sponsored by the National Mobilization Committee to End the War in Vietnam (Mobe). The Mobe rally promised to bring a motley crew of anti-war activists with approaches and philosophies that could be antithetical to King's, and his inner circle was concerned that his appearance with them might lead his allies to brand him as a renegade. He understood their concerns but decided that the risk was one he had to take. To try to play it safe, he agreed to first present his ideas to a group and in a setting with the veneer of respectability, a meeting of the National Emergency Committee of Clergy and Laymen Concerned about Vietnam, in New York City's Riverside Church. This way it would be difficult to confuse his message with the potential din of the Mobe event.

Clergy and Laymen Concerned about Vietnam was formed in 1965 as an interfaith pacifist group, and it engaged in demonstrations associated with the war in Vietnam abroad and advised young men who opposed the draft at home. As the decade progressed, chapters formed around the country, and King became the cochair of the organization's national committee. Their April 4, 1967, meeting took place at the Riverside Church in Upper Manhattan, New York City, where Rev. Dr. Robert James McCracken presided. Riverside opened in 1930 as a progressive, interdenominational church and is located on one of the highest points of elevation in the city, overlooking the scenic Hudson River. It was an ideal spot for King to deliver "Beyond Vietnam."

Vincent Harding, a professor at Spelman College in Atlanta, Georgia, wrote the first draft, and King's aids meticulously edited and added to the speech, making "Beyond Vietnam" King's best-known condemnation of the war, his most eloquent statement of conscience as well as his most controversial speech. He shared the dais with Henry Steele Commager, the noted historian and activist; John Bennet, the president of the Union Theological Seminary; and Rabbi Abraham Heschel, a professor at the Jewish Theological Seminary of America. Heschel had supported and marched with King in nonviolent demonstrations in the South. In his address, King characterized the Vietnam War as a "disgraceful commitment," a "nightmarish conflict," "hell" for the impoverished Vietnamese, "an enemy of the poor" in the United States, antirevolutionary, a "tragic war," and a "dreadful conflict." As a patriotic American and minister committed to the teachings of Jesus and nonviolence, he believed it was his duty to speak out against the war even in the face of mounting criticisms from those who wanted him to remain silent and solely focus on black civil rights. His commitment for peace took him "beyond national allegiances" to be concerned about the lives and well-being of voiceless people in Vietnam and America. He posited several suggestions for the Johnson administration: an immediate cessation of bombing on the peninsula, an end to American military action in Vietnam, a reevaluation and restriction of the American troop buildup in Laos and Thailand, and a clear deadline for American troop removal from Vietnam. He advised those young men who were drafted or in the process of being conscripted to become conscientious objectors and assert their right not to participate in violent military actions (King, "Beyond Vietnam," 1967).

The speech was well received by anti-war activists and those on the Left, but others condemned the speech, and King was lambasted from what seemed like every corner. White moderates who did not necessarily support the war but supported the soldiers there misunderstood King's message as un-American. White supporters of the war effort accused him of being a communist or supporting the Viet Cong. Unsurprisingly, white political leaders such as Strom Thurmond, the notorious segregationist and republican senator from South Carolina who had harangued King and his civil rights work, slammed him for his anti-war stance. In a statement, Thurmond suggested that King's efforts to connect domestic black civil rights with the war "retards the advancement of his people" ("Thurmond Praises Brooke" 1967). Scathing editorials were printed in major and minor newspapers around the country denouncing King's speech. Gene Roberts of the *New York Times* said that by speaking out against the Vietnam War, King had "dampened his prospects for becoming the Negro leader who might be able to get the nation 'moving again' on civil rights" (Roberts 1967). In "Dr. King's Error," the same paper stated that in trying to unify the civil rights and anti-war movements, King made a grand folly because "by drawing them together, Dr. King has done a disservice to both." Making a connection between domestic issues such as the war on poverty and the war in Vietnam, the editorial said, is overly simplistic. *Life* magazine said that King's speech "sounded like a script from Radio Hanoi" and was a "demagogic slander" that came "close to betraying the civil rights movement" ("King's Disservice to His Cause" 1967).

Black civil rights activists and writers also expressed their discontent. For whatever reasons, political maneuvering or expediency, organizational survival or self-aggrandizement, mainstream black civil rights leaders failed to understand King's logic of wedding the civil rights movement and the anti-war movement. The national board of the NAACP voted to oppose the fusion of the anti-war and civil rights movements. The *New York Times* ran an article a week after the speech, declaring, "NAACP Decries Stand of Dr. King on Vietnam" wherein the organization suggested that neither it nor King had any expertise in foreign policy and could not weigh in on the Vietnam War. Dr. Ralph J. Bunche, the United Nations under-secretary for political affairs and one of the directors of the NAACP, said that King was "making a serious tactical error which will do much harm to the civil rights struggle" (Sibley 1967). Writing for *Reader's Digest*, the well-known and respected black journalist Carl T. Rowan, under the veiled guise of journalistic objectivity, wrote that King had made "ill-advised announcements" about the war and "taken a tack that many Americans of all races consider utterly irresponsible" (Rowan 1967).

King knew people would criticize his opposition to the Vietnam War, but their rebukes had shaken him and at times he was overwhelmed with the burden he had to bear, especially when donations to the SCLC decreased because white liberal donors disliked the idea of King discussing foreign policy. Most blacks and whites had a myopic vision of the intersection of race, racism, and poverty in America and failed to see their relationship with the nation's overseas military ventures. But King's vision was larger, and he saw the world and the various interactions between races and nations through a much wider lens. Despite the criticism and the ire of the Johnson administration and the disappointment it caused him, King continued to speak out against the war and prepared to participate in one of the largest anti-war demonstrations of 1967.

His critique of American foreign policy, his calls for a unilateral cease-fire in Vietnam as well as his desire to bring together the peace movement and the civil rights movement did not preclude his discussing and condemning American racism and structural inequality. On April 14, he introduced a new speech, "The Other America," to a predominantly white and "enlightened" audience at Stanford University. It was a collection of ideas and approaches he had considered in other addresses over the years, updated now to include new developments in the struggle for racial equality. He would deliver it in various iterations throughout the nation in 1967 and 1968.

The United States was a nation of two societies. One was affluent and largely white, with all the creature comforts and delights of life. The other society consisted of many whites but was largely populated by people of color, especially black people who lived in "rat-infested, vermin-filled slums" who were "perishing on a lonely island of poverty in the midst of a vast ocean of material prosperity." To end poverty and racism throughout the nation, King again called for a guaranteed minimum income for every citizen and family, a radical change in the nation's moral landscape, and concrete, federally sponsored and insured programs. He explained

American race relations with evangelical Christian imagery. The United States was like a sinful Christian who took one step toward God and then reverted to their old sinful ways. The nation abolished slavery and granted black men citizenship rights with the Fourteenth and Fifteenth Amendments but then allowed poll taxes, grandfather clauses, and segregation clauses to be instituted throughout the South and de facto segregation in the North to subdue black people politically and economically. The Supreme Court outlawed racial segregation in schools in 1954, yet state and federal courts balked at the creation of integrated schools. By committing political apostasy, the nation historically took two steps forward and one step back on issues of racial justice. For the nation to live up to its pronouncements that all men are created equal and to create "a truly integrated society," King demanded that "men and women will have to rise to the majestic heights of being obedient to the unenforceable" (King, "The Other America," 1967).

On April 15, 1967, the Spring Mobilization Committee to End the War in Vietnam brought together close to four hundred thousand anti-war activists in New York and one hundred thousand in San Francisco to voice their concerns and outrage over the war. Coretta Scott King spoke at the San Francisco event where marchers walked from Market Street and merged on Golden Gate Park. Both demonstrations were predominantly white, but black people showed up. The Black Panther Party, only six months old at the time, attended the San Francisco rally to call attention to African American involvement in the war. King was present in New York City and joined marchers as they walked from Central Park to the United Nations building. The New York protest was a coming together of various factions and groups: a Harlem contingent of black youths carried signs reading "Black Men Should Fight Racism, Not Vietnamese Freedom Fighters" and "Black People: 53% of the Dead, 2% of the Bread . . . Why?" White males of draft age burned their draft cards, and progressive white women of all ages showed their support. King led the procession through the streets of Midtown Manhattan with Dr. Benjamin Spock, Harry Belafonte, David Dellinger, the Chicago-based pacifist and Christian socialist, and Monsignor Charles Rice, a Catholic priest from Pittsburgh and cofounder of Catholic Radical Alliance, a religious organization that supported union workers. The peaceful gathering assembled at the United Nations Plaza on East Forty-Second Street, overlooking the East River, to listen to a variety of speakers.

Spock spoke to the crowd, as did William Pepper of the National Conference of New Politics, Floyd McKissick, Stokely Carmichael, and James Bevel, who had worked with King in the Southern Christian Leadership Conference and helped organize the early spring event in New York, but King was the headliner. The crowd was eager to hear his ideas. His speech echoed his Riverside address, and he discussed the casualties of the war. He told the audience that as a person of conscience, it was his right and duty to speak out against the war, because the war in Vietnam had no long-term strategic goal, and Vietnam was not an existential threat to the United States. "We are arrogant in professing to be concerned about the freedom of foreign nations," he said, "while not setting our own house in order" with its racism, segregation, and poverty. "Stop the bombing," he and the crowd proclaimed. After the march, King and a delegation of anti-war activists met with Ralph Bunche and presented him with a petition that called for an immediate diplomatic end to the war.

He appeared on the current-affairs program *Face the Nation* the next day and repeated his thoughts about the need for a unilateral cease-fire and then went back to Atlanta to spend time with his family. There he began making plans for a Vietnam Summer, a "nationwide project designed to reach concerned citizens throughout the United States and to weld them into an organized and active constituency against the war in Vietnam" ("Swarthmore College Peace Collection" n.d.). On April 23, he spoke at the Christ Episcopal Church in Cambridge, Massachusetts, where he, Spock, and *Ramparts* magazine editor Robert Scheer held a press conference announcing the aims and objectives of the Vietnam Summer. He encouraged those concerned about the war to join the campaign and go door to door speaking with their neighbors and strangers to stimulate a healthy dialogue about the war and build the anti-war movement. Following the press conference, with reporters and cameramen in tow, he and Spock did some door knocking of their own and visited two homes to discuss the war and its effects on domestic programs. The following day, he crossed the Charles River and delivered "The Other America" in Jordan Hall at the New England Conservatory, his wife's alma mater.

King continued to be the copastor at Ebenezer Baptist Church with his father, but his work with the SCLC and in the civil rights movement nationwide with its constant traveling did not allow a great deal of time for him to work with his congregation. However, on April 30, he was back at his childhood church and in the Ebenezer pulpit, explaining his anti-war stance to the congregation, preaching, "Why I Am Opposed to the War in Vietnam." The text was taken from his April 4 speech at Riverside Church but tailored to a black Baptist congregation. Because the Vietnam War was an "unjust, evil, and futile war," it was the duty of every American concerned with justice and who took the teachings of Jesus seriously to stand up and speak out against the war. King said that being a minister and preacher of the gospel who believes that God is "deeply concerned . . . with His suffering and helpless and outcast children," he was obligated to speak for those who had been silenced and ignored, despite the negative publicity, criticisms, or growing disapproval within segments of white and black

> ### Cultural Connection: The Black Arts Movement
>
> In 1965, the passage of the Voting Rights Bill ended one phase of the civil rights movement, and, by October 1966, the emergent doctrine of black power had a concrete political form in the Black Panther Party for Self-Defense. Black power also had an artistic extension in the form of the Black Arts Movement (BAM). Positioning themselves as an alternative to the mainstream civil rights movement, BAM poets and black power activists replaced the ideal of integration with that of black cultural particularism.
>
> BAM was led by Amiri Baraka, Ed Bullins, Addison Gayle Jr., Hoyt Fuller, Larry Neal, Ishmael Reed, and James Stewart. It emerged out of Philadelphia, New York, and Oakland during the early 1960s, and by 1964, it had a literary center in the arts journal *Liberator*, founded by Neal and Askai Toure. In 1968, the publication of *Black Fire*, edited by Baraka and Neal, marked one of the major events in BAM's print culture. BAM reached the peak of its cultural influence in the late 1960s and early 1970s.
>
> Central to the movement was a belief that political action would come through artistic expression. Art had a social value, and the artist had a role in political transformation. Black nationalist cultural politics would help answer problems such as poverty, police brutality, and substandard education, because imaginative culture would alter the reality of oppressed peoples.
>
> The movement also stressed cultural heritage, the beauty of blackness, and a black aesthetic. It asked that black people no longer see through white eyes, and BAM poets therefore subverted traditional forms and accepted values. In 1968, Neal described BAM as a cultural revolution, adding that a whole new system of ideas was needed. As part of this revolution, BAM artists embraced the jazz avant-garde. They believed that music articulated an authentic black expression. Alongside this interest in music as a language of the people, BAM poets stressed the orality of poetry, focused on vernacular speech as a communicative medium, and tried to make art accessible.
>
> Yet for all their efforts, BAM writers failed to resonate beyond a limited group of black urbanites. Increasingly criticized for its anti-Semitism and chauvinism, as well as its exclusion of liberal whites and its strident form of nationalism, BAM faded from public view by the mid-1970s.
>
> Source: Zoe Trodd, "Black Arts Movement," in Leslie Alexander and Walter Rucker, ed., *Encyclopedia of African American History*, vol. 3 (Santa Barbara, CA: ABC-CLIO, 2010), 645.

America. He ended his homily with the African American spiritual "Down by the Riverside" and said that "I ain't gonna study war no more." The sermon is significant because it was the first time that he presented his antiwar stance to a predominantly black audience who previously had been more concerned with race and racism in the United States than a foreign war and its implications on domestic policies. "Beyond Vietnam" was delivered to a largely white, progressive audience, similar to that of the April 15 Mobe event, but returning to Ebenezer as a native son was an opportunity for King to talk to his people who knew him, nurtured him, and accepted his ideas and leadership. After his sermon, many in his congregation came around to his way of thinking that the Vietnam War was a mistake (King, "Why I Am Opposed to the War in Vietnam," 1967).

King traveled around the nation in May speaking about the war, the intersection of labor and civil rights, and his perspective on contemporary events. In New York City, he addressed an affiliate of the International Brotherhood of Teamsters, a union founded in 1903 which would later become one of the nation's largest and varied collective bargaining units. Close to one thousand people listened to his concerns about the war and domestic policies at the University of Wisconsin, Marathon County, in Wausau, Wisconsin, on the banks of the Wisconsin River. He reminded the predominantly youthful white audience that "I will not limit my morals to one area of life. If I see immorality anywhere, I will take a stand against it" (Freund 2017). At the University of California, Berkeley, the epicenter of the Free Speech Movement, seven thousand students, faculty, staff, and community members converged on Sproul Plaza in front of the university's administrative offices to hear King talk about the Vietnam War and ways to extricate the nation from the crisis. He spoke to a crowd of two thousand at the University of Denver in Colorado, while white racists burned crosses outside the arena where he spoke. His most penetrating appearance that month was a nationally televised NBC interview with prominent broadcast journalist Sander Vanocur.

The interview took place on May 8 in Atlanta at Ebenezer Baptist Church, and King elaborated on his journey to nonviolence, the effectiveness of nonviolent massive resistance in northern cities and southern states, economic deprivation, and slums. Poverty was a hallmark of black life throughout the nation, especially in the northern urban areas, he noted, over one hundred years after the end of slavery, because hypocritical northern white legislators were ready to condemn discrimination against black people in the South but failed to see the harmful economic segregation in their states. In addition, their white moderate and liberal supporters were opposed to the brutality meted out to blacks during civil rights campaigns in the South but were also opposed to genuine equality of opportunities for black people and an economic investment in northern cities. Consequently, it was necessary for the civil rights struggle to enter a new stage because "the vast majority of white American will only go so far ... for equality" (National Broadcasting Company n.d.)

King was asked about the dream he discussed at the March on Washington in 1963. In his response, he maintained that the optimism he and others felt during the early 1960s was superficial and perhaps premature, and as the 1960s unfolded, the combination of stalled progress in the field of racial and economic justice, the war in Vietnam, and growing white antipathy throughout the nation led his earlier dream to become a nightmare. As if seeing the future of race relations and poverty in the late twentieth and early twenty-first centuries, he said that the nation had a long way to go to reckon with racial injustice and poverty and would have to commit billions of dollars to bring about a fundamental change in the status quo (National Broadcasting Company n.d.).

King's anti-war stance was a concern to other civil rights leaders, who believed his position had fractured the civil rights movement and needlessly antagonized the Johnson administration, which they needed to further African American civil rights. So in mid-June, King sat down with them in Suffern, New York, at a confidential summit at the Motel on the Mountain to mend organizational rifts. Noted black psychologist Kenneth B. Clark, of the Metropolitan Applied Research Center, called the meeting and invited Jack Greenberg, the director of the NAACP Legal Defense and Educational Fund; Dorothy Haight, of the National Council of Negro Women; Floyd McKissick, national director of CORE; Bayard Rustin, executive secretary of the A. Philip Randolph Institute; Roy Wilkins, executive director of the NAACP; and Whitney Young, executive director of the National Urban League. The group had met in late May at Clark's home but could not come up with any substantive conclusions or recommendations. Their second conference on June 13, however, yielded a pact by the organizations to work together in Cleveland to organize the black community there and address potential violence during the long, hot summer.

Days after the secret civil rights summit, King began a national media campaign to promote his fourth book, *Where Do We Go from Here: Chaos or Community?*, which had been published earlier in June. On June 19, he appeared on the *Arlene Francis Show* in New York City. The next day, the ever-popular Merv Griffin interviewed him on his show, where King was a charming and ebullient guest sitting beside his friend and benefactor, Harry Belafonte. *Where Do We Go from Here?* is a meditation on race relations and the civil rights movement in the mid- to late 1960s. King declares that the civil rights movement to have entered a new phase of struggle. During the first phase, activists were concerned about breaking down legal barriers in public accommodations, especially in the South. The new phase, which began after the Memphis to Selma march in 1965, sought to bring about economic equality throughout the United States for every citizen, not just black people, and extend the movement to every section of the nation. During the first phase, the nation spent very little, because desegregation amounted to the enforcement of already existing laws, but with the new phase, King maintained, the nation would have to spend billions of dollars to be true to its ideal that everyone is entitled to life, liberty, and the pursuit of happiness.

Throughout the book, King questions white Americans' commitment to nationwide racial and economic justice and critiques African Americans' calls for black power. Having worked with whites in the struggle for over ten years, he was convinced that there were white Americans who were truly committed to racial and economic justice. However, he eventually concluded that they represented a clear minority of whites because of America's "strange ambivalence on the question of racial justice" and the "tendency of the nation to take one step forward on the question of racial justice then to take a step backward" (King, *Where*, 2010, 85, 87). To bring about true freedom and equality for all Americans, King argued that white liberals needed to "escalate . . . rather than de-escalate" their support for a revolutionary change of values and structures in the nation (King, *Where*, 2010, 97). To end the injustices blacks and their ancestors had suffered since the early 1600s, when the first Africans landed on the continent as slaves, King urged African Americans to be at the forefront of the nations' transformation of values and abandon contemporary calls for black power because of its "implicit and often explicit belief in black separatism" and its absence of concrete, programmatic responses to white supremacy (King, *Where*, 2010, 49). To transform and improve black life in America, King calls for a "worldwide war against poverty" (King, *Where*, 2010, 188), tapping into the growing black electorate in northern urban areas, a "revolution of values" (199), and a renewed commitment from the federal government to improve and invest in K–12 education, job training, and housing.

The Civil Rights Act of 1964 may have prohibited racial discrimination in many sectors of American life, and the Voting Rights Act bolstered African American participation in the electorate, but racism persisted, King declared, and Americans needed to recommit to the struggle to eradicate poverty and racism. As expected, *Where Do We Go from Here?* was received along racial lines. White critics were perturbed at King's assessment of them and white America and his seeming lack of gratitude and impatience for what the country had done for black people in the 1950s and 1960s. King was simply asking too much of them. For many black readers, the book was an important elucidation of the contemporary movement for freedom, even if black power advocates questioned his ideas.

King traveled throughout the summer discussing many of the issues he raised in *Where Do We Go from Here?* when his promotional book tour ended. He reminded an audience at the Charleston County Hall in Charleston, South Carolina, on July 30 that "[w]e have to face the fact that, honestly, racial discrimination is present. So don't get complacent. We made some strides. We made some progress here and there and it hasn't been

> ### Cultural Connection: The Shrine of the Black Madonna
>
> The Shrine of the Black Madonna is part of the Pan African Orthodox Christian Church (PAOCC), founded by Rev. Albert B. Cleage, in Detroit, Michigan. The Shrine gained national fame in 1967 when on Easter Sunday, Cleage unveiled an eighteen-foot-high and nine-foot-wide black Madonna and Child, which replaced a stained-glass window depicting the Pilgrims' landing at Plymouth Rock. With the Shrine as his institutional base, Cleage called for black churches to reinterpret the teachings of Christianity to address the social, economic, and political needs of the contemporary African American community.
>
> Formerly known as the Central Congregational Church, founded by Cleage in 1953, the Shrine of the Black Madonna has provided theological, philosophical, and institutional support for the African American community in Detroit and beyond. The Shrine became particularly prominent for its role in city politics following the 1967 riots in Detroit. As many whites fled the city to the suburbs, membership in black social and political organizations exploded, and the Shrine became one of the most important religious and civic organizations in the city. The Shrine actively campaigned to elect black public officials and was instrumental in the 1973 election of Detroit's first African American mayor, Coleman Young.
>
> In the midst of the social and cultural upheavals of the 1960s, many black activists began to question whether Christianity was a source of liberation or oppression for African Americans. Cleage was quite critical of the role played by white Christians in fostering racism, colonialism, and imperialism, but he forcefully countered claims of those such as Elijah Muhammad and Stokely Carmichael that Christianity was a white man's religion with a white man's God, inherently bankrupt and serviceable only in the propagation of white supremacy. Asserting that Christianity was rightfully a black religion, Cleage redefined Jesus and Christianity in new terms that sought to assure their continuing relevance in the modern black community.
>
> In 1968, Cleage expressed his theological views in a collection of sermons and other writings, titled *The Black Messiah*. He further articulated his views in *Black Christian Nationalism: New Directions for the Black Church* (1972). The Shrine of the Black Madonna has continued its active ministry and community work even after the death of its founder in 2000.
>
> Source: Patrick Q. Mason, "Shrine of the Black Madonna," in Leslie Alexander and Walter Rucker, ed., *Encyclopedia of African American History*, vol. 3 (Santa Barbara, CA: ABC-CLIO, 2010), 257–258.

enough. It hasn't been fast enough" ("Flashback" 2018). Back in Atlanta on August 12, he talked to the National Association of TV and Radio Announcers with a discourse called "Transforming a Neighborhood into a Brotherhood" wherein he told them what he had told listeners in Cleveland, Ohio, days before: "The roots of racism are very deep in America and they're still here, and that racial injustice is still the Black man's burden and the white man's shame." The next day he made another appearance on *Meet the Press* and discussed his position on Vietnam and recent black urban violence in Newark, New Jersey, which had left over one thousand jailed, six hundred injured, and twenty-three dead, and in Detroit, Michigan, which resulted in over seven thousand arrests, forty-three deaths, and the city ransacked with scores of buildings destroyed. He was reluctant to condemn those who participated in the riot, because he saw such violence as the consequence of local, state, and federal neglect of the poor, especially the black poor throughout the nation. Urban violence weighed heavy on his heart, however, and he often equated rioting with unnecessary black suicide.

At the annual meeting of the SCLC on August 16, he told the members and supporters of the organization that "the problem of racism, the problem of economic exploitation, and the problem of war are all tied together." Such problems could only be resolved through a creative synthesis of the best in capitalism, communism, and a continuing nonviolent movement (King, *Where*, 2010). He told the distinguished, largely white group of social scientists at their annual American Psychological Association convention in early September that "[i]f the Negro needs social sciences for direction and for self-understanding . . . [w]hite America needs to understand that it is poisoned to its soul by racism and the understanding needs to be carefully documented." Consequently, social scientists must be at the forefront of social change to examine society and "extirpate evil" (King, "The Role of the Behavioral Scientist," 1967). Educating his listeners was a critical aspect of King's work because he understood that most Americans were misinformed or were just too self-involved with the new technologies and creature comforts of the time to care about larger societal and world issues.

He persisted into the fall of 1967 trying to reach as many people as he could, because he believed that the Vietnam War, the summer's urban violence, and President Johnson's foreign policy failures would bring about more domestic problems and an international conflagration such as World War III. He talked about the connections between the labor movement and the civil rights movement to the International Longshore and Warehouse Union, a local of the American Federation of Labor and Congress of Industrial Organizations in San Francisco on September 21. The next day, he was back in Ohio with students and their families at Scott High School in Toledo, a community on the banks of Lake Erie, discussing contemporary race relations and the federal government's response to the racial upheavals of the summer. "I am leery," he said, "of a Congress that is so fast to pass a riot control bill and so slow to pass rat control bills, rent supplement bills, and a model cities program" ("Martin Luther King, Jr. in Toledo 1967" 2013). Other stops on his speaking tour that fall included Sacramento State

College, the University of Southern California, Grinnell College, and the University of Buffalo.

SCLC fundraising had suffered considerably since his "Beyond Vietnam" speech, so King continued to raise funds for the financially beleaguered organization. Throughout October, he joined stage, film, and music stars on a nationwide "Stars of Freedom" tour that stopped first in Oakland (October 15) and then in Chicago (October 20), Cleveland (October 21), Washington, DC (October 23), Philadelphia (October 26), and Boston (October 27). Harry Belafonte was present at every concert and was joined by different artists in different cities as their schedules allowed. In Oakland, "Mister Show Business," Sammy Davis Jr., appeared alongside Joan Baez. During the height of the 1963 Birmingham campaign, Davis raised thousands of dollars at a Los Angeles dinner party, and Baez, a longtime SCLC supporter, performed at the March on Washington. During the later concerts, Aretha Franklin, folk singer Esther Morrow, comedian Nipsy Russell, and actor Sidney Poitier entertained audiences. Bebop jazz trumpeter Dizzy Gillespie and his band were in Boston in late October as a last-minute addition to the Beantown concert lineup. King wanted more attendees, but every concert had thousands in the audience; Boston had the lowest turnout, with about nine thousand attendees, and Chicago the largest, with over twenty-five thousand concertgoers.

When the concert tour was over, King, Ralph Abernathy, Wyatt Walker, and King's brother A. D. unceremoniously turned themselves in to Alabama sheriffs to serve a five-day sentence for violating a prohibition on demonstrations during the 1963 Birmingham campaign. King was initially convicted by a lower court and appealed the verdict all the way to the U.S. Supreme Court, which upheld the conviction. On Monday, October 30, dressed in blue denim jeans and carrying the Bible, John Kenneth Galbraith's *The New Industrial State*, and William Styron's novel *The Confession of Nat Turner*, King entered Jefferson County Jail in Bessemer, Alabama, a steelmaking town sixteen miles southwest of Birmingham. King read and prayed as he did before, when he was jailed in Birmingham, and considered producing another treatise on race, racism, and race relations, such as "Letter from Birmingham Jail." Instead, he continued to contemplate the road ahead of him.

Lecturing and fundraising were necessary, but King was searching for more concrete and dramatic ways to force Congress and the Johnson administration to shake their political lethargy, see how the Vietnam War affected domestic policy, and implement far-reaching, progressive economic legislation. He considered a version of socialism, so he gathered the SCLC leadership and his advisers and brainstormed ideas shortly after Labor Day and again after Thanksgiving. The civil rights movement had changed over the last decade, but even the long, hot summers of violence and turmoil had not shaken the SCLC's commitment to nonviolence. Some called for a nationwide hunger strike; others called for a sit-in at labor secretary W. Willard Wirtz's office, a nationwide call-in to the White House, disrupting traffic on the nations' highways, occupying government buildings, simultaneous demonstrations throughout the nation with Washington, DC, as the epicenter of the campaign, poor people's tent cities in the nation's capital, and massive boycotts.

When the often-contentious deliberations ended, the organization decided to pursue Marian Wright Edelman's idea of a "Poor People's Campaign" and developed broad contours of a spring 1968 political project in Washington, DC, which King revealed at a press conference on December 4. The federal "government does not move to correct a problem involving race until it is confronted directly and dramatically" he announced, so, "the Southern Christian Leadership Conference will lead waves of the nation's poor and disinherited to Washington, D.C., next spring to demand redress of their grievances by the United States government and secure at last jobs or income for all" (King, "Statement by Dr. Martin Luther King Jr.," 1967). Johnson's administration was put on notice, but the SCLC still had major planning to do if it wanted to make the Poor People's Campaign a meaningful act of political protest and expression. As he got to work with his staff on the structure and extent of the Poor People's Campaign, King wrote and delivered a series of sermons and lectures for the Massey Lectures series, which were recorded and broadcast by the Canadian Broadcasting Corporation. The series was named in honor of Charles Vincent Massey, the Canadian lawyer, diplomat, and eighteenth governor-general of Canada. The five talks King delivered were published posthumously in *The Trumpet of Conscience* in 1968.

In the first lecture, "Impasse in Race Relations," King said that the Underground Railroad that took so many fugitive slaves from chattel bondage into Canada meant that African Americans and "the Great White North" were historically connected by the "freedom road." He goes on to detail the two phases of the mid-twentieth-century black freedom struggle. During the first phase, blacks challenged segregation, forced the nation to grapple with blatant racism, and won a host of legal victories and federal legislation, including the 1964 Civil Rights Act and the 1965 Voting Rights Act, but they always had the long-range goal of achieving equality under the law. Most white Americans saw those achievements as an end to white brutality against blacks and therefore the end of the struggle. During the second phase, when blacks began to demand economic equality, the logical outgrowth of the first phase, a large portion of white Americans, even those who marched and demonstrated with blacks during the first phase, began to resist African Americans' calls for changes in the American racial and caste system. This resistance, this backlash, was one of the primary causes of recent violent uprisings by blacks in urban areas. Being a prophet of nonviolence, King deplored the riots but understood them as the result of "greater crimes of the white society" that by law, custom, greed, and ignorance trapped black people in ghettos and slums and expected them to be satisfied. To push forward for full equality, King urges black people to participate in "mass civil disobedience," "formulate new tactics which do not count on government goodwill," recommit to nonviolent protest, and work to eradicate black ghettos. He urged Congress and the Johnson administration to "provide employment for everyone in need of a job" or "a guaranteed annual income" (King, *Trumpet*, 2010, 14–15).

The second address, "Conscience and the Vietnam War," is an abbreviated reiteration of his "Beyond Vietnam" speech. "Youth and Social Action," the third address, examines the alienation of contemporary American youth who he says possess an unprecedented "new quality of bitter antagonism and confused anger" that stems from misplaced American values associated with all the foreign wars from the early 1940s to the late 1960s, as well as misguided domestic policies that have failed to address racial and economic injustice.

American youth, he asserts, can generally be grouped into three categories: those who generally accept the economic and political status quo; radicals, who want systemic change; and hippies, who promote a counterculture in which many seek to escape reality using mind-altering drugs. Supporting and uniting young people and correcting the evils of society, King contends, requires strong, creative leadership and nonviolent active resistance to encourage and unite estranged and hostile youth. One need only look to the alliances of black and white youth in the early 1960s for encouragement. In "Nonviolence and Social Change" and "A Christmas Sermon on Peace," the fourth and fifth lectures in the Massey series, respectively, King returns to themes he had preached and discussed throughout his entire public ministry: the effectiveness of nonviolence in one's personal life, in national life, and in the international sphere, as well as the need to embrace and employ a deep Christian love in dealing with one's family, friends, and enemies.

Details of the Poor People's Campaign were slow to materialize during the winter of 1968, but King toured the nation informing people of the need for a new movement of the poor. At the January SCLC board meeting, he insisted, "I don't care if we don't name the demand, just go to Washington . . . because there is something wrong with this nation and the nation needs a movement now" (Statler 2021). Shortly thereafter, he held a brunch at Paschal's Motor Hotel and Restaurant, a local establishment so frequented by civil rights activists that it was often called the unofficial headquarters of the movement. There in the banquet hall were assembled a cross section of the Americans to whom he had appealed for the massive direct action in Washington. "We assembled here together today," he told the group, "with common problems bringing together ethnic groups that maybe have not been together in this type of meeting in the past . . . black people, Mexican-Americans, American Indians, Puerto Ricans, Appalachian whites all working together to solve the problem of poverty" (Kunhardt 2018). Weeks later he told reporters that three thousand to three hundred thousand white, black, Mexican American, Puerto Rican, and Native American demonstrators from rural and urban locations would descend upon the capital and create "nonviolent massive dislocation" throughout the city until Congress created a $10 billion-per-year program for jobs or guaranteed income. In February and March, he toured the nation visiting blacks in Mississippi, Chicano migrant workers in California, Native Americans on reservations, and poor whites in rural areas to listen to their concerns, show his support for them, and recruit people for his nonviolent army. During his listening tour and recruitment efforts, he agreed to go to Memphis, Tennessee, to assist black sanitation workers.

Situated on the banks of the Mississippi River, Memphis, Tennessee, is the home of blues music and the birthplace of rock and roll. In the late 1960s, over one-third of the city's population was African American and, despite federal legislation against racial discrimination and the achievements of the civil rights movement, African Americans in the city remained segregated, underemployed, underpaid, and disrespected by local whites and the city government. The sanitation department was primarily comprised of black men paid approximately $1 per hour when the national minimum wage was $1.60. In January and February, they unionized to collectively bargain for better pay and working conditions, but city officials, including Mayor Henry Loeb, dismissed their claims. When 2 black sanitation workers died on the job, 1,300 black sanitation workers decided to strike and for weeks attempted to negotiate with the city government and held demonstrations throughout the city but faced increasing police repression. Desperate to turn the tide in their favor, Rev. James Lawson, one of the leaders of the strike and a friend of King's, asked him to come to Memphis and offer any assistance he could: deliver a galvanizing speech, lead a march, or meet with workers. King's advisers, especially Andrew Young, did not want him to go to Memphis because the SCLC was heavily involved in organizing and recruiting for the Poor People's Campaign and because King was tired.

King saw the Memphis sanitation workers' struggle as part of larger movement for jobs, income, and worker dignity and agreed to go to Memphis, though he underestimated the time he would have to commit to that strike. He arrived in Memphis on March 18 and addressed a large mass meeting. There he decried the poor working conditions and inadequate pay of the sanitation workers, offered encouragement, and buoyed their spirits, telling them that it was criminal that they worked so hard in the most prosperous nation on the planet but could barely make enough money to feed their families. Ten days later, he returned and led a march that was marred by violent outbursts when a group of young toughs began breaking windows.

Although the SCLC did not plan the march, King and his associates were blamed for the violence. He was criticized by the national press, which had grown tired of him, and by other influential blacks, who felt that his time in leadership had passed. How could King lead a multiracial, nonviolent army of thousands in Washington for weeks at a time if he could not keep hundreds of his own people calm for an afternoon march? Some media outlets suggested that King should cancel the April Poor People's Campaign or, at the very least, postpone it to a later date. That bad publicity caused King to doubt himself and vacillate between despair and cautious optimism about the campaign's prospects. He did not want to return to Memphis but eventually decided that if the SCLC wanted to recruit people to Washington in a couple of weeks, he would have to change the public narrative and remind America of his commitment to nonviolence, the power of nonviolent mass action, and SCLC's ability to organize a peaceful demonstration. King was confident that his staff could organize a peaceful march in Memphis and continued promoting the Poor People's Campaign.

On Sunday, March 31, he preached at the National Cathedral, the nation's house of prayer for all people, in Washington, DC; it was to be his last Sunday sermon. The homily was a revision of "Remaining Awake through a Great Revolution," which he had delivered on other occasions, and this oration spoke to the issue of poverty and the need for major national reform. When speaking about the upcoming Poor People's Campaign, he declared, "We are coming to Washington . . . to demand that the government address itself to the problem of poverty. . . [and] to call attention to the gulf between promise and fulfillment," not to "engage in any histrionic gesture . . . [or] to tear up Washington." He conferred with several political leaders after the address to discuss the upcoming presidential election and then held a press conference, where he informed reporters that the campaign would continue unless Congress and the Johnson administration provided a robust economic plan with clear timetables and benchmarks.

He returned to Atlanta, met with SCLC staff about the second Memphis march the next day, and then flew to Memphis on Wednesday, April 3, where he, Ralph Abernathy, Jesse Jackson, and Andrew Young checked into the Lorraine Hotel. Initially called the Marquette Hotel, the hotel only served white patrons until World War II, when it was purchased in 1945 by Walter Bailey, a prominent African American businessman, who renamed it after his wife, Loree. The Lorraine Hotel was known to be a hospitable place for blacks to stay when traveling through the Jim Crow South or while visiting Memphis. It was also highlighted in Victor Green's *The Negro Motorist Green Book*, the African American traveler's guidebook. King met with attorneys about the city's injunction prohibiting the SCLC march and talked with young black Memphis residents about their role in the city's movement before attempting to retire for the evening.

It had been agreed that Abernathy would address the evening's mass meeting at Mason Temple Church of God in Christ, but the crowd wanted to hear from King. Despite the poor weather and threats of tornadoes, King dressed himself, left the Lorraine, and delivered what was to be his last speech, posthumously named "I've Been to the Mountaintop." The church was full when he arrived and, with neither script nor notes, told them that the city's injunction would not stop their march to freedom, because the U.S. Constitution and God allowed for freedom of speech and assembly even if, and especially when, it did not suit structures of racial and economic oppression. In the speech, King referenced the biblical prophet Moses, who had led the Israelites from slavery in Egypt to the Promised Land but who could not himself proceed into that land. King said he had seen the promised land of racial justice and equality, where racial discrimination was nonexistent and poverty was eradicated. Children had nourishment for their bodies, mind, and soul. Able-bodied working adults had well-paying and fulfilling jobs. He said that he might not have the chance to join black people and the nation in that land of plenty and ended the sermon quoting the "Battle Hymn of the Republic"—"Mine eyes have seen the glory of the coming of the lord."

The next morning, on April 4, King rested most of the day and waited as the injunction was brought before a federal judge. That evening, while he stood on the balcony outside his room, preparing to go to dinner, he was shot by James Earl Ray, a white racist and career criminal. He died shortly thereafter at St. Joseph's Hospital. Robert F. Kennedy, Democratic candidate for president, was in Indiana delivering a campaign address as part of his effort to win the Indiana Democratic primary. He was in a poor Indianapolis neighborhood speaking to mostly African American supporters who had not heard the news, and he announced King's death. Kennedy's announcement was heard throughout the nation: "I'm only going to talk to you just for a minute or so this evening, because I have some very sad news for all of you and, I think, sad news for all of our fellow citizens, and people who love peace all over the world; and that is that Martin Luther King was shot and was killed tonight in Memphis, Tennessee" (Kennedy 1968).

King was thirty-nine years old. He left behind a wife, four young children, and a nation trying to find its way. His thirteen-year ministry for justice, peace, love, and equality had ended, but his dream lives on.

# Why Martin Luther King Jr. Matters

King had an intersectional approach to examining black life in America before the phrase gained popularity in the academy and daily life. To be sure, he was no black feminist, he held chauvinistic beliefs and practices, and he was limited by the era within which he worked, but he examined overlapping structures of discrimination and privilege and sought to address them. When few others, including his black contemporaries, could see the link between racism, poverty, and war, King did and risked his reputation by making those connections.

He critiqued President Eisenhower's record on racial justice, guided and questioned President Kennedy's civil rights agenda, and advised President Johnson on the Civil Rights Act of 1964 and the Voting Rights Act of 1965. He was an expert in using the new medium of television to gain national attention for the movement. During the first phase of the civil rights movement that included the Montgomery bus boycott, the Prayer Pilgrimage, the March on Washington for Jobs and Freedom, the Birmingham Campaign, and the Selma March, he received support from blacks, liberal whites, and some moderate whites. He and other civil rights agencies appealed to the conscience of the nation and used the Constitution for legal support to undermine a system of segregation whose sole purpose was to degrade and dehumanize a certain segment of the population solely because of their color.

Only staunch segregationists, white racists including the Ku Klux Klan and the White Citizens' Councils, and white politicians who were trying to stay in power voiced their opposition to desegregation. In a speech at a White Citizen's Committee meeting in 1957 in Mississippi, U.S. senator James Eastland said that segregation would not be forced on a militant, proud southern people and maintained on the floor of the U.S. Senate that "the South will retain segregation" (Reinecke 1956). Klan leader J. B. Stoner, the Georgian segregationist, openly led segregation rallies in St. Augustine, Florida, when black residents and the SCLC challenged racism there. At one such event, he spoke to the audience standing beside a poster with an image of King and a caption reading "America's King Coon: Must Unwanted Man." Of course, there was also Alabama governor George Wallace's declaration in 1963: "In the name of the greatest people that have ever trod this earth, I draw the line in the dust and toss the gauntlet before the feet of tyranny . . . and I say . . . segregation today . . . segregation tomorrow . . . segregation forever" (Wallace, "Segregation Now, Segregation Forever," 2013).

For whites outside of the South in states without segregation statutes, it was easy to support King's efforts and the civil rights movement because it was abundantly clear that black people suffered discrimination at every turn in the South. After 1966, when King moved into what he called the second phase of the movement, which confronted economic issues outside of the South and the nation's war effort, he faced resistance. White moderates and liberals said he was out of order. The *Washington Post* and the *New York Times*, two national newspapers that had praised King's civil rights work and promoted his publications, said he was out of his depth when he tried to bring together the civil rights movement and the anti-war movement. Newspapers throughout the nation tried to either discredit him or weaken his influence. The *Kansas City Star* ran a tasteless political cartoon that depicted King sitting in a bar getting drunk from bottles of "Anti-Vietnam" liquor while his young daughter wears a civil rights movement placard and begs him to come home.

During the second phase of the civil rights movement, black leaders did not know what to do with King. Jackie Robinson wrote to President Johnson saying that King did not represent the view of most black Americans. He and other NAACP directors voted against King's ideas to merge the civil rights movement and the peace movement. Bayard Rustin, the activist who helped convince King about the value of nonviolent passive resistance during the Montgomery bus boycott and organized the 1963 March on Washington, questioned King's wisdom. African American leaders were primarily concerned about black people in America and how to best serve their needs and wrongly assumed that King was not. King saw black people's desires and needs as fundamentally tied up with bigger and interconnected needs of people outside of the nation.

It was during the second phase that King went to Chicago and faced down mobs waving Confederate flags and swastikas. When black residents in Los Angeles and other cities said they faced discrimination and police brutality, the white fathers of those cities and most whites denied any racism or maltreatment of blacks. Apparently, King and the black people he represented were misinformed about their situation and misunderstood white residents in their cities. Black people became the problem for asking for too much, not racism.

After his death, Coretta Scott King, activists, politicians, and celebrities worked to have a national holiday in his honor. Stevie Wonder, the international recording star and one of the celebrities involved in the effort to recognize King, recorded "Happy Birthday," which appeared on his 1980 *Hotter Than July* album in King's honor. Through their relentless work, President Ronald Reagan signed a law in 1983 making the third Monday in January Martin Luther King Jr. Day. Eleven years later, President Bill Clinton, signed the King Holiday and Service Act, making the King holiday a National Day of Service, where Americans of all backgrounds were to use their day off to participate in community service projects. In 2017, President Obama signed Proclamation 9568 urging Americans to use the federal holiday to work in their communities.

Almost every year since the inauguration of a holiday in his honor, the nation celebrates Martin Luther King Jr. on the days leading up to and after the third Monday in January. Colleges and universities hold their annual Martin Luther King Jr. Convocation, where black luminaries give their thoughts about King and his legacy and bestow their Martin Luther King Jr. Award. Grade school students color pictures of King and recite passages from his famous "I Have a Dream" speech, while middle school and high school students watch a documentary or two about King's life. I remember watching the 1978 King television miniseries in the auditorium of my middle school in the 1980s. Liberal white religious institutions and most middle-class black churches dedicate a day of worship to King. On that day, they sing spirituals from the civil rights movement and the worship leader usually talks about events in King's life and his dream of a beloved community. The Friday, Saturday, and Sunday before the Monday holiday, savvy shoppers get discounts on their purchases in King's honor from nationwide chain stores for what is now known as Martin Luther King Jr. Weekend.

While writing this portrait of King, a host of people, mostly those outside the academy, asked, "What are you working on?" or "What are you writing?" When I replied that I was working on a biography of Martin Luther King Jr., many said, "Oh, there must be many biographies about King." I often responded, "Yes, that is true, but what was the last one you read?" Invariably, the answer was none or that they read one a long time ago when King was more relevant than their day off shopping. Despite King's family, who has vigorously protected and promoted his legacy, most Americans, despite race, religion, class, or education, know little about King. And the little they know comes from Hollywood movies that are geared more for entertainment than education including recent box office hits such as *The Butler* (2013), *Selma* (2014), and *I Am King* (2018).

In a scene in Tim Story's *Barbershop* (2002), a barber named Eddie, played by the comedian Cedric the Entertainer, is discussing civil rights icons and says that King was a "ho," referring to King's numerous extramarital affairs. After the film was released, a maelstrom of criticisms emerged online and in print discussing how the scene was in poor taste and how it may have sullied King's legacy. Very few of those early twenty-first-century criticisms reference a biography about King, King's autobiography, or King's writings. Street historians and purveyors of African American and U.S. trivia saw the scene as fact and most viewers failed to take the next step and read about King's work.

Over the years, politicians and pundits, like the American public they claim to represent, similarly have not read King's works or biographies about him yet invoke his name for numerous causes against affirmative action, diversity initiatives, race-conscious policies, and other hot-button issues. Priests for Life says that King was antiabortion. *Ms.* magazine says that he believed in birth control and family planning and therefore a woman's right to choose an abortion. In 2022, Ron DeSantis, Republican governor of Florida, referenced King in his opposition to the teaching of critical race theory in public schools, as did Texas senator Ted Cruz during the confirmation of U.S. Supreme Court justice Ketanji Brown Jackson, the first black, female Supreme Court justice. When this happens, liberal media outlets produce short reports such as the one by Adrian Florido on National Public Radio report, "Important Parts of Martin Luther King Jr.'s Legacy Are Often Glossed Over" or Amy Goodman's "He Gave His Life in the Labor Struggle." Such well-meaning reports try to rescue King from portrayals as an innocuous humanitarian and present him as a radical freedom fighter, as Jenn Jackson suggests in her January 2021 Aljazeera article, "Martin Luther King, Jr. Was Radical: We Must Reclaim That Legacy."

King was murdered in 1968 at the age of thirty-nine, so why does he matter over a half century after his death? He matters because his social and political agenda has largely been unfulfilled.

King matters because public education and housing matter. In his addresses, he constantly referred to the 1954 *Brown* decision and believed that it would usher in a new era for African American children attending public schools. According to a 2022 report, however, a large portion of black and brown children continue to attend segregated schools "that have less resources available to them" than predominantly white schools (Carrillo and Salhotra 2022). One of the reasons that they attend segregated schools is segregation in residential housing. African Americans and Latinos tend to live in neighborhoods with a high representation of people of color; whites do not. It bears repeating that the same Chicago neighborhoods that King sought to integrate during his Chicago campaign eventually let blacks and Latinos purchase homes and rent apartments, and then whites fled. In 2022, African Americans were denied mortgage loans at twice the rate of the general population. So even if black families want to move to an area with better schools, they have limited means to do so.

King matters because higher education matters. Poorly funded public schools mean that African American students have difficulty meeting college admission requirements or require remedial help in college. Black students enrolled in traditional, four-year, publicly funded institutions of higher education graduate at a rate of 45.9 percent. African American males' graduation rate is 40 percent, the lowest of any ethnic and racial group. King graduated from Morehouse College, a historically black college, which prepared him for his education at Crozer Theological and Boston University. Today, black colleges and universities graduate close to 20 percent of all black college students, though they only make up 3 percent of colleges and universities nationwide. A college education is an important route out of intergenerational poverty and into the middle class, but historically black colleges and universities have been chronically underfunded for decades, and many of their students must take out more loans to pay for their education because their parents either do not own a home or do not have the same intergenerational wealth tied up in their homes as middle-class white families do (Bridges n.d.). A quote commonly attributed to King states that "the function of education is to teach one to think intensively and to think critically." One way to honor King's life and legacy, to make his work matter in the twenty-first century, is to invest in higher education for African Americans and create more black critical thinkers.

King matters because police brutality matters. One of the many causes of the violent urban uprisings during the long, hot summers was police brutality. King pointed this out when he toured the Watts neighborhood of Los Angeles and called for remedies such as a civilian review board. In 2022, according to the *Washington Post*, blacks are killed by police at a higher rate than whites were. Black motorist Rodney King's police beating was caught on tape in 1992 and sparked riots in Los Angeles. In 2014, Michael Brown, an unarmed black man, was gunned down by police in Ferguson, Missouri, and Eric Garner was choked to death by police in New York City. Breonna Taylor was killed by police in her Louisville, Kentucky, home during a botched raid in 2020. That same year, George Floyd was murdered by police when a white Minneapolis officer knelt on his neck for close to ten minutes. Their deaths and others caused public outcry and some reforms in police departments nationwide. Adults and children enjoy quoting the "I Have a Dream" speech in which King says he wants his offspring to be judged by their character and not their color. There is another important line from that speech, where he says, "We can never be satisfied as long as the Negro is the victim of the unspeakable horrors of police brutality" (King, "I Have a Dream," 1963).

King matters because white supremacy matters. The recent upswing in white supremacist rhetoric and racially motivated killings has led to a racial reckoning in some areas of the nation, and organizations are revisiting systemic racism, white supremacy, and white privilege for a new generation. The National Education Association offered a toolkit in 2020 called "White Supremacy Culture Resources" which aimed to define white supremacy and offer educators strategies to counter the privileging of whiteness in their classroom. They define white supremacy culture as a "form of racism centered upon the belief that white people are superior to people of other racial backgrounds and that whites should politically, economically, and socially dominate non-whites" (National Education Association 2020). As early as 1961, in "The American Dream," King called for the complete eradication of the ideology of white supremacy in which white Americans and white Europeans are understood to be superior to every other racial group in the nation and on the planet. One year later, he urged white religious leaders to use their position to refute the idea that there are superior and inferior races of people. King matters because we did not listen to him then. We should listen to him now.

King matters because poverty matters. In 1967 and 1968, he brought poverty to the nation's attention. How could such a prosperous nation allow for such poverty? The Center on Poverty & Social Policy at Columbia University notes that "in 1970, Black children were more than three times as likely to live in poverty than White children and the gap is nearly as large today" (2022). In 2021, 19.5 percent of African Americans lived under the poverty line. Looking at historical data, the *Journal of Blacks in Higher Education* argues that "the Black-White family poverty rate gap, where African American families are about three times as likely to be poor as White families, has remained virtually unchanged for the past half century" (2022). The Center on Poverty & Social Policy calls for robust federal policies, including federal child tax credits as one way to end poverty. The Poor People's Campaign, a movement led by Repairers of the Breach and the Kairos Center for Religions, Rights, and Social Justice, has picked up where King and the SCLC ended and "demand[s] the immediate implementation of federal and state living wage laws that are commensurate for the 21st century economy, guaranteed annual incomes, full employment and the right for all workers to form and join unions" (n.d.). King and the SCLC called for a Bill of Rights for the Disadvantaged, and the Poor People's Campaign called for a Third Reconstruction. So long as poverty persists, King matters.

King matters because American international warfare continues. In his Nobel lecture, he said that wars only result in bloodshed, destruction for the vanquished, hatred for the victors, and worldwide instability. He often argued that if nonviolence works in personal and national matters, it can work in the international arena. King was in a minority of those who opposed the Vietnam War in 1967; six years later, when the United States ended direct military action in Vietnam, most Americans had come around to his way of thinking. He also said that the Vietnam War reallocated money that could have been used to eradicate poverty. In 2021, the United States ended its twenty-year war in Afghanistan, the nation's longest war with no clear resolution or victory. The Brown University Watson Institute for International and Public Affairs estimated that the cost of the Afghanistan War from 2001 to 2022 was $2.313 trillion. During the same period, the poverty rate gap between blacks and whites remained unchanged. If we follow King's line of thinking, some of that $2.313 trillion could have been spent to expand food assistance and child tax credits, invest in poor schools, or give direct cash payments to poor families.

King matters because of our nation's impulse to idolize and because our children continue to learn, and most Americans believe in, Great Man's history. George Washington, Abraham Lincoln, John F. Kennedy, and others are all great men beyond reproach. From this perspective, King was a natural-born leader and a great man who could do no wrong and deserves our reverence, a reverence that has often turned into hero worship. So when we learn that King was often uneasy in his role as a leader, had self-doubt, was unfaithful to Coretta, had mistresses in different cities, and, if we believe the FBI intelligence, had a child with another woman, we either deny the information or reject King outright because he was a flawed man and failed to live up to the standards that we created for him. On numerous occasions, King characterized himself as a sinner trying to do God's work. King deserves our attention, and his life and work have merit; otherwise, this book would not have been written. The more I read about him and his influence on so many aspects of the movement for social justice in the 1950s and 1960s, the more amazed I am. King was a flawed person who made mistakes and missteps, and canonizing him among saints does not afford us opportunities to understand him as a man.

King matters because African American Christianity matters. African Americans adopted and transformed Christianity in the early to mid-nineteenth century, and since then it has been a liberating force for them, both during and after bondage. Black ministers have always been spiritual and political leaders in their community. King was born and raised in the bosom of black Baptists in Atlanta and followed his father and grandfather and generations of black Christian ministers. His family was so steeped in the Baptist denomination that when he met Coretta, one of his parents' concerns about her was that she was a black Methodist. There are plenty of studies indicating that nationwide church membership is in decline among whites. However, African Americans remain a deeply religious and churchgoing people. Even when we take into consideration those younger than thirty, black churchgoing folk are mostly affiliated with a predominantly black Protestant denomination and see their church as an important institution in fighting racism, just as their ancestors did when they put their lives on the line during the civil rights movement. Like King, most black people—even those who do not go to church—regularly pray to and have faith in God or a higher power, because their faith is anchored in something that goes beyond the fancies and ephemeral tastes of the times. King matters because Sunday mornings in America continue to be the most segregated time of the week.

King matters because black people are still looking for a brighter day, and as they move toward it, as the nation moves toward it, King's hopes and work for racial justice are a guiding light on their faces. King matters because when it comes to creating a just and equitable society, a beloved community, as he often said, America has a long way to go.

# Timeline

**1929**

January 15: Rev. Dr. Martin Luther King Jr. is born in Atlanta, Georgia.

**1954**

May 12: *Brown v. Board of Education of Topeka*. U.S. Supreme Court unanimously agrees that racial segregation in public education is unconstitutional.

September 1: At age twenty-five, King assumes the pastorate at Dexter Avenue Baptist Church.

**1955**

January 18: President Dwight Eisenhower signs Executive Order 10590 prohibiting racial discrimination in federal employment.

August 28: Emmett Till, a teenager from Chicago, Illinois, is beaten, shot, and dumped in the Tallahatchie River outside of Money, Mississippi, for allegedly whistling at a white woman.

December 5: King becomes the president of the Montgomery Improvement Association, the leader of the Montgomery bus boycott. The yearlong boycott ends segregation on intrastate transit in Alabama.

**1956**

January 30: King's house is bombed.

April 4: Jazz singer and pianist Nat King Cole is assaulted after performing for an integrated audience in Birmingham, Alabama.

September 30: King's house is bombed for the second time in less than a year.

**1957**

January–February: King, Rev. Ralph Abernathy, Rev. Fred Shuttlesworth, and another clergy from southern states form the Southern Christian Leadership Conference.

May 17: The SCLC and other civil rights groups stage the Prayer Pilgrimage for Freedom in Washington, DC, seeking enforcement of the 1954 *Brown* Decision.

September 9: President Dwight Eisenhower signs the Civil Rights Act of 1957 into law. The act marked the first of such laws since Reconstruction. The law established the Civil Rights Commission and made it illegal to prevent citizens from practicing their right to vote.

**1958**

June 29: Bethel Baptist Church in Birmingham, Alabama, is bombed by the Ku Klux Klan.

September 20: Izola Ware Curry stabs King in the chest at Blumstein's Department Store in Harlem, New York, during a book-signing event.

**1959**

June 26: Rather than desegregate its schools, school officials in Prince Edward County, Maryland, dismantle the public school system.

December: Berry Gordy founds Motown Records in Detroit, Michigan. Employing some of the best-known rhythm and blues and soul artists of the 1960s and 1970s, the company helped produce the soundtrack for the 1960s.

**1960**

February 1: Students from North Carolina Agricultural and Technical College stage a sit-in at a local Woolworth's segregated lunch counter, which begins a wave of sit-ins around the country.

April: Black college students meet to create the Student Nonviolent Coordinating Committee. The Student Nonviolent Coordinating Committee is founded at Shaw University in Raleigh, North Carolina.

November 14: Ruby Bridges integrates William Frantz Public School in New Orleans, Louisiana.

**1961**

March 6: President John F. Kennedy signs Executive Order 10925. The Order establishes the President's Committee on Equal Employment Opportunity and prohibits racial discrimination in employment by all government contracting agencies.

May: An interracial group of activists affiliated with the Congress of Racial Equality embarks on Freedom Rides to challenge continued segregation in interstate transit. In Alabama, their bus is attacked by a white mob. In Mississippi, riders are jailed when they attempt to integrate a whites-only rest area.

**1962**

June: The SCLC starts Operation Breadbasket, the economic wing of the organization, to change discriminatory hiring practices and boycott stores that continued to practice segregation.

June 24: James Meredith becomes the first black student to enroll at the University of Mississippi.

**1963**

June 12: Medgar Evers, field secretary for the National Association for the Advancement of Colored People in Jackson, Mississippi, is murdered by Byron De La Beckwith.

August 28: King delivers the "I Have a Dream" address at the March on Washington for Jobs and Freedom to an audience of 250,000.

November 22: Lee Harvey Oswald assassinates President John F. Kennedy in Dallas.

**1964**

January 23: The Twenty-Fourth Amendment to the Constitution is ratified, eliminating the use of poll taxes as a prerequisite for voting.

June 2: President Lyndon B. Johnson signs the Civil Rights Act of 1964 into law.

December 10: King is awarded the Nobel Peace Prize in Oslo, Norway.

**1965**

February 21: Malcom X is assassinated in New York City.

March 7: Scores of protesters are beaten by police while trying to cross the Edmund Pettus Bridge in Selma, Alabama, on their way to the state's capital.

March 16–25: King, members of the SCLC, and the Student Nonviolent Coordinating Committee lead thousands of activists on a march from Selma to Montgomery, Alabama.

**1966**

June 6: James Meredith is shot and injured in Hernando, Mississippi, on his March against Fear.

October: The Black Panther Party is founded in Oakland, California, by Huey P. Newton and Bobby Seale.

November: Edward William Brooke III is elected to the U.S. Senate as a Republican from Massachusetts. He is the first African American since the Reconstruction era to be elected to the U.S. Senate. He served until 1979.

**1967**

April 4: King delivers his address, "Beyond Vietnam: A Time to Break Silence," at Riverside Church in New York City.

June 12: The U.S. Supreme Court unanimously decides in *Loving v. Virginia* that state laws prohibiting interracial marriage are unconstitutional.

August 30: Thurgood Marshall is confirmed by the U.S. Senate and becomes the first African American Supreme Court Justice.

November: Carl Stokes becomes the fifty-first mayor of Cleveland, Ohio, and the first African American mayor of a major U.S. city.

**1968**

April 3: King delivers "I've Been to the Mountaintop" in Memphis, Tennessee, to support black sanitation workers.

April 4: King is shot by James Earl Ray while on the balcony outside his room at the Lorraine Motel in Memphis. King dies an hour later at St. Joseph's Hospital.

Senator Robert F. Kennedy addresses a crowd in Indianapolis, Indiana, informs them of King's death, and encourages them to embrace compassion and justice.

April 4–April 14: Riots erupt in cities throughout the United States during the aftermath of King's murder.

April 5: King's first funeral is held at R. S. Lewis Funeral Home in Memphis.

April 7: President Johnson declares a National Day of Mourning.

April 8: Forty thousand mourners, including many participating in the Memphis sanitation workers strike, join King's family in a march for economic justice through Memphis.

April 9: Family and friends hold a funeral for King at Ebenezer Baptist Church, followed by a public funeral at Morehouse College with over fifty thousand attendees. Television and radio stations broadcast the public funeral to millions of people across the United States.

April 11: Congress passes and President Johnson signs the Civil Rights Act of 1968, also known as the Fair Housing Act.

May 12: The SCLC establishes Resurrection City. Three thousand poor people from across the nation set up temporary residence on the National Mall until police disperse them with tear gas a month later.

June 8: Authorities arrest James Earl Ray in London and quickly extradite him to the United States.

June 26: Coretta Scott King starts a nonprofit organization called the Martin Luther King Jr. Center for Nonviolent Social Change, now known as the King Center.

**1969**

January 15: Ebenezer Baptist Church holds a memorial service for King to honor what would have been his fortieth birthday.

March 10: Ray confesses to murdering King and accepts a plea deal. He is sentenced to ninety-nine years in prison.

**1977**
July 12: President Jimmy Carter posthumously awards King the Presidential Medal of Freedom. Coretta Scott King accepts the award on his behalf.

**1980**
October 10: Congress establishes the Martin Luther King Jr. National Historical Park, to be operated by the National Park Service, in Atlanta.

**1983**
November 2: President Ronald Reagan signs Congress's "King Holiday Bill" to establish Martin Luther King Jr. Day starting in 1986.

**1991**
September 28: The National Civil Rights Museum officially opens, with the Lorraine Motel serving as its primary attraction.

**1998**
April 23: James Earl Ray dies from medical complications at Columbia Nashville Memorial Hospital.

**2011**
August 22: The Martin Luther King Jr. Memorial opens in Washington, DC.

# PRIMARY DOCUMENTS

## Lincoln Memorial Program, March on Washington for Jobs and Freedom, August 28, 1963

*The March on Washington was one of the largest demonstrations of the modern civil rights movement. More than 250,000 Americans, blacks and whites, poor and affluent, assembled to be inspired by, to bear witness to, and ultimately be changed by such a demonstration of unity and hope. The speakers that day were African American and white religious and political leaders committed to racial harmony, social justice, and the American democratic ethos. The March forced the president of the United States and Congress to move forward with new civil rights legislation.*

1. The National Anthem
   Led by Marian Anderson.
2. Invocation
   The Very Rev. Patrick O'Boyle, Archbishop of Washington
3. Opening Remarks, A. Philip Randolph, Director, March on Washington for Jobs and Freedom.
4. Remarks
   Dr. Eugene Carson Blake, Stated Clerk, United Presbyterian Church of the U.S.A.; Vice Chairman, Commission on Race Relations of the National Council of Churches of Christ in America.
5. Tribute to Negro Women Fighters for Freedom
   Daisy Bates
   Diane Nash Bevel
   Mrs. Medgar Evers
   Mrs. Herbert Lee
   Rosa Parks
   Gloria Richardson
6. Remarks
   John Lewis, National Chairman, Student Nonviolent Coordinating Committee.
7. Remarks
   Walter Reuther, President, United Automobile, Aerospace and Agricultural Implement Workers of America, AFL-CIO; Chairman, Industrial Union Department, AFL-CIO.

8. Remarks
   James Farmer, National Director, Congress of Racial Equality.
9. Selection
   Eva Jessye Choir.
10. Prayer
    Rabbi Uri Miller, President Synagogue Council of America.
11. Remarks
    Whitney M. Young, Executive Director, National Urban League.
12. Remarks
    Matthew Ahmann, Executive Director, National Catholic Conference for Interracial Justice.
13. Remarks
    Roy Wilkins, Executive Secretary, National Association for the Advancement of Colored People.
14. Selection
    Miss Mahalia Jackson.
15. Remarks
    Rabbi Joachim Prinz, President American Jewish Congress.
16. Remarks
    The Rev. Dr. Martin Luther King, Jr., President, Southern Christian Leadership Conference.
17. The Pledge
    A. Philip Randolph.
18. Benediction
    Dr. Benjamin E. Mays, President, Morehouse College.
    "We Shall Overcome"

**Source:** Papers of John F. Kennedy, Presidential Papers, President's Office Files, January 20, 1961–November 22, 1963.

---

# Robert F. Kennedy, On the Death of Martin Luther King Jr., April 4, 1968

*When Martin Luther King Jr. was assassinated on April 4, 1968, Robert F. Kennedy, Democratic candidate for president, was in Indiana delivering a campaign address as part of his effort to win the Indiana Democratic primary. He stopped in a poor black Indianapolis neighborhood and told them of King's death.*

I have bad news for you, for all of our fellow citizens, and people who love peace all over the world, and that is that Martin Luther King was shot and killed tonight.

Martin Luther King dedicated his life to love and to justice for his fellow human beings, and he died because of that effort.

In this difficult day, in this difficult time for the United States, it is perhaps well to ask what kind of a nation we are and what direction we want to move in. For those of you who are black—considering the evidence there evidently is that there were white people who were responsible—you can be filled with bitterness, with hatred, and a desire for revenge. We can move in that direction as a country, in great polarization—black people amongst black, white people amongst white, filled with hatred toward one another.

Or we can make an effort, as Martin Luther King did, to understand and to comprehend, and to replace that violence, that stain of bloodshed that has spread across our land, with an effort to understand with compassion and love.

For those of you who are black and are tempted to be filled with hatred and distrust at the injustice of such an act, against all white people, I can only say that I feel in my own heart the same kind of feeling. I had a member of my family killed, but he was killed by a white man. But we have to make an effort in the United States, we have to make an effort to understand, to go beyond these rather difficult times.

My favorite poet was Aeschylus. He wrote: "In our sleep, pain which cannot forget falls drop by drop upon the heart until, in our own despair, against our will, comes wisdom through the awful grace of God."

What we need in the United States is not division; what we need in the United States is not hatred; what we need in the United States is not violence or lawlessness; but love and wisdom, and compassion toward one another, and a feeling of justice toward those who still suffer within our country, whether they be white or they be black.

So I shall ask you tonight to return home, to say a prayer for the family of Martin Luther King, that's true, but more importantly to say a prayer for our own country, which all of us love—a prayer for understanding and that compassion of which I spoke.

We can do well in this country. We will have difficult times; we've had difficult times in the past; we will have difficult times in the future. It is not the end of violence; it is not the end of lawlessness; it is not the end of disorder.

But the vast majority of white people and the vast majority of black people in this country want to live together, want to improve the quality of our life, and want justice for all human beings who abide in our land.

Let us dedicate ourselves to what the Greeks wrote so many years ago: to tame the savageness of man and make gentle the life of this world.

Let us dedicate ourselves to that, and say a prayer for our country and for our people.

Source: Papers of Robert F. Kennedy. Senate Papers, Speeches and Press Releases, Box 4, "4/1/68–4/10/68." John F. Kennedy Presidential Library.

# U.S. Congress, Commemorating the Fiftieth Anniversary of the Southern Christian Leadership Conference, 2007

*Fifty years after the founding of the Southern Christian Leadership Conference, members of the House of Representatives spoke to honor the lasting legacy of the SCLC and its founding members. The following excerpts share insights from the House of Representative members Nancy Pelosi, Charles Rangel, Bobby Rush, and Al Green. In their public comments, these individuals reiterated the SCLC's role in the civil rights movement, noting how the organization and individuals involved with it helped end segregation and gave African Americans a stronger more widely respected voice as voters and citizens of the United States.*

HON. NANCY PELOSI
Of California
In the House of Representatives
Tuesday, July 31, 2007

Ms. PELOSI. Madam Speaker, 50 years ago next month, a group of courageous champions of civil rights united to form the Southern Christian Leadership Conference (SCLC), which became a driving force behind the fight for equality and economic opportunity for African Americans. Led by the Rev. Dr. Martin Luther King, the SCLC's commitment to nonviolent civil disobedience exposed the evils of segregation and the violence and intimidation necessary to enforce this immoral policy.

The heroic efforts of the SCLC and the great faith and courage of its members were indispensable to the epic and defining struggle of our history: to secure rights for all and to live up to the purpose for which this nation was founded—equality and justice for all.

At the March on Washington for Freedom and Jobs, where Dr. King delivered his famous "I Have a Dream" speech, the SCLC created a turning point in the national debate over civil rights, helping propel passage of the Civil Rights Act of 1964 and the Voting Rights Act of 1965. These twin victories shattered the policy of segregation and reaffirmed our nation's commitment to equality for all of our citizens. The SCLC changed the nation with a vision of justice, equality, and opportunity for all.

Today, the SCLC continues its commitment to improving the lives of African Americans, focusing on issues of economic empowerment, access to health care, and opportunity through education. On the occasion of its 50th anniversary, I honor the SCLC for its commitment to positive social change through direct action and non-violence, and I look forward to the victories we will achieve together in the name of equal justice and equality for all Americans.

HON. CHARLES RANGEL
Of New York
In the House of Representatives
Tuesday, July 31, 2007

Mr. RANGEL. Madam Speaker, I rise today to acknowledge the 50th anniversary of the
Southern Christian Leadership Conference.

This year marks the anniversary of the creation of the civil rights organization that contributed to significant change in the United States. Founded by Dr. Martin Luther King, Ralph Abernathy, and other ministers whose moral vision led to them becoming civil rights leaders, the organization was originally named the Southern Leadership Conference on Transportation and Nonviolent Integration. The original name embodied the spirit of addressing civil rights issues nonviolently, Christian beliefs, and the goal of desegregating buses in Montgomery, Alabama. The organization's strength and support was rooted in the Black church community.

Through mobilizing the black community in Montgomery to walk and share car rides to destinations for almost a year, this organization successfully led a bus boycott which resulted in desegregation of buses. This event was a landmark victory for the civil rights movement. Another success for the organization came with the 1963 demonstration held in downtown Birmingham to desegregate local businesses. Thousands of people, including schoolchildren, attending the demonstration were sprayed by high-pressure fire hoses and attacked by police dogs. Many were arrested and jailed. The inhumane and unjust attack on demonstrators was aired on national TV and around the world. The massive outcry from Americans urged the Kennedy administration to act.

A settlement was reached whereby the downtown Birmingham businesses were desegregated and addressed discriminatory hiring practices.

Montgomery and Birmingham were catalysts for a Civil Rights Movement that ended legal segregation in this nation and opened doors of opportunity for an oppressed Black people. The Southern Christian Leadership Conference under the leadership of Dr. King became the agent of change to make a just society that is more in keeping with the promise of the U.S. Constitution.

On this day, I pay honor and thank the Southern Christian Leadership Conference for their contribution to the Civil Rights Movement. I admire the nonviolent approach taken by the organization to address discrimination. I urge my colleagues to learn about the contributions of this great organization.

HON. BOBBY L. RUSH
Of Illinois
In the House of Representatives
Tuesday, July 31, 2007

Mr. RUSH. Madam Speaker, we are here tonight to pay tribute to an historic American institution. This August the Southern Christian Leadership Conference, the SCLC, will celebrate its 50th anniversary.

The SCLC is one of the oldest and most influential civil rights organizations in American history. From its storied beginning, under the leadership of Dr. Martin Luther King, Jr., the SCLC has practiced the cornerstone of its founding principles: nonviolence in the fight for civil and human rights.

Originating from the Montgomery Bus Boycott that began after Rosa Parks was arrested for refusing to give up her seat, the SCLC has been a stalwart [force] in the struggle for equal rights and human dignity for all.

The bus boycott organized under the leadership of Dr. King and Ralph David Abernathy signaled to Black America the beginning of a new phase in the long struggle in what has come to be known as the modern civil rights movement.

Bombings, threats, and arrests could not dissuade church leaders from all over the Deep South from coming together and organizing under a simple mission and platform.

At its first convention in Montgomery, Alabama in August 1957, the Southern Leadership Conference adopted the current name, the Southern Christian Leadership Conference, and the newly-formed group issued a document declaring that civil rights were essential to democracy, that segregation must end, and that all Black people should reject segregation absolutely and nonviolently.

Founders at these early meetings adopted nonviolent mass action as the centerpiece of their strategy against segregation and inequality. Additionally, the organization made the determination to open up the SCLC movement to people of all races, religions, and backgrounds.

At that time in American history there were many of us who questioned solely using nonviolent protest as a tactic in the fight for civil rights. However, today there can be no question that the strategy was effective.

One of the most dramatic moments in America history occurred during a SCLC campaign in Birmingham, Alabama. On May 2, 1957, more than 1,000 Black school children joined in the peaceful demonstrations where hundreds were arrested. The following day, 2,500 more students showed up, and Public Safety Commissioner Bull Connor met them with police dogs and high-pressure fire hoses.

That evening, television news programs showed the nation, and the world, scenes of fire hoses knocking down school children and dogs attacking individual demonstrators, who had no means of protecting themselves.

Public outrage led the Kennedy administration to intervene more forcefully. A settlement was announced on May 10, under which the downtown Birmingham businesses would desegregate and eliminate discriminatory hiring practices, and the city would release the jailed protesters.

During this turbulent episode, the brutal response of local police and "Bull" Connor stood in stark contrast to the nonviolent civil disobedience of the activists, and public sentiment came down on the side of justice.

Madam Speaker, I take pride in doing my part to continue the work of Dr. King and other prominent SCLC members and moving the civil rights agenda forward.

Tonight my colleagues and I would like to salute the efforts and hard work of the SCLC. The world is a better place today because of their actions throughout these past fifty years. I want to extend my heartfelt congratulations and gratitude for the legacy the SCLC has established, here in America and around the globe.

HON. AL GREEN
Of Texas
In the House of Representatives
Saturday, August 4, 2007

Mr. AL GREEN of Texas. Madam Speaker, I wish to commemorate the Southern Christian Leadership Conference's, SCLC, 50th Anniversary.

Committed to obtaining and securing equal rights for African Americans and human rights for all people, the SCLC is a prominent body of influence. The organization, along with others including the National Association for the Advancement of Colored People (NAACP) and the Student Nonviolent Coordinating Committee (SNCC), gave African Americans and other minorities a sense of pride when times seemed dismal and bleak.

Beginning with the Montgomery Bus Boycott in December 1955, the then Southern Leadership Conference on Transportation and Nonviolent Integration was founded by Dr. Martin Luther King, Jr., and Ralph David

Abernathy. Although it was initially thought by some to be of an antagonist nature, in its early years the organization prided itself on education initiatives and voter registration campaigns to ensure that their young people had a voice in the political process. With the successful conclusion of the Montgomery Bus Boycott in February 1957, the group changed its name to the Southern Leadership Conference, widening their scale to reach a much larger audience. In August of the same year, the name was once again changed to the Southern Christian Leadership Conference, the name the organization bears today.

The initiatives and beliefs of the group, along with those of several others, culminated in the March on Washington for Jobs and Freedom on August 28, 1963, where an estimated 250,000 demonstrators came to the Mall, making the march the largest political rally of its time. At this historic march, Dr. King delivered his famous "I Have a Dream" speech, inspiring the masses in attendance and those viewing at home. The march was later seen as an integral part to the passing of the Civil Rights Act of 1964 and the National Voting Rights Act of 1965.

Committed to the philosophy of its founding president, Dr. Martin Luther King, the SCLC has always prided itself on nonviolent protests and rallies, allowing the message to overshadow the brutality they were often met with.

Madam Speaker, I urge my colleagues to join me in celebrating this marvelous organization and wishing them great success in the next 50 years.

**Source:** *Congressional Record* 153, nos. 123 and 125 (July 30, 2007, and August 1, 2007).

## President Barack Obama, Proclamation 9568, 2017

*On January 13, 2017, President Barack Obama issued Proclamation 9568, proclaiming January 16, 2017, as the Martin Luther King, Jr., Federal Holiday. He encouraged Americans to use the holiday to remember King's legacy and honor his life by performing acts of public service and volunteering throughout their communities.*

BY THE PRESIDENT OF THE UNITED STATES OF AMERICA
A PROCLAMATION

When the Reverend Dr. Martin Luther King, Jr., shared his dream with the world atop the steps of the Lincoln Memorial, he gave mighty voice to our founding ideals. Few could have imagined that nearly half a century later, his iconic profile would forever be memorialized in stone, standing tall and gazing outward, not far from where he stirred our collective conscience to action. In summoning a generation to recognize the universal threat of injustice anywhere, Dr. King's example has proven that those who love their country can change it.

A foot soldier for justice and a giant of the Civil Rights Movement, Dr. King lifted the quiet hopes of our Nation with the powers of his voice and pen. Whether behind his pulpit in Montgomery, at a podium on the National Mall, or from his jail cell in Birmingham, he beckoned us toward justice through non-violent resistance and oratory skill. Dr. King fought not merely for the absence of oppression but for the presence of opportunity. His soaring rhetoric impelled others to take up his cause, and with struggle and discipline, persistence and faith, those who joined him on his journey began to march. America was watching, and so they kept marching; America was listening, and so they kept sounding the call for justice. Because they kept moving forward with unwavering resistance, they changed not only laws but also hearts and minds. And as change rippled across the land, it began to strengthen over time, building on the progress realized on buses, in schools, and at lunch counters so that eventually, it would reverberate in the halls of government and be felt in the lives of people across our country.

[...]

As we reflect on Dr. King's legacy, we celebrate a man and a movement that transformed our country, and we remember that our freedom is inextricably bound to the freedom of others. Given the causes he championed—from civil rights and international peace to job creation and economic justice—it is right that today we honor his work by serving others. Now more than ever, we must heed his teachings by embracing our convictions. We must live our values, strive for righteousness, and bring goodness to others. And at a time when our politics are so sharply polarized and people are losing faith in our institutions, we must meet his call to stand in another person's shoes and see through their eyes. We must work to understand the pain of others, and we must assume the best in each other. Dr. King's life reminds us that unconditional love will have the final word—and that only love can drive out hate.

[...]

NOW, THEREFORE, I, BARACK OBAMA, President of the United States of America, by virtue of the authority vested in me by the Constitution and the laws of the United States, do hereby proclaim January 16, 2017, as the Martin Luther King, Jr., Federal Holiday. I encourage all Americans to observe this day with appropriate civic, community, and service projects in honor of Dr. King and to visit www.MLKDay.gov to find Martin Luther King, Jr., Day of Service projects across our country.

IN WITNESS WHEREOF, I have hereunto set my hand this thirteenth day of January, in the year of our Lord two thousand seventeen, and of the Independence of the United States of America the two hundred and forty-first.

BARACK OBAMA

Source: Barack Obama, Presidential Proclamation 9568, January 19, 2017, Office of the Federal Register, Code of Federal Regulations. Washington, DC: Government Printing Office, 2018, 7615–7616.

# President Barack Obama, Presidential Proclamation 9565, 2017

*On January 12, 2017, President Barack Obama issued Proclamation 9565, establishing a national monument in Birmingham, Alabama, to commemorate and honor the Project C, the civil rights campaign in that city. In his remarks, he dedicates the monument in honor of individuals' struggles against racial injustice, and "the heroism of those who worked so hard to advance the cause of freedom."*

ESTABLISHMENT OF THE BIRMINGHAM CIVIL RIGHTS
NATIONAL MONUMENT BY THE PRESIDENT OF THE UNITED
STATES OF AMERICA
A PROCLAMATION

The A.G. Gaston Motel (Gaston Motel), located in Birmingham, Alabama, within walking distance of the Sixteenth Street Baptist Church, Kelly Ingram Park, and other landmarks of the American civil rights movement (movement), served as the headquarters for a civil rights campaign in the spring of 1963. The direct action campaign—known as "Project C" for confrontation—challenged unfair laws designed to limit the freedoms of African Americans and ensure racial inequality. Throughout the campaign, Dr. Martin Luther King, Jr., and Reverend Ralph David Abernathy of the Southern Christian Leadership Conference (SCLC), Reverend Fred L. Shuttlesworth of the Alabama Christian Movement for Human Rights (ACMHR), and other movement leaders rented rooms at the Gaston Motel and held regular strategy sessions there. They also staged marches and held press conferences on the premises. Project C succeeded in focusing the world's attention on racial injustice in America and creating momentum for Federal civil rights legislation that would be enacted in 1964.

[. . .]

The events at the Gaston Motel drew attention to State and local laws and customs that—a century after the Civil War—promoted racial inequality.

[...]

*Whereas*, section 320301 of title 54, United States Code (known as the "Antiquities Act"), authorizes the President, in his discretion, to declare by public proclamation historic landmarks, historic and prehistoric structures, and other objects of historic or scientific interest that are situated upon the lands owned or controlled by the Federal Government to be national monuments, and to reserve as a part thereof parcels of land, the limits of which shall be confined to the smallest area compatible with the proper care and management of the objects to be protected;

*Whereas*, the Birmingham Civil Rights Historic District (Historic District) was listed in the National Register of Historic Places (NRHP) in 2006, as a nationally significant property associated with the climax of the civil rights struggle during the 1956–63 period; and the Historic District contains three key areas and the streets that connect them, covering 36 acres throughout the city; and the Gaston Motel, located in the African American commercial and cultural area known as Northside, is deemed a "major significant resource" in the Historic District;

*Whereas*, many other Birmingham places have been listed and recognized for their historic roles in the Birmingham civil rights story, including by designation as National Historic Landmarks;

*Whereas*, the City of Birmingham has donated to the National Trust for Historic Preservation fee and easement interests in the Gaston Motel . . .

*Whereas*, the National Trust for Historic Preservation has relinquished and conveyed all of these lands and interests in lands associated with the Gaston Motel to the Federal Government for the purpose of establishing a unit of the National Park System;

*Whereas*, the designation of a national monument to be administered by the National Park Service would recognize the historic significance of the Gaston Motel in the Birmingham civil rights story and provide a national platform for telling that story;

*Whereas*, the City of Birmingham and the National Park Service intend to cooperate in the preservation, operation, and maintenance of the Gaston Motel, and interpretation and education related to the civil rights struggle in Birmingham;

*Whereas*, it is in the public interest to preserve and protect the Gaston Motel in Birmingham, Alabama and the historic objects associated with it within a portion of the Historic District;

*Now, Therefore, I, Barack Obama*, President of the United States of America, by the authority vested in me by section 320301 of title 54, United States Code, hereby proclaim the objects identified above that are situated upon lands and interests in lands owned or controlled by the Federal Government to be the Birmingham Civil Rights National Monument (monument) and, for the purpose of protecting those objects, reserve as a part thereof all lands and interests in lands owned or controlled by the Federal Government within the boundaries described on the accompanying map, which is attached to and forms a part of this proclamation.

[. . .]

The National Park Service is directed to use applicable authorities to seek to enter into agreements with others, including the City of Birmingham, the Birmingham Civil Rights Institute, the Sixteenth Street Baptist Church, and the Bethel Baptist Church, to address common interests and promote management efficiencies, including provision of visitor services, interpretation and education, establishment and care of museum collections, and preservation of historic objects.

[. . .]

Warning is hereby given to all unauthorized persons not to appropriate, injure, destroy, or remove any feature of this monument and not to locate or settle upon any of the lands thereof.

*In Witness Whereof,* I have hereunto set my hand this twelfth day of January, in the year of our Lord two thousand seventeen, and of the Independence of the United States of America the two hundred and forty-first.

BARACK OBAMA

**Source:** Barack Obama, Presidential Proclamation 9565, January 12, 2017, Office of the Federal Register, Code of Federal Regulations. Washington, DC: Government Printing Office, 2018, 23–28.

# Bibliography

Albert, Peter J., and Ronald Hoffman. *We Shall Overcome: Martin Luther King, Jr. and the Black Freedom Struggle.* New York: Da Capo Press, 1993.
"Alfred Nobel's Will." n.d. https://www.nobelprize.org/alfred-nobel/alfred-nobels-will. Accessed July 29, 2022.
"America's Gandhi: Rev. Martin Luther King, Jr." *Time.* January 3, 1964. https://content.time.com/time/subscriber/article/0,33009,940759-1,00.html. Accessed July 8, 2022.
Arnold, Martin. "Rights Leaders Hold Unity Talks; Map Effort to Ease Tension in Cleveland." *New York Times.* June 15, 1967, 31.
Baldwin, Lewis V. *The Legacy of Martin Luther King, Jr.: The Boundaries of Law, Politics, and Religion.* Notre Dame, IN: University of Notre Dame Press, 2002.
Bennett, Lerone, Jr. *What Manner of Man: A Memorial Biography of Martin Luther King, Jr.* New York: Pocket Books, 1968.
"Books and Authors." *New York Times.* May 25, 1963, 12.
"Books—Authors." *New York Times.* May 22, 1964, 32.
Branch, Taylor. *Parting the Waters: America in the King Years, 1954–1963.* New York: Simon and Schuster, 1988.
Branch, Taylor. *Pillar of Fire: American in the King Years, 1963–1965.* New York: Simon and Schuster, 1998.
Bridges, Brian. "African American Education and College Education by the Numbers." United Negro College Fund. n.d. https://uncf.org/the-latest/african-americans-and-college-education-by-the-numbers. Accessed December 7, 2022.
Brown, William Adams. *How to Think of Christ.* New York: Scribner, 1948.
Buckwalter, Tim. "Quotes from the Rev. Martin Luther King Jr.'s 1963 Speech in Lancaster." *LancasterOnline.* January 21, 2019. https://lancasteronline.com/news/local/quotes-from-the-rev-martin-luther

-king-jr-s-1963-speech-in-lancaster/article_af377212-bbba-11e5-b635-6bde14686fac.html. Accessed June 24, 2022.

Burrow, Rufus. *A Child Shall Lead Them: Martin Luther King Jr., Young People, and the Movement*. Minneapolis: Fortress, 2014.

Carrillo, Sequoia, and Pooja Salhotra. "The U.S. Student Population Is More Diverse, but Schools Are Still Highly Segregated." NPR. July 14, 2022. https://www.npr.org/2022/07/14/1111060299/school-segregation-report. Accessed December 7, 2022.

Carson, Clayborne. *Martin's Dream: My Journey and the Legacy of Martin Luther King, Jr.: A Memoir*. New York: Palgrave Macmillan, 2013.

Carson, Clayborne, ed. *The Autobiography of Martin Luther King, Jr*. New York: Grand Central Publishing, 1998.

Carson, Clayborne, and Tenisha Armstrong, eds. *The Papers of Martin Luther King*. Vol. 7, *To Save the Soul of America*. Oakland: University of California Press, 2014.

Carson, Clayborne, Tenisha Armstrong, Susan Carson, Adrienne Clay, and Kieran Taylor, eds. *The Papers of Martin Luther King*. Vol. 5, *Threshold of a New Decade*. Berkeley: University of California Press, 2005.

Carson, Clayborne, Stewart Burns, Susan Carson, Dana Powell, and Peter Holloran, eds. *The Papers of Martin Luther King*. Vol. 3, *Birth of a New Age*. Berkeley: University of California Press, 1997.

Carson, Clayborne, Susan Carson, Adrienne Clay, Virginia Shadron, and Kieran Taylor, eds. *The Papers of Martin Luther King*. Vol. 4, *Symbol of a Movement*. Berkeley: University of California Press, 2000.

Carson, Clayborne, Susan Carson, Susan Englander, Troy Jackson, and Gerald L. Smith, eds. *The Papers of Martin Luther King*. Vol. 6, *Advocate of the Social Gospel*. Berkeley: University of California Press, 2007.

Carson, Clayborne, and Peter Holloran. *A Knock At Midnight: Inspiration from the Great Sermons of Reverend Martin Luther King, Jr*. New York: Warner Books, 2000.

Carson, Clayborne, Ralph E. Luker, and Penny A. Russell, eds. *The Papers of Martin Luther King*. Vol. 1, *Called to Serve*. Berkeley: University of California Press, 1992.

Carson, Clayborne, Ralph E. Luker, Penny A. Russell, and Pete Holloran, eds. *The Papers of Martin Luther King*. Vol. 2, *Rediscovering Precious Values*. Berkeley: University of California Press, 1994.

Center on Poverty & Social Policy at Columbia University. "The Black-White Child Poverty Gap Persist. Can We Close It?" March 10, 2022. https://www.povertycenter.columbia.edu/news-internal/2022/black-white-child-poverty-gap. Accessed March 31, 2023.

Crawford, Vicki. "Coretta Scott King and the Struggle for Civil and Human Rights: An Enduring Legacy." *Journal of African American History* 92, no. 1 (Winter 2007): 106–117.

Del Signore, John. "Listen to the Newly-Released Speech Martin Luther King Jr. Made in NYC in 1962." Gothamist. January 20, 2014. https://gothamist.com/news/listen-to-the-newly-released-speech-martin-luther-king-jr-made-in-nyc-in-1962. Accessed May 15, 2022.

"Dignity Event to Have Dr. King at Coliseum." n.d. https://www.lacoliseum.com/timeline/human-dignity-event-to-have-dr-king-at-coliseum/. Accessed July 21, 2022.

"Dr. King Is Freed: Peace Plan Set in Georgia City." Special to the *New York Times*. December 19, 1961, 1.

"Dr. King Leads Chicago Peace Rally." *New York Times*. March 26, 1967, 44.

"Dr. King's Error." *New York Times*. February 7, 1967, 36.

"Dr. King's Speech at E.C. Glass High School." Lynchburg Public Library. March 27, 1962. https://lynchburgpubliclibrary.org/martin-luther-king-jr-center/dr-kings-speech-at-e-c-glass-h-s. Accessed March 30, 2022.

"Dr. Martin Luther King Jr. 1963 WMU Speech Found." Western Michigan University Archives and Regional History Collections and University Libraries. n.d. https://wmich.edu/sites/default/files/attachments/MLK.pdf. Accessed June 24, 2022.

"Dr. Martin Luther King's Visit to Cornell College." n.d. https://news.cornellcollege.edu/dr-martin-luther-kings-visit-to-cornell-college. Accessed May 17, 2022.

Dudley, Uncle. "Dr. King Strikes Home." *Boston Globe*. April 24, 1965, 4.

Edgell, Holly. "A Monumental Figure: 4 Times Martin Luther King, Jr. Spoke in St. Louis." St. Louis Public Radio. January 14, 2018. https://news.stlpublicradio.org/arts/2018-01-14/a-monumental-figure-4-times-martin-luther-king-jr-spoke-in-st-louis. Accessed July 28, 2022.

Farmer, James. "James Farmer Oral History Interview." By John F. Stewart. JFK Library. March 10, 1967. https://www.jfklibrary.org/sites/default/files/archives/JFKOH/Farmer,%20James%20L/JFKOH-JLF-01/JFKOH-JLF-01-TR.pdf. Accessed April 26, 2022.

Farris, Christine King. *Through It All: Reflections on My Life, My Family, and My Faith*. New York: Atria Books, 2009.

Farris, Christine King. "The Young Martin." *Ebony* 41 (January 1986): 56–58.

"Flashback: Dr. King Visited Charleston in 1962, July 1967." January 15, 2018. https://www.live5news.com/story/37266288/flashback-dr-king-visited-charleston-in-1962-july-1967/. Accessed November 16, 2022.

Florido, Adrian. "Important Parts of Martin Luther King, Jr.'s Legacy Are Often Glossed Over." NPR. January 17, 2022. https://www.npr.org/2022/01/17/1073661284/important-parts-of-martin-luther-king-jr-s-legacy-are-often-glossed-over. Accessed November 24, 2022.

Frady, Marshall. *Martin Luther King, Jr.: A Life.* New York: Penguin Group, 2002.

Freund, Win. "When Martin Luther King, Jr. Visited Wausau." *Wausau Daily Herald.* January 17, 2017. https://www.wausaudailyherald.com/story/news/local/2017/01/16/when-martin-luther-king-jr-visited-wausau/96621590/. Accessed November 10, 2022.

"From the Archives: Martin Luther King Spoke to San Diegans in 1964." *San Diego Union-Tribune.* January 21, 2019. https://www.sandiegouniontribune.com/news/local-history/sd-me-archive-king-1964-speech-20190118-story.html. Accessed July 19, 2022.

Garrow, David J. *Bearing the Cross: Martin Luther King, Jr., and the Southern Christian Leadership Conference.* New York: Harper Collins, 1986.

Garrow, David J. *The FBI and Martin Luther King: From "SOLO" to Memphis.* New York: W. W. Norton, 1981.

Gibson, David. "David T. Howard: From Georgia Slave to Atlanta Philanthropist." *Atlanta Journal-Constitution.* February 2, 2017. https://www.ajc.com/lifestyles/david-howard-from-georgia-slave-atlanta-philanthropist/BlsNK0GcM6WPKVGIf43SBK/. Accessed November 25, 2022.

Goodman, Amy. "He Gave His Life in the Labor Struggle: MLK's Forgotten Radical Message for Economic Justice." April 3, 2018. https://www.democracynow.org/2018/4/3/he_gave_his_life_in_the. Accessed April 14, 2023.

Harding, Vincent. *Martin Luther King: The Inconvenient Hero.* Maryknoll, NY: Orbis Books, 1996.

Harding, Vincent. *The Other American Revolution.* Los Angeles: Center for Afro American Studies, 1980.

Harvey, Paul. *Martin Luther King: A Religious Life.* Lanham, MD: Rowman & Littlefield, 2021.

Herbers, John. "Dr. King and 770 Others Seized in Alabama Protest." *New York Times.* February 2, 1965, 1.

"Here's What Dr. King Told Vast Thousands." *Chicago Daily Defender.* July 11, 1966, 1.

Hitchcock, William. *The Age of Eisenhower: America and the World in the 1950s.* New York: Simon & Schuster, 2018.

Hobbs, Chuck. "Dr. Martin Luther King and President John F. Kennedy's Tense 1963 Meeting." *Insight News.* June 9, 2022. https://www.insightnews.com/opinion/columnists/dr-martin-luther-king-and

-president-john-f-kennedys-tense-1963-meeting/article_6743500a-e856-11ec-923d-db7b301c49a4.html. Accessed on June 16, 2022.

Hoffman, Paul. "Pope and Dr. King Confer on Rights." *New York Times*. September 19, 1964, 3.

Hughes, C. Alvin. "A New Agenda for the South: The Role and Influence of the Highlander Folk School, 1953–1961." *Phylon* 46, no. 3 (1985): 242–250.

Isaacs, Harold R. "Civil Disobedience in Montgomery." *New Republic*. October 10, 1958, 19–20.

Ivory, Luther D. *Toward a Theology of Radical Involvement: The Theological Legacy of Martin Luther King, Jr.* Nashville: Abingdon Press, 1997.

Jackson, Jenn. "Martin Luther King, Jr. Was Radical: We Must Reclaim That Legacy." January 18, 2021. https://www.aljazeera.com/features/2021/1/18/martin-luther-king-jr-was-radical-we-must-reclaim-that-legacy. Accessed April 14, 2023.

Jackson, Thomas F. *From Civil Rights to Human Rights: Martin Luther King, Jr., and the Struggle for Economic Justice.* Philadelphia: University of Pennsylvania Press, 2007.

Jenks, Jayson. "When MLK Came to Seattle, a Young Teacher's Life Changed." *Seattle Times*. April 3, 2018. https://www.seattletimes.com/seattle-news/when-mlk-came-to-seattle-a-young-teachers-life-changed/. Accessed March 3, 2022.

*Ka Leo* Staff. "King Optimistic on Civil Rights Progress, Warns against Dangerous Complacency." *Ka Leo O Hawai'i*. February 25, 1964. https://www.hawaii.edu/news/wp-content/uploads/2016/01/24277998741_af76c810b8_k.jpg. Accessed July 15, 2022.

Kennedy, John F. "Executive Order 11063." November 20, 1962. https://www.archives.gov/federal-register/codification/executive-order/11063.html#1. Accessed December 1, 2022.

Kennedy, John F. "Statement by the President upon Signing the Manpower Development and Training Act." March 15, 1962. https://www.presidency.ucsb.edu/documents/statement-the-president-upon-signing-the-manpower-development-and-training-act. Accessed April 15, 2022.

Kennedy, Robert F. "Statement on the Assassination of Martin Luther King, Jr., Indianapolis, Indiana, April 4, 1968." April 4, 1968. https://www.jfklibrary.org/learn/about-jfk/the-kennedy-family/robert-f-kennedy/robert-f-kennedy-speeches/statement-on-assassination-of-martin-luther-king-jr-indianapolis-indiana-april-4-1968. Accessed April 26, 2023.

King, Coretta Scott. *My Life with Martin Luther King, Jr.* New York: Henry Holt and Company, 1993.

King, Dexter Scott. *Growing Up King: An Intimate Memoir.* New York: Warner Books, 2003.
King, Martin Luther, Jr. "Address of Reverend Doctor Martin Luther, Jr. Delivered to a Joint Convention of the Two Houses of the General Court of Massachusetts." April 25, 1965. https://archives.lib.state.ma.us/bitstream/handle/2452/70100/ocn701908905.pdf?sequence=1&isAllowed=y. Accessed August 24, 2022.
King, Martin Luther, Jr. "Address to the Chicago Freedom Festival." March 12, 1966. https://www.crmvet.org/docs/6603_sclc_mlk_cfm.pdf. Accessed September 18, 2022.
King, Martin Luther, Jr. "Beyond Vietnam: A Time to Break Silence." April 4, 1967. https://www2.hawaii.edu/~freeman/courses/phil100/17.%20MLK%20Beyond%20Vietnam.pdf. Accessed April 14, 2023.
King, Martin Luther, Jr. "The Boycott Explained." *New York Amsterdam News.* April 10, 1965, 16.
King, Martin Luther, Jr. "Can We Ever Repay Them?" *New York Amsterdam News.* June 9, 1962, 11.
King, Martin Luther, Jr. "The Case against Tokenism." *New York Times.* August 5, 1962, 164.
King, Martin Luther, Jr. "The Casualties of the War in Vietnam." African-American Involvement in the Vietnam War. February 25, 1967. https://www.aavw.org/special_features/speeches_speech_king02.html. Accessed October 17, 2022.
King, Martin Luther, Jr. "Equality Now: The President Has the Power." *The Nation* 192, no. 5 (February 4, 1961): 91–95.
King, Martin Luther, Jr. "Feeling Alone in the Struggle." *New York Amsterdam News.* August 28, 1965, 1.
King, Martin Luther, Jr. "Fumbling on the New Frontier." *The Nation.* March 3, 1962.
King, Martin Luther, Jr. "'I Have a Dream' Speech by the Rev. Martin Luther King Jr. at the 'March on Washington,' 1963 (Excerpts)." August 28, 1963. https://www.gilderlehrman.org/sites/default/files/inline-pdfs/king.dreamspeech.excerpts.pdf. Accessed April 14, 2023.
King, Martin Luther, Jr. "A Letter from Martin Luther King from a Selma, Alabama Jail." *New York Times.* February 5, 1965, 15.
King, Martin Luther, Jr. "Literacy Bill Dies." *New York Amsterdam News.* May 26, 1962, 11.
King, Martin Luther, Jr. "Most Abused Man in Nation." *New York Amsterdam News.* March 31, 1962, 9.
King, Martin Luther, Jr. "My Dream." *Chicago Defender.* February 12, 1966, 10.
King, Martin Luther, Jr. "New Harassment." *New York Amsterdam News.* June 23, 1962, 11.

King, Martin Luther, Jr. "New Negro Battling for Rights in Albany." *Chicago Daily Defender*. August 14, 1962, 1.
King, Martin Luther, Jr. "Nobel Lecture." December 11, 1964. https://www.nobelprize.org/prizes/peace/1964/king/lecture. Accessed August 9, 2022.
King, Martin Luther, Jr. "Nothing Changes Unless." *New York Amsterdam News*. April 28, 1962, A9.
King, Martin Luther, Jr. "The Other America." April 14, 1967. https://www.crmvet.org/docs/otheram.htm. Accessed October 31, 2022.
King, Martin Luther, Jr. "Pathos and Hope." *New York Amsterdam News*. March 3, 1962, A9.
King, Martin Luther, Jr. "A Prayer for Chicago." *Chicago Defender*. April 16, 1966, 10.
King, Martin Luther, Jr. "The President's Record." *New York Amsterdam News*. February 17, 1962, A9.
King, Martin Luther, Jr. "Religious Witness for Human Dignity." Arizona State University Library. n.d. https://prism.lib.asu.edu/items/173/view. Accessed July 21, 2022.
King, Martin Luther, Jr. "Remaining Awake Through a Great Revolution." March 31, 1968. https://www.seemeonline.com/history/mlk-jr-awake.htm. Accessed April 15, 2023.
King, Martin Luther, Jr. "Rev. M.L. King's Diary in Jail." *Jet*. August 23, 1962.
King, Martin Luther, Jr. "The Role of the Behavioral Scientist in the Civil Rights Movement." American Psychological Association. September 1, 1967. https://www.apa.org/monitor/features/king-challenge. Accessed November 16, 2022.
King, Martin Luther, Jr. "The Role of the Church." *New York Amsterdam News*. September 15, 1962, 11.
King, Martin Luther, Jr. "Speech on South Africa in London." December 1964. http://www.rfksafilm.org/html/speeches/pdfspeeches/13.pdf. Accessed August 6, 2022.
King, Martin Luther, Jr. "Statement by Dr. Martin Luther King Jr." December 4, 1967. https://www.crmvet.org/docs/6712_mlk_ppc-anc.pdf. Accessed November 21, 2022.
King, Martin Luther, Jr. *Strength to Love*. Minneapolis: Fortress Press, 2010.
King, Martin Luther, Jr. *Stride toward Freedom*. Boston: Beacon Press, 2010.
King, Martin Luther, Jr. "The Time for Freedom Has Come." *New York Times*. September 10, 1961, SM25.
King. Martin Luther, Jr. "Transforming a Neighborhood into a Brotherhood." Speech to The National Association of TV and Radio Announcers. August 12, 1967. https://www.rimaregas.com/2015/09

/12/transcript-martin-luther-kings-speech-to-natra1967-second-half-racism-on-blog42. Accessed December 5, 2022.

King, Martin Luther, Jr. *The Trumpet of Conscience.* Boston: Beacon Press, 2010.

King, Martin Luther, Jr. "Turning Point of Civil Rights." *New York Amsterdam News.* February 3, 1962, 1.

King, Martin Luther, Jr. "Unknown Heroes." *New York Amsterdam News.* May 12, 1962, 11.

King, Martin Luther, Jr. "Virginia's Black Belt." *New York Amsterdam News.* April 14, 1962, 9.

King, Martin Luther, Jr. "What Is the World's Greatest Need?" *New York Times.* April 2, 1961, SM7.

King, Martin Luther, Jr. "Where Do We Go from Here?" August 16, 1967. https://kinginstitute.stanford.edu/where-do-we-go-here. Accessed November 16, 2022.

King, Martin Luther, Jr. *Where Do We Go from Here: Community or Chaos?* Boston: Beacon Press, 2010.

King, Martin Luther, Jr. "Why Chicago Is the Target." *New York Amsterdam News.* September 11, 1965, 16.

King, Martin Luther, Jr. "Why I Am Opposed to the War in Vietnam." April 30, 1967. https://www.youtube.com/watch?v=PRk81CuUKwI. Accessed April 14, 2023.

King, Martin Luther, Jr. "Why We Are in Chicago." *New York Amsterdam News.* March 12, 1966, 21.

King, Martin Luther, Jr. *Why We Can't Wait.* New York: Signet Classic 1964.

"King, Realty Forces Reach Agreement." *Chicago Defender.* August 27, 1966, 1.

"King Wins Approval." *Chicago Defender.* January 15, 1966, 11.

"King's Disservice to His Cause." *Life.* April 21, 1967, 4.

Krieg, Gregory. "When MLK Turned on Vietnam, Even Liberal 'Allies' Turned on Him." CNN. April 4, 2018. https://www.cnn.com/2018/04/04/politics/martin-luther-king-beyond-vietnam-speech-backlash. Accessed October 25, 2022.

Levey, Robert. "Dr. King Appeals for Brotherhood: 50,000 Expected on Common for Rally." *Boston Globe.* April 23, 1965, 1.

Levey, Robert. "A Mile of Marchers." *Boston Globe.* April 24, 1965, 1.

Lewis, David L. *King: A Biography.* Champaign: University of Illinois, 1978.

Ling, Peter. "Local Leadership in the Early Civil Rights Movement: The South Carolina Citizenship Education Program of the Highlander Folk School." *Journal of American Studies* 29, no. 3 (1995): 399–422.

"Los Angeles Freedom Rally, 1963." California African American Museum. n.d. https://caamuseum.org/exhibitions/2018/los-angeles-freedom-rally-1963. Accessed June 14, 2022.

Lynd, Staughton. "*Strength to Love*, by Martin Luther King Jr.; *The Negro Leadership Class*, by Daniel C. Thompson; The New World of Negro Americans." September 1963. https://www.commentary.org/articles/staughton-lynd/strength-to-love-by-martin-luther-king-jr-the-negro-leadership-class-by-daniel-c-thompson-the-new-world-of-negro-americans-by-ha/. Accessed June 6, 2022.

"Lyndon B. Johnson and Richard J. Daley on 19 July 1966." Conversation WH6607-02-10414-10415, *Presidential Recordings Digital Edition*. Vol. 2, *Lyndon B. Johnson and Civil Rights*, ed. Kent B. Germany. Charlottesville: University of Virginia Press, 2014. http://prde.upress.virginia.edu/conversations/4006262. Accessed April 6, 2023.

"Man with a Dream." *New York Times*. October 15, 1964, 14.

"Martin Luther King and Economic Justice, 1966." n.d. https://college.cengage.com/history/ayers_primary_sources/king_justice_1966.htm. Accessed October 2, 2022.

"Martin Luther King, Jr. in Toledo 1967." *The Blade*. August 27, 2013. https://www.toledoblade.com/gallery/martin-luther-king-jr-in-toledo-1967. Accessed November 19, 2022.

Martin Luther King Press Conference. June 5, 1963. https://www.c-span.org/video/?403151-1/reel-america-martin-luther-king-press-conference-1963. Accessed June 20, 2022.

McKnight, Gerald. *The Last Crusade: Martin Luther King Jr., the FBI, and the Poor People's Campaign*. Boulder, CO: Westview Press, 1998.

Miller, Keith. *Voice of Deliverance: The Language of Martin Luther King, Jr., and Its Sources*. New York: Free Press, 1992.

Miller, Perry. "The Mind and Faith of Martin Luther King." *The Reporter*. October 30, 1958, 40–42.

Miskewicz, Jennifer. "Clarendon Co. Residents Tell of Martin Luther King, Jr. Visit." WIS News 10. January 15, 2006. https://www.wistv.com/story/4369032/clarendon-co-residents-tell-of-martin-luther-king-jr-visit/. Accessed April 20, 2022.

Monjeau, Julianna. "Archivist's Angle: Martin Luther King, Jr. at NYU, a Catalyst for Change." January 15, 2021. https://www.nyu.edu/alumni/news-publications/nyu-connect-newsletter/january-2021/archivist-angle-mlk-nyu.html. Accessed November 30, 2022.

Moore, Ray. "Martin Luther King on JFK Murder: 'Shocking.'" CBS News. November 19, 2013. https://www.cbsnews.com/video/martin-luther-king-on-jfk-murder-shocking/#x. Accessed June 23, 2022.

Moran, Chuck. "The Day I Met MLK." January 16, 2017. https://medium.com/@chuckmoran/the-day-i-met-mlk-7ce3a639c007. Accessed April 15, 2022.

Muir, Hugh. "Martin Luther King in London, 1964: Reflections on Landmark Visit." *The Guardian*. December 2, 2014. https://www.theguardian.com/us-news/2014/dec/02/martin-luther-king-in-london-1964-reflections-on-a-landmark-visit. Accessed August 6, 2022.

National Broadcasting Company. "Meet the Press." August 21, 1966. https://www.crmvet.org/info/660821_mtp_ckmmwy.pdf. Accessed September 30, 2022.

National Broadcasting Company. "MLK Talks 'New Phase' of Civil Rights Struggle, 11 Months before His Assassination." n.d. https://www.youtube.com/watch?v=2xsbt3a7K-8. Accessed November 5, 2022.

National Education Association. "White Supremacy Culture Resources." 2020. https://www.nea.org/resource-library/white-supremacy-culture-resources. Accessed December 8, 2022.

"News Summary and Index." *New York Times*. December 19, 1961, 35.

"News Summary and Index." *New York Times*. August 6, 1966, 19.

"The Next 25 Years." *Look* 26, no. 2 (January 16, 1962): 17–20.

Pearson, Hugh. *When Harlem Nearly Killed King: The 1958 Stabbing of Dr. Martin Luther King Jr.* New York: Seven Stories Press, 2002.

"The Persistent Black-White Poverty Gap Hinders African American Access to Higher Education." *Journal of Blacks in Higher Education*. September 26, 2022. https://www.jbhe.com/2022/09/the-persistent-black-white-poverty-gap-hinders-african-american-access-to-higher-education-2. Accessed December 8, 2022.

Plenn, Abel. "The Cradle Was Rocked: The Montgomery Story." *New York Times*. October 12, 1958, BR24.

Poor People's Campaign. "Our Demands." n.d. https://www.poorpeoplescampaign.org/about/our-demands/. Accessed December 8, 2022.

Przybys, John. "Martin Luther King, Jr. Spoke in Las Vegas 54 Years Ago." *Las Vegas Review-Journal*. April 1, 2018. https://www.reviewjournal.com/local/local-las-vegas/martin-luther-king-jr-spoke-in-las-vegas-54-years-ago/. Accessed July 18, 2022.

Reddick, L. D. *Crusader without Violence: The Biography of Martin Luther King, Jr.* Montgomery, AL: New South Books, 2018.

Redding, Saunders. "To Lift the Siege of Denial." *New York Times*. July 26, 1964, BR1.

Regents of the University of California. "Martin Luther King, Jr. Speaks at UCLA." April 27, 1965. https://100.ucla.edu/timeline/martin-luther-king-jr-speaks-at-ucla. Accessed August 25, 2022.

Reinecke, John. "Eastland in His Own Words." *Honolulu Record* 9, no. 12 (October 18, 1956): 2. Center for Labor Education & Research, University of Hawaii—West Oahu: Honolulu Record Digitization

Project. https://www.hawaii.edu/uhwo/clear/HonoluluRecord/articles/v9n12/Eastland%20in%20His%20Own%20Words.html. Accessed December 12, 2022.

"Rev. King Says 'We Will Fight to the Death.'" *New York Amsterdam News.* December 30, 1961, 4.

Roberts, Gene. "Dr. King and the War." *New York Times.* April 14, 1967, 21.

Robinson, Jo Ann. *The Montgomery Bus Boycott and the Women Who Started It.* Knoxville: University of Tennessee Press, 1987.

Rowan, Carl T. "Martin Luther King's Tragic Decision." *Reader's Digest* 91 (September 1967): 37–42.

Sams, Tonya. "Crowds Packed Cleveland Venues Where the Rev. Martin Luther King, Jr. Spoke." January 18, 2010. https://www.cleveland.com/plain-dealer-library/2010/01/in_1963_dr_martin_luther_king_jr_delivers_speech_at_st_paul_episcopal_church_cleveland_heights.html. Accessed June 14, 2022.

Sharif, Hasan. "The Day Dr. King Visited Boston." *Bay State Banner.* January 10, 2012. https://www.baystatebanner.com/2012/01/10/the-day-dr-king-visited-boston-common-in-1965-3/. Accessed August 25, 2012.

Sibley, John. "Bunche Disputes Dr. King on Peace." *New York Times.* April 13, 1967, 1.

Sitton, Claude. "Dr. King Is Jailed Again at Prayer Rally in Georgia." *New York Times.* July 28, 1962, 1.

Smiley, Tavis, and David Ritz. *Death of a King: The Real Story of Dr. Martin Luther King Jr.'s Final Year.* New York: Little, Brown and Company, 2014.

Smith, Lillian. "And Suddenly Something Happened." *Saturday Review.* September 20, 1958, 21.

Southern Christian Leadership Conference. "The Chicago Plan." January 6, 1966. https://www.crmvet.org/docs/6601_sclc_mlk_chicagoplan.pdf. Accessed September 5, 2022.

Stateside Staff. "The Legacy of Martin Luther King, Jr.'s 1963 Visit to Detroit." Michigan Radio. January 20, 2020. https://www.michiganradio.org/stateside/2020-01-20/the-legacy-of-martin-luther-king-jr-s-1963-visit-to-detroit. Accessed June 17, 2022

Statler, Rick. "Listen to Dr. Martin Luther King, Jr. Speaking to the SCLC Board in 1968." March 19, 2021. https://www.swanngalleries.com/news/printed-and-manuscript-african-americana/2021/03/listen-to-dr-martin-luther-king-jr-speaking-to-the-sclc-board-in-1968/. Accessed November 23, 2022.

Sundquist, Eric J. *King's Dream.* New Haven, CT: Yale University Press, 2009.

"Swarthmore College Peace Collection." n.d. https://www.swarthmore.edu/library/peace/DG051-099/dg067vietnamsum.html. Accessed November 1, 2022.

Tenkotte, Paul. "Our Rich History: Dr. Martin Luther King Jr. and Our Regions; A Remarkable Legacy, Visionary Leader." January 21, 2019. https://www.nkytribune.com/2019/01/our-rich-history-dr-martin-luther-king-jr-and-our-region-a-remarkable-legacy-visionary-leader/. Accessed November 18, 2022.

Thiselton, Anthony. "The Theology of Paul Tillich." *Churchman* 88, no. 1 (1974): 86–107.

"Thurmond Praises Brooke." *Boston Globe.* April 7, 1967, 26.

Tisby, Jemar. "Martin Luther King's Eulogy of the Four Girls Killed in a Birmingham Church Bombing." The Witness, September 15, 2017. https://thewitnessbcc.com/martin-luther-kings-eulogy-four-girls-killed-birmingham-church-bombing. Accessed June 21, 2022.

Wallace, George. "Segregation Now, Segregation Forever." January 22, 2013. https://www.blackpast.org/african-american-history/speeches-african-american-history/1963-george-wallace-segregation-now-segregation-forever/. Accessed December 12, 2022.

Washington, Betty. "King Group Unveils Novel Slum Rescue Plan." *Chicago Daily Defender.* February 24, 1966, 1.

Washington, James M., ed. *A Testament of Hope: The Essential Writings of Martin Luther King, Jr.* San Francisco: Harper & Row, 1986.

Wettland, Georgia. "'Integration Still Far Away' Says Martin Luther King." *The Vanguard.* November 10, 1961. https://library.pdx.edu/news/martin-luther-king-at-portland-state-in-1961/. Accessed November 30, 2022.

"What Happened to Hell." *Ebony.* January 1961, 47–48, 50–52.

"White Clergymen Urge Local Negroes to Withdraw from Demonstrations." *Birmingham News.* April 13, 1963. https://bplonline.contentdm.oclc.org/digital/collection/p4017coll2/id/746. Accessed June 7, 2022.

"Why M.L. King Is Leaving Montgomery: Leader Says Time Is Ripe to Extend Work in Dixie." *Jet.* December 17, 1959, 12–17.

Young, Andrew. *An Easy Burden: The Civil Rights Movement and the Transformation of America.* New York: HarperCollins, 1996.

YWCA. "A History of the YWCA Mission." n.d. https://www.ywca.org/about/. Accessed April 15, 2023.

## MEDIA

Bagwell, Orlando, and W. Noland Walker, dirs. *Citizen King.* Boston: WGBH Educational Foundation, 2004. DVD.

Blackside, prod. *Eyes on the Prize—America's Civil Rights Movement*, episode "Ain't Scared of Your Jails 1960–1961." Aired February 4, 1987.

Transcript available at https://www-tc.pbs.org/wgbh/americanexperience/media/filer_public/b9/02/b902b327-70e0-4a4c-80d4-db9ca54941ab/eyes_on_the_prize_transcript.pdf. Accessed April 6, 2023.

Blackside, prod. *Eyes on the Prize—America's Civil Rights Movement*, episode "The Time Has Come 1964–1966." Aired January 15, 1990. Transcript available at https://www-tc.pbs.org/wgbh/americanexperience/media/filer_public/b9/02/b902b327-70e0-4a4c-80d4-db9ca54941ab/eyes_on_the_prize_transcript.pdf. Accessed April 6, 2023.

Blackside, prod. *Eyes on the Prize—America's Civil Rights Movement*, episode "Two Societies 1965–1968." Aired January 22, 1990. Transcript available at https://www-tc.pbs.org/wgbh/americanexperience/media/filer_public/b9/02/b902b327-70e0-4a4c-80d4-db9ca54941ab/eyes_on_the_prize_transcript.pdf. Accessed April 6, 2023.

Hudson, Robert, and Robert Houston, dirs. *Mighty Times: The Children's March*. Montgomery, AL: Southern Poverty Law Center, 2011. DVD.

Kunhardt, Peter W., dir. *King in the Wilderness*. Written by Chris Chuang. Burbank, CA: HBO Home Box Office, 2018. https://www.youtube.com/watch?v=9eQXD_44Kso. Accessed April 26, 2023.

"November 23, 1963—Martin Luther King, Jr., following the Assassination of President John F. Kennedy." https://www.youtube.com/watch?v=Fay1_QI_0uE. Accessed June 23, 2022.

Pritchett, Laurie. "Interview with Laurie Pritchett." By James A. DeVinney. Blackside Inc., November 7, 1985. Available in the Washington University Film & Media Archive. http://mavisweb.wulib.wustl.edu:81/mavisDetail/TitleWork/key/208. Accessed on March 30, 2022.

# Index

Abernathy, Juanita, 33, 133
Abernathy, Ralph
   Albany Movement, 87, 95–96
   arrest and jailing of, 87, 95
   audience with Pope Paul VI, 133
   bail posted for King, 28
   Birmingham Campaign,
     106, 172
   Chicago Movement, 153
   freedom rides rally, 83
   Green, Al, on, 199–200
   hate crimes against, 38
   meeting with Nixon, 44
   in Memphis, 176–177
   Montgomery Improvement
     Association and, 25, 29
   Obama, Barack, on, 202
   "People to People" tour, 91–92
   Rangel, Charles, on, 197
   Rush, Bobby L., on, 198
   Selma March, 139
   Southern Christian Leadership
     Conference founding, 187
   vacation with Kings, 33
Abyssinian Baptist Church (Harlem),
   42, 145
Acoba, Simeon R., Jr., 125
Addams, Jane, 30
African American Christianity,
   185–186
Ahmann, Matthew, 194

Alabama Christian Movement for
   Human Rights, 105
Alabama Council on Human Relations
   (ACHR), 25
Alabama Voters League, 19
Albany Movement, 86–88, 95–96
Alford, William Frank, 24
Alpha Phi Alpha, 29, 34
American Baptist Home Missions
   Societies (ABHMS) Conference,
   34–35
Anderson, James H., 90
Anderson, Marian, 3
Anderson, William G., 86–88
Apartheid, 134–135, 160
Arnold, Melvin, 49, 111
Aubrey, Edwin, 7
Augustine of Hippo, 14
Azikewe, Nnamdi, 69–70

Baez, Joan, 119, 152, 172
Bagley, James H., 25
Baker, Ella, 64
Ballenger, Milton Cornelius, 26
Baraka, Amiri, 166
*Barbershop* (film), 182
Barth, Karl, 7, 10, 14
Bates, Daisy, 193
Batten, Charles, 8
Battle, H. H., 15–16
Beat Generation, 152

Belafonte, Harry, 64, 148–149, 164, 168, 172
Bell Street Baptist Church (Montgomery), 24
Bennet, John, 161
Bennett, L. Roy, 23
Berdyaev, Nicholas, 10–11
Berkeley, George, 15
Berry, Chuck, 47
Berry, Edwin, 155
Beulah Baptist Church (Montgomery), 24
Bevel, James, 108, 128, 137, 146, 164
Big Bethel AME Church (Atlanta), 37
Billingsley, Orzell, Jr., 31
Birmingham, Alabama
  bombing of Sixteenth Street Baptist Church, 119–120
  bombings of churches, homes, and businesses, 91, 105, 188
  "Letter from Birmingham Jail" (King), 107, 117, 131, 172
Birmingham Campaign, 104–110, 119–120, 172, 179, 197
Birmingham Civil Rights National Monument, 202–204
Bishop College, 58
Black Arts Movement, 166
Black nationalism, 111, 117, 119, 126, 127, 166
Black Panther Party, 164, 166, 189
Black Power, 151, 153
Blake, Eugene Carson, 193
Bloomsbury Central Baptist Church (London), 80
Bowne, Borden Parker, 7, 10
Branch, Taylor, 68
Brandt, Willy, 133
Bridges, Ruby, 188
Bright Hope Baptist Church (North Philadelphia), 56, 120
Brightman, Edgar S., 7, 9–11
Britton, Milton, 29
Brock, James, 130
Brooke, Edward William, III, 189
Brooks, Phillips, 32

*Browder v. Gayle*, 32, 35
Brown, Edmund, 143
Brown, Michael, 183
Brown, Oscar, 153
Brown, Theodore E., 49
Brown, William Adam, 6
Brown Chapel AME Church (Selma), 137–139
*Brown v. Board of Education*, 22, 31, 39, 42, 44–45, 62, 65, 67, 70, 75, 85, 90, 94, 101, 182, 187, 188
Bryant, C. Farris, 130
Bryant, Carolyn, 20
Bryant, Clory, 156
Bryant, Roy, 20
Bullins, Ed, 166
Bunche, Ralph J., 41, 163, 165
Burks, Mary Fair, 21
*Butler, The* (film), 182

Calvin, John, 11, 14
Carey, Archibald James, Jr., 27
Carmichael, Stokely, 151, 155, 164, 170
Carr, Leonard, 16
Carter, Eugene, 31, 35
Carter, James, 65
Carter, Jimmy, 191
Carter, Marmaduke, 86
Carver, George Washington, 53
Cassity, John, 52
Cathedral of St. John the Divine (New York City), 32–33
Chandler, Hugh Storer, 153
*Chicago Daily Defender*, 96, 146–147, 150
Chicago freedom movement, 145–156
Civil Rights Act of 1957, 188
Civil Rights Act of 1968 (Fair Housing Act), 190
Civil Rights Act of 1964, 94, 110, 130, 135, 137–138, 169, 173, 179, 189, 196, 200
Clark, Dick, 99
Clark, Jim, 138
Clark, Kenneth, 59, 168

Clark, Septima, 22
Clarke, Charles Arden, 40
Cleage, Albert B., 111, 170
Clergy and Laymen Concerned about Vietnam, 161
Clinton, Bill, 181
COINTELPRO, 127
Cold War, 8, 112, 115
Cole, Nat King, 64, 187
Collins, John F., 142
Colvin, Claudette, 21, 25
Commager, Henry Steele, 161
Congress of Racial Equality (CORE), 30, 67, 73, 82, 98, 118, 131, 151, 168, 188, 194
Connor, Theophilus Eugene "Bull," 106–107, 108, 131, 199
Cooper, Annie Lee, 138
Coordinating Council of Community Organizations (CCCO), 143, 146–148, 150, 153–155
Cordice, John, 52
Cotton, Dorothy, 91
Crenshaw, Jack, 25
Crockett, Roosevelt, 15
Crozer Theological Seminary, 5–9, 18, 29, 34, 86, 183
Cruz, Ted, 182
Curry, Izola, 51–52, 55, 72, 188

Daley, Richard J., 146, 149, 153–155
Dangerfield, Maudestine, 2
Daves, Joan, 48, 49
Davis, Abraham L., Jr., 39
Davis, George W., 29
Davis, Ossie, 118
Davis, Sammy, Jr., 109–110, 172
Dawson, William, 27
DeSantis, Ron, 182
DeWolf, L. Harold, 9–11, 18
Dexter Avenue Baptist Church (Montgomery), 14–18, 23, 26, 28, 30, 41, 48, 53, 55, 58–64, 72, 111, 187
Dialectical Society, 9, 11
Dickerson, Earl Burrus, 27

Dillard College (later Dillard University), 58
Dozier, Lamont, 79
Du Bois, W. E. B., 2, 30, 53
Duckett, Al, 130
Dungee, Erna, 24

Eastland, James, 180
Ebenezer Baptist Church (Atlanta)
  King as copastor of, 60, 68, 71, 73, 77, 84, 86–87, 90, 102, 165, 167
  King's early sermons at, 12
  King's father as pastor of, 1–2
  King's funeral and memorial service, 190
  King's maternal grandfather as pastor of, 1
*Ebony* (magazine), 40, 59, 86, 107
  "Advice for Living" (King column), 45–48, 59, 89
  "My Trip to the Land of Gandhi," 58
Edelman, Marian Wright, 173
Edmund Pettus Bridge, 138–139, 189
Eichelberger, James William, Jr., 27
Eisenhower, Dwight D., 37–39, 42, 43–44, 67, 78, 117, 179, 187, 188
Emancipation Proclamation, 44, 75, 81, 101
Emerson, Ralph Waldo, 113, 160
Emrich, Richard, 44
Enninful, George, 116
Enslin, Morton Scott, 8
Evers, Medgar, 189
Evers, Mrs. Medgar, 193

Farmer, James, 98, 124, 194
FBI, 85, 124, 127, 134, 185
Fellowship of Reconciliation (FOR), 30–31
Fichte, Johann Gottlieb, 15
Fields, Uriah J., 23–24
Fifteenth Amendment, 164
First African Baptist Church (Tuscaloosa), 125
First Baptist Church (Birmingham), 90, 107

First Baptist Church (Chattanooga), 14–16
First Baptist Church (Montgomery), 25, 28, 29, 38, 42, 83
Fisk, Clinton B., 29–30
Fisk University, 29–30, 34, 84
Fleming, Bobby, 93
Fleming, William, 93
*Fleming v. South Carolina Electric and Gas Company*, 32
Florido, Adrian, 182
Floyd, George, 183–184
Fourteenth Amendment, 106, 164
Fox, George, 14
Franklin, Aretha, 110, 111, 172
Franklin, C. L., 111
Free Speech Movement (FSM), 136, 167
Freedman's Bureau, 29, 58, 62, 85
Freedom rides, 30, 73, 82–84, 86, 90, 96, 180, 188
Freedom Summer, 131–132
Freeman, John, 80
French, Edgar Nathaniel, 24, 25, 27
Friendship Baptist Church (Harlem), 16–17
Fuller, Hoyt, 166

Gaines, Ida, 126
Gandhi, Mahatma, 7–8, 30–31, 49, 54
Garner, Eric, 183
Garroway, David, 51
Garvey, Marcus, 71
Gayle, Addison, Jr., 166
Gayle, William A. "Tacky," 25, 27–29, 32, 35
Gayton, Carver, 74
Ghana, 40–41, 57, 67
Gibson, John, 128
Gordy, Berry, Jr., 79, 99, 188
Graham, Billy, 45, 48, 89
Gray, Fred D., 23, 27, 31, 64
Gray, William H., Jr., 56
Great Man's history, 185
Great Migration, 13, 42, 71
Green, Al, 199–200

Greenberg, Jack, 168
Gregory, Dick, 109, 110, 148, 149, 153
Gregory, Frank J., 42
Gruening, Ernest, 159

Haight, Dorothy, 168
Hall, Peter, 31
Hallahan, Paul, 133
Harding, Vincent, 105, 161
Harlem Hospital, 51–52
Hatfield, Mark, 159
Hegel, George Wilhelm Friedrich, 11
Helstein, Ralph, 153
Henderson, Clarence, 61
Henderson, J. Raymond, 33
Henry, Aaron, 132
Heschel, Abraham, 161–162
Highlander Folk School, 21, 22
Hippies, 152
Historically black colleges and universities (HBCUs), 62
   ABHMS's support for, 35
   Arkansas Agricultural, Mechanical and Normal College, 50
   Bethune-Cookman College, 50
   Bishop College, 58
   Central State College, 50
   Dillard College (later Dillard University), 58
   Erma Hughes Business College, 50
   Fisk University, 29–30, 34, 84
   King's speaking tours of, 29–30, 50, 58
   Lincoln University, 40, 73
   Maryland State College, 58
   Meharry Medical College, 30, 52
   Morehouse College, 2, 4–8, 43, 58, 124, 183, 190
   Morgan State College, 50
   Talladega College, 58
   Tennessee State University, 30
Hobb, Charles, 110
Hocking, William Ernest, 10
Holland, Bryan, 79
Holland, Eddie, 79
Holmes, John Haynes, 33

Holt Street Baptist Church (Montgomery), 23, 24, 31–32, 35–36
Hoover, J. Edgar, 124
Horton, Myles, 22
*Hour of Faith* (radio program), 15
Howard University, 3, 7, 31, 41, 43–44, 49, 58
Hughes, Langston, 64
Huie, William Bradford, 20
Hume, David, 15
Humphrey, Hubert, 138
Hutchinson Street Baptist Church (Montgomery), 35

*I Am King* (film), 182
Ickes, Harold, 3
Interdenominational Ministerial Alliance, 23, 26, 120
International politics, 48, 104, 113
Interracial marriage, 46, 48, 189
Isaacs, Harold, 51

Jackson, Abraham P., 160
Jackson, Jenn, 182
Jackson, Jesse, 150, 156, 176
Jackson, Joseph Harrison, 27
Jackson, Ketanji Brown, 182
Jackson, Mahalia, 34, 43, 110, 148–149, 194
Jackson Street Baptist Church (Montgomery), 27
James, C. L. R., 41
Jefferson, Thomas, 113
Jemison, Theodore Judson, 25, 38
Jenkins, Esau, 93
Jenkins, William A., 106
*Jet* (magazine), 20, 34, 39, 40–42, 60, 96, 134
Jim Crow, 2, 7
 Great Migration and, 13
 King on, 75, 82, 91
 origins of, 4, 115
 support for, 94
 traveling in Jim Crow South, 176–177

Johnson, Bernice, 119
Johnson, Frank, 139
Johnson, James Weldon, 30
Johnson, John Harold, 40, 59
Johnson, Lyndon B.
 Chicago movement and, 155
 Civil Rights Act of 1968 (Fair Housing Act), 190
 Civil Rights Act of 1964, 121, 124, 130, 179, 189
 Great Society programs, 124, 137, 160
 King's relationship with and criticisms of, 146, 157, 159, 162, 163, 168, 172, 173, 174, 176, 179
 meetings with King, 110, 121, 124, 130
 Mississippi Freedom Democratic Party and, 132
 National Day of Mourning declared by, 190
 presidential election of 1964, 132, 134, 135
 protection orders for Selma to Montgomery march, 139
 response to "Long, Hot Summer" riots, 144
 Vietnam War and, 160, 171
 Voting Rights Act of 1965, 138, 140
Johnson, Mordecai W., 7–8, 41, 43–44
Johnson Publishing Company, 40, 59
Jones, Rufus, 7
Jones, Walter B., 32

Katzenbach, Nicholas, 138
Kelsey, George D., 5, 49, 124
Kennedy, John F., 66–69, 78, 81–83, 89–91, 97–100, 104
 assassination of, 120–121, 189
 Executive Order 10925 (President's Committee on Equal Employment Opportunity), 90–91, 188
 Executive Order 11063 (equal opportunity in housing), 97–98
 King on legacy of, 120–121
 presidential election of 1960, 66–69

Kennedy, Robert F., 69, 83, 110
  assassination of, 190
  remarks on the death of King, 177, 194–196
Kent, Herb, 153
Kilpatrick, James J., 70
King, Alberta Williams (King's mother), 1–2, 12
King, Alfred Daniel (King's brother), 2, 172
King, Bernice Albertine (King's daughter), 105, 121
King, Christine (King's sister), 2
King, Coretta Scott
  accepts Presidential Medal of Freedom on Martin's behalf, 191
  anti-war activism, 145–146, 164
  bombing of home, 28–29, 187
  Chicago Movement, 146, 147, 153, 157
  childhood and education of, 11–12
  King Center founded by, 190
  March against Fear, 151
  marriage to Martin, 12
  move to Atlanta, 61
  student at Antioch College, 11–12
  student at New England Conservatory, 12, 14
  trip to India, 54, 55
  vacation with Abernathys, 33
King, Dexter Scott (King's son), 89, 121, 157
King, Ed, 132
King, Joel Lawrence (King's paternal uncle), 15
King, Martin Luther, Jr.
  as "American Gandhi," 123
  on *Arlene Francis Show*, 168
  arrested and jailed in Montgomery, 28
  assassination of, 177
  audience with Pope Paul VI, 133
  awards and honors, 33–34, 39–40, 43–45, 123–124, 133–135, 137, 189
  baptism of, 5
  birth of, 187
  bombing of home, 28–29, 187
  Chicago freedom movement, 145–156
  childhood of, 1–3
  copastor at Ebenezer Baptist Church, 60, 68, 71, 73, 77, 84, 86–87, 90, 102, 165, 167
  dissertation of, 14, 16, 17–18
  early experiences of racial discrimination, 3
  early work experiences, 3
  on *Face the Nation*, 165
  on *Face to Face*, 80
  Fisk University's first Distinguished Service Award granted to, 34
  funeral of, 190
  in Georgia State Prison, 69–70, 72
  Holmes-Weatherly Prize awarded to, 33–34
  legacy of, 179–186
  marriage to Coretta Scott, 12
  on *Meet the Press*, 65, 155, 171
  on *The Merv Griffin Show*, 168
  on *The Mike Wallace Interviews*, 78, 80
  Montgomery trial, 31–32
  National Press Club address, 100
  on *The Nation's Future*, 70
  on *Open Circuit*, 81
  on *Open End*, 117
  ordination of, 5
  pastor of Dexter Avenue Baptist Church, 187
  perjury arrest and trial, 63–66
  qualifying exams, 14, 15
  resignation from Dexter Avenue Baptist Church, 60–61
  Senate hearing testimony, 156–157
  Southern Christian Leadership Conference founded by, 26
  stabbed during book-signing event, 51–54, 55, 72, 188
  Stars of Freedom tour, 172
  student at Booker T. Washington High School, 2–4

student at Boston University, School
   of Theology, 9–18
student at Crozer Theological
   Seminary, 5–8
student at David T. Howard
   Elementary School, 2
student at Laboratory High School
   (Atlanta University), 2
student at Morehouse College,
   4–5, 8
student at Yonge Street Elementary
   School, 2
*Time* magazine "Man of the Year,"
   123–124
trip to Ghana, 40–41, 57, 67
trip to India, 53–54, 55–60, 71–74,
   76–77
U.S. Information Program press
   conference, 116–117
Vanocur interview, 167
visit to Nigeria, 69–70, 74
work on tobacco farm, 4
*See also* King, Martin Luther, Jr.,
   published writings; King, Martin
   Luther, Jr., speeches and sermons
King, Martin Luther, Jr., published
   writings
"Advice for Living" (*Ebony* column),
   45–48, 59, 89
*Autobiography*, 51, 53–54, 57, 96–97,
   120, 129, 182
"The Case against Tokenism" *(New
   York Times)*, 98
*Chicago Daily Defender* articles, 96,
   147, 150
"Equality Now: The President Has
   the Power" *(The Nation)*, 81
"Fumbling on the New Frontier"
   *(The Nation)*, 98–99
"Letter from Birmingham Jail," 107,
   117, 131, 172
*New York Amsterdam News* articles,
   88–100, 116, 141, 145, 147, 149
"The Rising Tide of Racial
   Consciousness" *(YWCA
   Magazine)*, 70–71

*Strength to Love,* 50, 59, 111, 113, 116
*Stride toward Freedom,* 48–51,
   130–131
"The Time for Freedom Has Come"
   *(New York Times Magazine),* 81,
   82
"What Is the World's Greatest
   Need?" *(New York Times
   Magazine),* 81, 82
*Where Do We Go from Here: Chaos
   or Community?,* 157, 168–170
*Why We Can't Wait,* 107,
   130–131, 133
King, Martin Luther, Jr., speeches and
   sermons
"Address to the Chicago Freedom
   Festival," 149
"The American Dream," 73–75, 92,
   124, 184
"Beyond Vietnam: A Time to Break
   Silence," 161–163, 166–167, 172,
   174, 189
"The Birth of a Nation," 41
"Can a Christian Be a Communist?,"
   102, 103–104, 113
"A Christmas Sermon on Peace," 174
"A Comparison of the Conceptions
   of God in the Thinking of Paul
   Tillich and Henry Nelson
   Wieman" (dissertation), 14, 16,
   17–18
"Conscience and the Vietnam
   War," 174
"A Creative Protest," 63
"The Death of Evil upon the
   Seashore," 32–33, 112
"Facing the Challenge of a New
   Age," 37
"Farewell Statement" (All India
   Radio), 57
"The Future of Integration," 42–43,
   55, 73, 75
"Give Us the Ballot," 43, 49
"Going Forward by Going
   Backward," 30
"How Long? Not Long," 139

"I Have a Dream," 73, 118, 167, 181, 184, 189, 196, 200
"Impasse in Race Relations," 173–174
"It's Hard to Be a Christian," 29, 114
"I've Been to the Mountaintop," 177, 190
"A Knock at Midnight," 50, 112
"Levels of Love," 102–103
"Love in Action," 115
"Loving Your Enemies," 16
"The Man Who Was a Fool," 73, 76, 113
Massey Lecture series, 173–174
"The Negro and the Constitution" (first public address), 3
Nobel Peace Prize lecture, 135, 137, 185
"Nonviolence and Social Change," 174
"On Being a Good Neighbor," 114
"The Other America," 163–164, 165
"Paul's Letter to American Christians," 73, 77–78, 82
"Problems of the South," 55
"Progress toward Desegregation," 125
"Recommendations to the Dexter Avenue Baptist Church for the Fiscal Year 1954–1955," 17
"Rediscovering Lost Values," 15, 30
"Remaining Awake through a Great Revolution," 176
"The Secret of Adjustment," 84, 86
"Segregation Must Die," 142
"Speech on South Africa," 134–135
"The Summer of Our Discontent," 124
"The Three Dimensions of a Complete Life," 14–15, 30, 134
"A Tough Mind and a Tender Heart," 59–60, 112
"Transformed Nonconformist," 113
"What Is Man?," 16, 29–30
"What Then Are Some of the Secrets of a Happy Marriage?," 84
"When Peace Becomes Obnoxious," 32
"Why I Am Opposed to the War in Vietnam," 165, 167
"Youth and Social Action," 174
King, Martin Luther, Sr. (King's father), 1–2, 5, 12, 60
King, Martin Luther, III (King's son), 89, 121, 157
King, Rodney, 183
King, Yolanda Denise (King's daughter), 19, 24, 26, 28, 89, 121, 157
King Holiday and Service Act, 181
Kitt, Eartha, 64
Ku Klux Klan, 75, 82–83, 85, 94, 120, 129, 138, 179–180, 188

Lamar, Nat, 130
Lamming, George, 41
Lands, Elizabeth, 148–149
Langford, Charles D., 31, 64
Langston, Esther, 126
Lawson, James, 175
Lee, Bernard, 95, 129, 157
Lee, Mrs. Herbert, 193
Lenud, Philip, 11
Levison, Stanley, 49, 130
Lewis, John, 138, 193
Liberty Life Insurance, 27
Lincoln, Abraham, 37, 81, 101, 129, 160, 185
Lincoln University, 40, 73
Livingston, David, 8
Locke, John, 15
Lodge, Robert, 116–117
Loeb, Henry, 175
"Long, Hot Summer" riots, 144
Longfellow, Henry Wadsworth, 113
Lorraine Hotel
　King's assassination at, 176–177, 190
　National Civil Rights Museum, 191
*Loving v. Virginia*, 189
Lowell, Russell, 37, 113
Lowenstein, Al, 132

Luther, Martin, 11
Lynd, Staughton, 116

Maitland, Leo, 52
Malcolm X, 126, 127
Mandela, Nelson, 134
Mann, Horace, 11
Manpower Development and Training Act of 1962, 92–93
March against Fear, 150–153, 189
March on Washington for Jobs and Freedom, 117–121, 179, 180
   "I Have a Dream" (King), 73, 118, 167, 181, 184, 189, 196, 200
   Kennedy and, 110
   performers at, 172
   program for, 193–194
   SCLC fiftieth anniversary speakers on, 196, 200
Maritain, Jacques, 11
Marshall, Thurgood, 7, 31, 189
Martin Luther King Jr. Center for Nonviolent Social Change, 190
Martin Luther King Jr. Day, 181, 191
Martin Luther King Jr. National Historical Park, 191
Maryland State College, 58
Massey, Charles Vincent, 173
Mayer, Helen, 52
Maynard, Aubré, 52
Mays, Benjamin, 5, 37, 86, 194
McCaffery, John, 70
McCain, Franklin, 61
McCarthy, Eugene, 159
McCracken, Robert James, 161
McFall, Benjamin, 111
McGovern, George, 159
McKissick, Floyd, 151, 155, 164, 168
McNeil, Joseph, 61
McTaggart, J. M. E., 10
Meharry Medical College, 30, 52
Memphis sanitation workers' strike, 175–177, 190
Men's Day, 16, 34, 77
Meredith, James, 150–151, 155, 189

Milam, J. W., 20
Miller, Perry, 51
Miller, Uri, 194
Mississippi Freedom Democratic Party (MFDP), 132
Mitchell, James P., 44
Mitchell, Oscar, 68–69
Monson Motor Lodge protests, 129–130
Montgomery bus boycott, 21–36
Montgomery Bus Lines, 26–27
Montgomery Improvement Association (MIA), 23–29, 31–33, 35, 38, 41–42, 49, 55–56, 61, 63, 187
Moore, Douglass, 63
Moore, Ray, 120–121
Moran, Chuck, 92
Morehouse, Henry Lyman, 4–5
Morehouse College
   founding and history of, 4–5
   honorary doctor of humane letters given to King, 43
   King's commencement address, 58
   King's funeral at, 190
   King's studies and teachers at, 4–8, 124, 183
   sponsor of Laboratory High School, 2
Moses, Robert, 126
Motown, 79, 99, 148, 188
Mount Zion AME Zion Church (Montgomery), 23
Mount Zion Baptist Church (Albany), 95
Muhammad, Elijah, 148, 170
Murchison, H. I., 120
Music, civil rights, 119
Muste, A. J., 30

Naclerio, Emil, 52
Namboodiripad, E. M. S., 57
Nash, Diane, 84, 193
Nation of Islam, 117, 126, 127, 148

National Association for the Advancement of Colored People (NAACP), 21, 33, 37, 42–44, 66–67, 78, 90, 118, 131, 162–163, 189, 194, 199
National Baptist Convention, 12, 17, 27, 55, 148
National Cathedral (Washington, DC), 176
National City Lines, 25, 27
National Civil Rights Museum, 191
National Mobilization Committee to End the War in Vietnam (Mobe), 161, 167
National Urban League, 67, 118, 168
Neal, Larry, 166
Negro American Labor Council, 118
Negro Ministers of Montgomery and Their Congregations, 26–27
*Negro Motorist Green Book, The*, 177
Nehru, Jawaharlal, 56
Nelson, William Stuart, 58
New Bethel Baptist Church (Detroit), 111, 145–146
New Hope Baptist Church (Niagara Falls), 34
New School, 124–125
*New York Amsterdam News*, 88–100, 116, 141, 145, 147, 149
New York State Convention of Universalists, 35
New Zion Baptist Church (New Orleans), 39
Newton, Huey P., 189
Niebuhr, Reinhold, 10, 14
Nixon, E. D., 19, 21–24, 30, 63
Nixon, Richard M., 38, 39, 41, 44, 66, 67
Nkrumah, Kwame, 40–41
North Carolina Agricultural and Technical College, 61, 188
Nygren, Anders, 11

Obama, Barack
  Presidential Proclamation 9565, 202–204
  Presidential Proclamation 9568, 181, 200–202
O'Boyle, Patrick, 193
Organization of Afro-American Unity (OAAU), 126, 127
Oswald, Lee Harvey, 189

Pacifism, 8, 30–31, 33, 56, 161, 164
Pan African Orthodox Christian Church (PAOCC), 111, 170
Parasuram, T. V., 116
Parker, Wheeler, 20
Parker, William, 143, 144
Parks, Frank Warren, 25
Parks, Rosa, 19, 21, 23, 31, 33, 63, 193, 198
Paul of Samosta, 14
Paul VI, Pope, 133
Pelosi, Nancy, 196–197
Pitt, David, 41
Pitts, Lucius, 120
*Plessy v. Ferguson*, 4, 42, 101
Poitier, Sidney, 64, 148, 172
Police brutality, 109, 138, 144, 166, 167, 181, 183–184
Poor People's Campaign, 173–176, 184–185
Pope, Roslyn, 68
Popper, Hermine, 49, 130–131
Powell, Adam Clayton, Jr., 41–43, 145
Powell, Mary, 12
Prayer Pilgrimage for Freedom, 39, 42–43, 179, 188
president of Montgomery Improvement Association, 187
Presidential election of 1960, 66–69
Prince Edward County, Maryland, 92, 188
Prinz, Joachim, 194
Pritchett, Laurie, 87–88, 95, 96

Quinn Chapel AME Church (Chicago), 27

Raby, Al, 143, 147, 148, 153, 154, 155
Ramachandran, C., 54

Randolph, A. Philip, 19, 33, 39, 41, 42, 49, 51, 64, 67, 71, 117–118, 168, 193, 194
Rangel, Charles, 197–198
Ray, James Earl, 177, 190, 191
Ray, Sandy, 52
Rayner, Ahmed "Sammy," Jr., 160
Reagan, Ronald, 181, 191
Reagon, Bernice Johnson, 119
Reagon, Cordell, 86
Reconstruction, 75, 85, 137, 188, 189
Red Summer of 1919, 13
Reddick, Lawrence, 54, 56–57
Redding, Saunders, 131
Reed, Ishmael, 166
Reuther, Walter, 56, 111, 193
Ribicoff, Abraham, 156–157
Richardson, Gloria, 193
Riverside Church (New York City), 77, 161, 165–166, 189
Roberts, Gene, 162
Robinson, Bernice, 22
Robinson, Jackie, 51, 66–67, 130, 180
Robinson, Jo Ann, 21–22, 28
Robinson, Smokey, 79
Rock and roll, 46, 47, 99, 175
Rockefeller, Nelson, 51, 101, 131
Rodell, Marie, 48–49
Rogers, Theophilus, Jr., 125
Roosevelt, Eleanor, 53, 64
Roosevelt, Franklin, 71, 81, 131
Rowan, Carl T., 27, 59, 163
Ruah, Joseph, 132
Rumford Fair Housing Act, 128–129
Rush, Bobby L., 198–199
Rustin, Bayard, 30–31, 38, 49, 64, 67, 118, 132, 134, 144, 168, 180

Savio, Mario, 136
Scheer, Robert, 165
Schilling, S. Paul, 18
Schopenhauer, Arthur, 15
Schweitzer, Albert, 8
Scott, John B., 23
Seale, Bobby, 189
Second Baptist Church (Detroit), 15

Second Baptist Church (Los Angeles), 33
Second Morrill Act, 62
Sellers, Clyde Chapman, 25, 27–29, 32, 35
*Selma* (film), 182
Selma March, 137–142, 168, 179, 189
Sherrod, Charles, 86
Shiloh Baptist Church (Englewood, Chicago), 29
Shores, Arthur D., 31, 64
Shrine of the Black Madonna, 170
Shurtleff College, 26
Shuttlesworth, Fred, 38, 91–92, 105, 109, 120, 187, 202
Simone, Nina, 119
Simpkins, Cuthbert O., 95
Sit-in movement, 61–72, 84, 90, 96, 105–109, 136, 188
Sixteenth Street Baptist Church bombing (Birmingham), 119–120
Smiley, Glenn, 31
Smith, Billy, 61
Smith, Lillian, 50–51
Southern Christian Leadership Conference (SCLC)
  Alabama boycott, 141
  Albany Movement and, 87, 95–96
  Birmingham Campaign, 105–110
  Chicago freedom movement, 145–156
  Children's Crusade, 108–110
  Democratic Party and, 68
  FBI and, 124
  fiftieth anniversary commemoration, 196–200
  founding of, 26, 39, 187
  freedom rides and, 83
  goal of, 137
  Green, Al, on, 199–200
  King as president of, 39, 90
  King's relocation to Atlanta, 60
  NAACP and, 78
  naming of, 39
  Operation Breadbasket, 150, 156, 188

Pelosi, Nancy, on, 196–197
"People to People" tours, 91–93
Poor People's Campaign, 173–176, 184–185
Prayer Pilgrimage for Freedom, 39, 42–43, 179, 188
Project C, 105–106, 108, 202
Rangel, Charles, on, 197–198
Resurrection City, 190
Rush, Bobby L., on, 198–199
Selma March, 137–138
sit-in movement and, 63, 64, 66–67
St. Augustine Movement, 128–131
Southern Negro Leaders Conference on Transportation and Nonviolent Integration, 38
Spingarn, Joel E., 44
Spock, Benjamin, 160, 164–165
Spring Mobilization Committee to End the War in Vietnam, 164
St. Paul's Cathedral (London), 134
Stanley, Frank, 29
Steele, C. K., 38
Stephen Wise Free Synagogue (New York City), 42–43
Stewart, James, 166
Stokes, Carl, 190
Stoner, J. B., 129, 180
Student Nonviolent Coordinating Committee (SNCC), 22, 65–66, 68, 86, 118, 126, 131, 137–138, 151, 188, 189, 199
Susskind, David, 117

Talladega College, 58
Taylor, Breonna, 183
Taylor, Gardner, 64
Tennessee State University, 30
Thetford, William H., 31
Thoreau, Henry David, 80, 160
Thurmond, Strom, 162
Till, Emmett, 20, 40, 187
Tillich, Paul, 17–18
Tindley, Charles Albert, 119
Tokenism, 82, 98, 117
Toure, Askia, 166

Truman, Harry, 71, 81
Twelfth Baptist Church (Roxbury), 9, 29
Twenty-Fourth Amendment, 189

Union Baptist Church (Cambridge), 16
Union Baptist Church (Lansing), 15
Unitarian Fellowship for Social Justice, 33–34
United Auto Workers (UAW), 56, 111
University of California, Berkeley, 33, 136, 167

Vanocur, Sander, 167
Vietnam War, 137, 144, 145–146, 156–157, 159–168, 171–174, 185
Vine Memorial Baptist Church (Philadelphia), 16, 56
Voting Rights Act of 1965, 94, 140, 169, 173, 179, 196, 200

Walk to Freedom, 110–111
Walker, Arnold, 142
Walker, Wyatt T., 87, 91, 95, 106, 118, 128–129, 172
Wallace, George, 138, 180
Wallace, Henry A., 12
Wallace, Mike, 78, 80
Walls, William Jacob, 27
War Resisters League (WRL), 56
Ware, J. L., 120
Warren, Earl, 39
Washington, Booker T., 2, 59, 71
Watts riots, 143–145
Weatherly, Arthur, 33–34
Webb, James E., 68
Weiss, Theodore, 52
Wells, Ida B., 30
Whitaker, H. Edward, 12, 34
White, Walter, 3, 112
White Citizens' Councils, 75, 94, 95, 179–180
White Rock Baptist Church (Durham), 63
White Rock Baptist Church (Philadelphia), 77

White supremacy, 44, 74–76, 93, 105, 145, 151, 169, 170, 184. *See also* Apartheid; Jim Crow; Ku Klux Klan; White Citizens' Councils
Wieman, Henry Nelson, 17–18
Wilkins, Roy, 42, 43, 90, 124, 132, 155, 168, 194
Williams, Hosea, 128, 138
Williams, Jennie Celeste Parks (King's maternal grandmother), 1
Wirtz, W. Willard, 173
Wise, Stephen, 42–43
Wofford, Harris, 49
Women's Political Council (WPC), 21, 23–24
Wonder, Stevie, 79, 181
Wood, Marcus Garvey, 29
Woods, Virgil, 142
Woodstock Music and Art Fair, 152
Wright, Moses, 20
Wright, Richard, 56

Yancey, Asa, 133
Young, Andrew, 87, 118, 154, 155, 156, 175, 176
Young, Coleman, 170
Young, Whitney, 124, 155, 168, 194
Young Women's Christian Association (YWCA), 70–71

**About the Author**

**Jamie J. Wilson** is Professor of History at Salem State University in Salem, Massachusetts. He is the author of *Building a Healthy Black Harlem* (2009), *Civil Rights Movement* (2013), *The Black Panther Party of Connecticut* (2014), and *The Black Panther Party: A Guide to an American Subculture* (2018). He is also the editor of *50 Events That Shaped African American History: An Encyclopedia of the American Mosaic* (2019).

www.ingramcontent.com/pod-product-compliance
Lightning Source LLC
Chambersburg PA
CBHW060949230426

43665CB00015B/2128